SUBVERTING THE PRESENT, IMAGINING THE FUTURE

CLASS, STRUGGLE, COMMONS

SUBVERTING THE PRESENT, IMAGINING THE FUTURE

CLASS, STRUGGLE, COMMONS

Werner Bonefeld, Editor

Werner Bonefeld

George Caffentzis

Harry Cleaver

Patrick Cuninghame

Mariarosa Dalla Costa

Massimo De Angelis

Ana Cecelia Dinerstein

Nick Dyer-Witherford

Leeds May Day Group

Midnight Notes Collective

Stevphen Shukaitis

Sergio Tischler

Paul Zarembka

Autonomedia

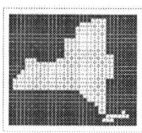

This publication is made possible in part with public funds
from the New York State Council on the Arts, a state agency.

Autonomedia
POB 568 Williamsburgh Station
Brooklyn, New York 11211-0568 USA

info@autonomedia.org
www.autonomedia.org

Printed in the United States of America

TABLE OF CONTENTS

Subverting the Present, Imagining the Future
Insurrection, Movement & Commons

Werner Bonefeld

It is Man, who, as a single individual, as a group, or as a mass, understands herself as subject and who defends herself against a merely objective existence — in politics, in religion, in philosophy. One can say that subversion is a truly human phenomenon. Man objects to be a mere football of the almighty. Here s/he is mere object. Similarly, as a servant of the master s/he is mere object, regardless of whether we conceive this in social or religious terms. Man is never at the centre of politics (as the political parties say), but s/he is a means of politics...And an object s/he remains most of all when s/he is kept in a state of ignorance...Subversion operates against systems of thought, against political and economic systems, that threaten nature and therewith always also the human being (Agnoli, 1996, p.29).

The earliest record of a subversive figure can be found in the Bible. Here one reads about the story of Eve who, unlike self-satisfied Adam for whom God's word was law, rebelled against her existence as a mere object. She not only plucked the forbidden apple — the apple of knowledge — she also ate it and found it tasty.

On finding out, and executing the first recorded act of summary punishment, God is said to have expelled human kind from paradise, condemning them to live in darkness. But God had not reckoned with Lucifer, his most beloved angel. Lucifer is said to have brought the light to human kind, so that they can be warm, so that they can see, and so that they can conduct their affairs in a state of general illumination and enlightenment. God's wrath was almighty. He expelled Lucifer from his entourage and condemned the bringer of light, of illumination and enlightenment, by one frightful world: the devil. From the view of constituted power, God's action makes sense. What would happen to power if the governed were to govern themselves?

Eve and Lucifer are more than just a figment of recorded imagination. They present legends of our past struggles against the grasping overlords of former times. Their legend has to be demystified. Enlightenment can only be provided by us by means of everyday struggle, now and here, in practical recognition of our collective being, our solidarity, and our desire to build a hospitable world — a world of general human illumination, and that is, the world of the "communist individual" (cf. Marcuse, 2000).

Subversion is the great laboratory of social knowledge and imaginary consciousness. This knowledge has many facets, chief among them the insight that "the tradition of the oppressed teaches us that the "state of emergency" in which we live, is not the exception but the rule. We must attain to a conception of history that is in keeping with this insight" (Benjamin 1965, p. 84). However, the history of the oppressed is also a history of the struggle for an alternative entelechy of human development — that is, to use a phrase from the *Communist Manifesto*, the "society of the free and equal." We thus have to attain an understanding of history as a history of class struggle. That is to say, history does nothing, does not "possess vast wealth," does not "fight battles"! History is nothing but the activity of Man pursuing his ends. Given where we are, what ends can we realistically hope for? We live now, have to sell our labour power and get a wage so that we can live. That is to say, the necessity to sell one's labour power is absolute. At best (!) there is only economic compulsion. And at best, there is a meaningful job that pays! Is this what a "realistic" conception of attainable ends ultimately boils down to? No. We have to attain a conception of realism that knows how to dream and sing, and dance. Imaginative realism is not just an art-form — it is subversion-in-practice. Paris 1968 — "be realistic, demand the impossible" — articulated an important insight. Realism left to work without imagination creates monsters. Imagination unalloyed by the power of reason gives rise to futile ideas. "United with reason, imagination is the mother of all art and the source of all its beauty" (Goya).

This volume is dedicated to the communist individual, her imagination and subversive cunning and reason. It is about the beauty of human values — freedom and equality of individual human needs, human dignity and respect, solidarity and collectivity, affection and warmth, democracy and social autonomy. And it is about subversive knowledge: What do we have to know to prevent misery?; what can be done to achieve conditions of human dignity, what can we hope for? Historically these questions inspired the Workers Inquiry approach. What is the composition of the working class, what are its forms of struggle, and what outcome of struggle can be hoped for?

Part I explores the contemporary meaning of primitive accumulation and the struggle for a new Commons. Part II analyses subversion in everyday struggle, assesses the meaning of movement, and examines theories of revolutionary currents and change. Part III assesses the insurrection of the Argentinean Piqueteros, the Other Campaign in Mexico, and the struggles of the US American working class. The concluding chapter returns to the issue of a Workers Inquiry. It argues that the struggle for a new Commons now entails the multitude and that a Workers Inquiry amounts to a Compositional Analysis of the multitude. What, then, can we hope for?

REFERENCES

Agnoli, J. (1996), *Subversive Theorie — Die Sache selbst und ihre Geschichte*, Ça ira, Freiburg.

Benjamin, W. (1965), "Geschichtsphilosphische Thesen," in *Zur Kritik der Gewalt und andere Aufsätze*, Suhrkamp, Frankfurt, English version published as "Theses on the Philosophy of History," in *Illuminations*, Harcourt, Brace & World, New York, 1968.

Marcuse, H. (2000), *Reason and Revolution*, Routledge, London.

PART I

PRIMITIVE ACCUMULATION
A DEBATE ON HISTORY, SOCIAL CONSTITUTION & STRUGGLE

1

The New Enclosures[1]

Midnight Notes Collective

... the historical movement which changes the producers into waged workers, appears on the one hand as their emancipation from serfdom and from the fetters of the guilds, and this side alone exists for our bourgeois historians. But on the other hand these new freedmen became sellers of themselves only after they had been robbed of all their own means of production and all the guarantees of existence offered by the old feudal arrangements. And the history of this, their expropriation, is written in the annals of mankind in letters of blood and fire.
— Karl Marx, *Capital*, Vol. 1.

The docile Sambo could and did become the revolutionary Nat Turner overnight. The slaves, under the leadership of those from the more complex African societies, fought and ran away, stole and feigned innocence, malingered on the job while seeming to work as hard as possible. And they lived to fight another day.
— George Rawick, *From Sundown to Sunup.*

Glasnost, end of the cold war, united Europe, we are the world, save the Amazon Rain Forest... these are typical phrases of the day. They suggest an age of historic openness, globalism, and breakdown of political and economic barriers. In the midst of this expansiveness, however, Midnight Notes poses the issue of "The New Enclosures." For a corrosive secret is hidden in the gleaming idols of globalism, the end of the blocs and Gaian ecological consciousness: the last decade has seen the largest Enclosure of the worldly Common in history. The essay explains the meaning and importance of Enclosures, both Old and New, in the planetary struggle of classes. The Old Enclosures were a counter-revolutionary process whereby, after a century of high wages and breakdown of feudal authority, beginning in the late 1400s, farmers in England were expropriated from their land and commons by state officials and landlords. They were turned into paupers, vagabonds and beggars, and later into waged workers, while the land was put to work to feed the incipient international market for agricultural commodities. According to the Marxist tradition, the Enclosures were the starting point of capitalist society. They were the basic device of "original ac-cumulation" which created a population of workers "free" from any means of re-production and thus compelled (in time) to work for a wage. The Enclosures, however, are not a one time process exhausted at the dawn of capitalism. They are a regular return on the path of accumulation and a structural component of class struggle. Any leap in proletarian power demands a dynamic capitalist re-sponse: both the expanded appropriation of new resources and new labor power and the extension of capitalist relations, or else capitalism is threatened with ex-tinction. Thus, Enclosure is one process that unifies proletarians throughout cap-ital's history, for despite our differences we all have entered capitalism through the same door: the loss of our land and of the rights attached to it, whether this loss has taken place in Front Mill, England, in southern Italy, in the Andes, on the Niger Delta, or in the Lower East Side of New York City.

THE APOCALYPSE OF THE TRINITY OF DEALS

Today, once again, the Enclosures are the common denominator of proletarian experience across the globe. In the biggest diaspora of the century, on every continent millions are being uprooted from their land, their jobs, their homes through wars, famines, plagues, and the IMF ordered devaluations (the four knights of the modern apocalypse) and scattered to the corners of the globe.

In Nigeria, for example, people currently are being thrown off communally-owned land by troops to make way for plantations owned and managed by the World Bank. The reason? The government points to the "debt crisis" and the In-ternational Monetary Fund dictated "Structural Adjustment Program" (SAP) allegedly devised for its solution. The SAP for Nigeria is similar to SAPs being implemented throughout Asia, Africa and Latin America. They invariably in-clude the commercialization of agriculture and the demonetarization of the econ-omy via massive devaluations which reduce money wages to a paper value. The result is destruction of village communities, emigration to nearby cities and then, for the desperate, clever or lucky, a chance to work in New York or Naples.

In the United States, millions are homeless and on the move. The immedi-ate reasons are highly publicized: the farm crisis, the steep rise of rental and mortgage payments relative to wages, the warehousing of apartments and gen-trification, the collapse of the social safety net, union busting. Behind these rea-sons, however, is a fact: the decline, since 1973, of real wages for the mass of workers. The post-WWII inter-class deal that guaranteed real wage increases is now definitively over and the homeless are the shock(ed) troops of this fact. But even those whose wages have escaped the deal's collapse complain of the con-comitant loss of the natural Commons due to a series of Big Catastrophes from the vanishing ozone layer to the burnt-out rain forests.

In China, the transition to a "free market economy" has led to the displace-ment of one hundred million from their communally operated lands. Their urban counterparts are facing the loss of guaranteed jobs in factories and offices and the prospect of emigrating from one city to another to look for a wage. The "iron rice bowl" is to be smashed while a similar scenario is developing in the Soviet Union and Eastern Europe. The post-WWII OECD (Western European–North American–Japanese), socialist, and third-worldist deals are all now null and void, as the examples of the US, China and Nigeria show. We refuse to mourn them. For who first voided them but brother and sister proletarians around the planet who desired and demanded more, much more than what was settled for? Not surprisingly, the old python of Capital has reacted instinctually and "originally" with a new lunge and the bite of Enclosures. The "debt crisis," "homelessness," and "the collapse of socialism" are frequently treated as different phenomena by both the media and left journals. For us at Midnight they but deceptively name aspects of a single unified process: the New Enclosures, which must operate throughout the planet in differing, divisive guises while being totally interdependent.

Under the logic of capitalist accumulation in this period, for every factory in a free-trade zone in China privatized and sold to a New York commercial bank, or for every acre enclosed by a World Bank development project in Africa or Asia as part of a "debt for equity" swap, a corresponding enclosure must occur in the US and Western Europe. Thus when communal land in Nigeria is expropriated or when the policy of free housing for workers is abolished in China, there must be a matching expropriation in the US be it the end of a "good paying" factory job in Youngstown, the destruction of a working class community in Jay, Maine, or the imposition of martial law in New York City's parks. With each contraction of "communal rights" in the Third World or of "socialist rights" in the Soviet Union and China, comes a subtraction of our seemingly sacred "social rights" in the US. Indeed, this subtraction has gone on so thoroughly in the 1980s that even the definition of what it means to be human is being revised by both capital and the proletariat.

This mutual contraction of the "right to subsist" in the Third World, the socialist countries and in the US is no accident. In no way could capital have won in any place if it had not operated in every place. Only if Filipinos thrown off the land could be used in "free enterprise zones" in Manila or as "shit" workers in Italy could capital reduce real wages in the US or sustain chronically high unemployment rates in Europe. Third world and socialist enclosures, apparently so distant and exotic from Boston or New York, inevitably become First World ones, equally distant and exotic from Lagos or Beijing.

The New Enclosures are so radical in their attack on what proletarian struggles in the course of history have imposed as human rights because capital confronted a life-and-death crisis that precluded any social-democratic deal. At the end of WWII, capital (in its Western and Eastern modes) offered a variety of slogans to the world proletariat: from "collective bargaining" and "racial integration" in the US, to the family "social wage" in the USSR, to "colonial emancipation" in

Asia and Africa. An enormous struggle ensued to determine the content of these slogans; but between 1965 and 1975, proletarian initiatives transcended the limits of capital's historic possibilities. From the Watts riot to the "Prague Spring" to Italy's "hot autumn" to the last US helicopter escaping from the fall of Saigon, the profit picture internationally turned sour and capital was facing euthanasia. Consequently, all deals were off and capital went on the attack everywhere.

At the end of the 1980s, capital seems to have gotten the better of the nullification of these various social contracts. For example, the US Left currently looks at "collective bargaining" and "racial integration" as utopias, while the Soviet workers anxiously watch as their "social wage" rapidly recedes into the past. Indeed, "colonial emancipation" is a phrase that, if any one has the bad taste to bring it up, can only cause derision. How have these "inalienable rights" been so rapidly alienated? Through the operation of the New Enclosures which attempt to eliminate any "traditional," "organic" or institutionalized relation between proletarians themselves and the powers of the earth or of their past.

These New Enclosures, therefore, name the large-scale reorganization of the accumulation process which has been underway since the mid-1970s. The main objective of this process has been to uproot workers from the terrain on which their organizational power has been built, so that, like the African slaves transplanted to the Americas, they are forced to work and fight in a strange environment where the forms of resistance possible at home are no longer available.

Thus, once again, as at the dawn of capitalism, the physiognomy of the world proletariat is that of the pauper, the vagabond, the criminal, the panhandler, the street peddler, the refugee sweatshop worker, the mercenary, the rioter.

THE PENTAGON OF ENCLOSURES

How have the New Enclosures been worked? First and foremost the New Enclosures operate exactly as the Old Enclosures did: by ending communal control of the means of subsistence. There are very few groups today who still can provide directly with their land and their work for their own needs. Even the last "aboriginals" from Indonesia to the Amazonas are being violently enclosed in governmental reservations. More commonly, the so-called "peasant" in the Third World today is a person who survives thanks to remittances from a brother or sister who has emigrated to New York; or by growing, in the most dangerous work conditions, poppies or coca leaves for export; or by prostituting him/herself to the carriers of hard-currencies (the great and perhaps only aphrodisiac of the age); or by migrating to the nearby cities to join the swelling ranks of day laborers, street peddlers or "free enterprise zone" workers, where conditions are often more dangerous than in the poppy fields back home.

The second major method of the New Enclosures is again similar to the Old: seizing land for debt. Just as the Tudor court sold off huge tracts of monastery and communal land to their creditors, so too modern African and Asian governments agree to capitalize and "rationalize" agricultural land in order to satisfy IMF auditors who will only "forgive" foreign loans under those conditions. Just as heads of clans in the Scottish Highlands of the eighteenth century connived with local merchants and bankers to whom they were indebted in order to "clear the land" of their own clansmen and women, so too local chiefs in Africa and Asia exchange communal land rights for unredeemed loans. The result now as then is enclosure: the internal and external destruction of traditional rights to subsistence. This is the secret hidden in the noise of the "debt crisis."

Third, the New Enclosures make mobile and migrant labor the dominant form of labor. We are now the most geographically mobile labor force since the advent of capitalism. Capital keeps us constantly on the move, separating us from our countries, farms, gardens, homes, workplaces because this guarantees cheap wages, communal disorganization and maximum vulnerability in front of law courts and police.

Fourth, the New Enclosures require the collapse of socialism from the USSR, to Poland to China. The aim of Enclosure could not be realized unless there was a dramatic increase in the international competition of workers and thus an enormous expansion of the world labor market. One third of the world's proletariat could no longer be kept out of competition with the rest of the world proletariat while socialist capital could no longer repress the socialist working class' desire to be able to appropriate universal wealth... even though this wealth be embodied in the commodity form.

For a long time socialism has ceased to be a pole of proletarian attraction. The anti-colonial revolutions of the 1960s and the primary commodities boom of the 1970s gave it some breathing space, but by the 1980s the game was up. The reasons for socialism's collapse are, in retrospect at least, rather obvious. Socialism is another name for a class "deal" that normally exchanges a guaranteed job at a lower level of exploitation for lower wages. "Lower," of course, is a relative term and it presupposes a comparison with a capitalist standard. The deal works as long as the guarantees, the exploitation and the wages are in synch.

By the 1980s, especially with the collapse of energy prices, socialist wages became too low on an international standard for the socialist working class to tolerate. But the exploitation rate the state demanded was simultaneously too high, while its guarantees were looking less and less promising to the proletariat. For with the computer-based technological leap, the expansion of production into the low waged Third World, and the end of the energy crisis in the OECD countries, the value of socialist work on the world market collapsed. It was not merely lower, it was almost nil. The "deal" fell apart at the seams and the piece-meal attempts to patch it worsened the tear. For example, the loans taken out by Eastern European countries in the 1970s (similar to the Third World loans of the time) to allow them to take part in the technological leap has required an enormous increase in exploitation and decrease in wages. The result: rebellion, disgruntlement and emigration.

Should we shed tears for this fallen deal? Hardly. For the collapse of social-ism provides the definitive answer to the riddle of the Great Twentieth Century Sphinx: the socialist working class. How many tomes have been written to de-termine whether this rough beast really is a working class? We can now consign them to the archives, for the socialist working class has come out of the closet. The fairy tale of "opposing blocs" is finished and we can directly see the class struggle from Berlin to Ho Chi Minh City. We now have the same bosses and can compare, on the same jobs, the relative merits of the different systems. If anything, the working class "virtues of socialism" will especially be tested in the next decade. When the new class struggles of the 1990s erupt in Eastern Europe, the Soviet Union and China, we will then see if the values of "solidarity," "co-operation" and "internationalism" have really sedimented.

The fifth aspect of the New Enclosures' operation is in its attack on our re-production: making us mutants as well as migrants! The highly advertised dis-appearance of the rain forest, the much commented upon hole in the ozone layer, the widely lamented pollution of air, sea and beach, along with the obvious shrinking of our living spaces, are all a part of the destruction of the earthly commons. Even the high seas have been enclosed in the 1980s with the dramatic extension of the traditional territorial limits. You need not be a science fiction freak to feel that we are guinea pigs in a capitalist experiment in non-evolution-ary species change. Human proletarians are not alone in this speed-up and shrink-down. Animals, from protozoa to cows, are being engineered and patented to eat oil spills, produce more eggs per hour, secrete more hormones. Increasingly, land is no longer valued for how much food it can grow or what kind of buildings it can support but for how much radioactive waste it can "safely" store. Thus a tired earthly commons, the gift of billions of years of labor-less transformation, meets tired human bodies.

Capital has long dreamed of sending us to work in space, where nothing would be left to us except our work-machine and rarefied and repressive work relations (see "Mormons in Space," Computer State Notes, Midnight Notes #5). But the fact is that the earth is becoming a space station and millions are already living in space-colony conditions: no oxygen to breathe, limited social/physical contact, a desexualized life, difficulty of communication, lack of sun and green ... even the voices of the migrating birds are missing.

The sentimental horror of this aspect of the New Enclosures has turned a profit for many a publisher and film corporation but we would like to point out its purgative value. For the bodily and personal common, which for most of the proletariat had been free, is now increasingly being enclosed for all to see. Ap-pearance and attitude are increasingly aspects of the work process in the so-called "service industries" from restaurants to hospitals. In the past how a worker looked or what s/he felt on the assembly line, farm or in the mine was im-material to the wage relation. This has definitively changed. Those who "work with the public" are now continually monitored from their urine to their sweat glands to their back brains. Capital now treats us as did the inquisitors of old, looking for the devil's marks of class struggle on our bodies and demanding that we open it up for alienation. The most "extreme" case of this enclosure is in the personal-political debates around the increasing recourse to reconstructive surgery in the working class. The siliconed breasts of the recent Miss America are the concrete universals of this trend. Are we to lament or condemn them? No, for they simply point out that though the bourgeoisie had long lost its body, the working class is now being forced to follow suit. Not only "beauty queens" and "male leads" must buy and re-buy their bodies piece-by-piece, reconstructive surgery is now a must for many jobs in the "service economy" and exposes for all of us to see and evaluate the commodity nature of capitalist relations.

These five aspects of capital's response to class struggle have been at least partially successful due to their ability to recapitulate proletarian desires. After all, even during the period of the Old Enclosures many were attracted to the possibilities of universal consumption offered by urban life and did not wait for the state thugs' arrival on the village green to head for the city. A similar point can be made about present-day socialism. For the socialist workers' desire to participate in the exchange of universal labor has been a crucial factor in the "battering down" the walls of socialism. Indeed, the allure of the world market lies not in its evident exploitative consequences but rather in the energies it unleashes for travel, communication and wealth appropriation. Post-WWII socialism was certainly unable to generate alternative models of international exchange and reproduction either in the form of a Comintern bureaucracy or Che Guevara's ideals, hence socialist internationalism on the economic plane evaporated in the current crisis.

THE SPIRAL OF STRUGGLE

Though the New Enclosures have been able to entice and divide, they have been fiercely fought and have brought about, unintentionally, an increased proletarian knowledge and autonomy. Most obviously, the planet has rung and reverberated with anti-IMF demonstrations, riots and rebellions. In 1989 alone, the streets and campuses of Venezuela, Burma, Zaire, Nigeria, and Argentina have seen confrontations between armed troops and students and workers who chant "Death to the IMF," loot foreign commodities markets, excarcerate prisoners, and burn banks. Though access to universal wealth is desired, the institutional forms of the world market that are using the "debt crisis" to create the New Enclosures are physically under a self-conscious attack throughout Africa, Latin America and Asia.

Not only is the money form of the New Enclosures being resisted, there has been a worldwide land war taking place in the 1980s. Up the Andes into Central America and Mexico there has been desperate and chronic armed struggle over the control of land (frequently referred to in the US as an aspect of the "drug problem"). In West Africa there is a micro-level of armed struggle against land seizures by the state and development banks (frequently discussed as anachronistic "tribal war"). In southern Africa, the battle over land and its control, both in town and country, is included as an aspect of "the struggle against apartheid," while in East Africa it is considered a "problem of nationalities." Land War is, of course, what the "Palestinian issue" is about, while from Afghanistan through India to Sri Lanka, the Philippines and Indonesia, proletarians have taken up arms against the New Enclosures in a wide variety of forms. But in the 1980s this Land War has not only been a rural, "third world-ist" struggle. From West Berlin, to Zurich, to Amsterdam, to London, to New York, squatters, street people and the "homeless" have battled against police, arsonists in the pay of real estate developers, and other agents of "spatial deconcentration" not simply for "housing" but for land and all that it means.

These direct, violent and frequently armed confrontations have certainly limited the pace and scope of the New Enclosures but there have been other, often unintended, consequences of the New Enclosures that will perhaps be even more central to their universal leveling. First, the New Enclosures have led to an enormous increase and intensification of proletarian knowledge of the international class composition. For example, the average West African farmer in the 1980s knows about the deals that can go down in Brooklyn, London and Venice. Second, the New Enclosures have forced an internationalism of proletarian action, since the proletariat has never been so compelled to overcome its regionalism and nationalism, as people are losing not just their plot of land but their stake in their countries. Third, the very extremities of the debt crisis and the need to organize reproduction outside of the money relation has often forced workers to develop their autonomy by imposing the task of creating a whole system of production and reproduction outside of the standard operating procedures of capitalist society.

THE MARXIST GHOST AT MIDNIGHT

These unintended consequences of the New Enclosures and their possibilities are themes near and dear to the work of Marx and Engels, and it is time now to speak of them. For one of the central ironies of the present is that at the very time when socialism is collapsing, Marx's predictions concerning the development of capitalism are being verified. Though "postist" intellectuals are now dancing on Marx's grave while "Marxists" are desperately trying to revise their curriculum vitae, Marx's theory has never been so true. What are we seeing now but the famous "immiseration of the working class," "the expansion of the world market," "universal competition among workers," and "rising organic composition of capital"? How can we understand anything about this world without using the axioms of Marx's theory of work, money and profit? Capitalists certainly cannot!

Theoretically, then, Marx's ghost still speaks truly at midnight. Strategically, however, Marx and Engels fail at this moment of the New Enclosures. It is worthwhile to explain why. The Marx of *Capital*, while recognizing the complexity of the situation, would have most likely understood the New Enclosures as he did the Old: they were fundamentally a stage in the "progressive nature" of capitalist development as it prepares the material conditions for a communist society. The two decisive tendencies in this development are: (1) it breaks down local barriers and the separation of town and country, thus producing a truly universal human being capable of benefiting from the world-wide production of cultural and material wealth, and (2) it unifies the international working class which increasingly recognizes and acts on its common interest. Consequently, for all the pain and death, the "blood and fire" of the Old Enclosures, they were inevitable and ultimately historically positive, for they accomplished "the dissolution of private property based on the labor of its owner."

By destroying the mode of production "where the laborer is the private owner of his own means of labor set in action by himself: the peasant of the land which he cultivates, the artisan of the tool which he handles as a virtuoso," the Enclosures set the stage for the creation of "capitalist private property, already practically resting on socialized production." The Enclosures, therefore, are the "protracted, violent, and difficult" transformation that makes possible the easier "expropriation of a few usurpers by the mass of people" in the communist revolution.

The problem with this analysis is simple: the New Enclosures (and probably many of the Old) are not aimed only at petty private producers and their property. They also aim to destroy communal land and space that forms an energy well of proletarian power. A Quiche Indian village in the Guatemalan hills, a tract of communally operated land in the Niger Delta, an urban neighbourhood like Tepito in Mexico City, a town surrounding a paper mill controlled by striking paperworkers like Jay, Maine, do not fit into the classic Marxist model of the Enclosures. In each of these examples we are not confronted with a number of isolated, petty producers but a staging point for proletarian attack or a logistical locus. It is plain madness to accept the demise of such villages, tracts of land, neighbourhood and towns as necessary and ultimately progressive sacrifices to the destruction of capitalism and the development of truly "universal" proletarians. Universal or not, real, living proletarians (that do not live on air) must put their feet some place, must strike from some place, must rest some place, must retreat some place. For class war does not happen on an abstract board toting up profit and loss, it is a war that needs a terrain.

Marx's righteous horror of "petty producers" and their disgusting behavior must not lead us to a loss of strategic reality under the rubric of honorific formulae. He did not see in 1867 the possibilities of proletarian power, however contradictory, in the intact communal life of millions in Africa, Asia, Oceania and the Americas. One certainly cannot find in *Capital* a call for the European proletariat to fight against the Enclosure of these communal peoples.

Similarly, Engels could not see a new communal power developing in the proletarian quarters of the new industrial cities of Europe that needed to be struggled for. To understand this strategic failure, let us look at a truly remarkable work of Engels, *The Housing Question* (1872), written a year after the Paris Commune. It is lucid, trenchant and more insightful than anything the housing and homelessness movement has recently produced. Engels seems to be describing, as if in a vision, New York of the 1980s by drawing on his observations of nineteenth-century London, Manchester, Paris and Berlin. He even describes a nineteenth century version of "spatial deconcentration" he attributes to Haussman, a Bonapartist urban developer. Haussman apparently planned "breaking long straight and broad streets through the closely-built workers' quarters and erecting big luxurious buildings on both sides of them, the intention thereby, apart from the strategic aim of making barricade fighting more difficult, being also to develop a specifically Bonapartist building trades proletariat dependent on the government and to turn the city into a pure luxury city."

But in the midst of these acute observations, Engels' actual discussion of the "housing question" is disappointing. Why? Because he puts aside his strategic standpoint, namely, how does the spatially defined class composition in a city determine working class power, to deal with two other classic Marxist points: (a) the average house rent paid by workers is simply a redistribution of surplus value between industrial capitalists and rentiers, (b) the "solution" to the housing question cannot be the promotion of home ownership since that would "bourgeoisify" workers and delay the coming of the real solution, revolution. The first point is abstract and, more or less, true, while the second reflects the horror-of-the-petty-proprietor-vacuum typical of Marx and Engels. Therefore, he nowhere takes up the defense of workers' quarters as an essential aspect of the "housing question" and an important strategic consideration of class thought.

It appears that in Engels' judgement, the housing market can totally transform the spatial composition of an urban working class and yet be irrelevant to "the housing question." Aside from being absurd, this is certainly not the view of capital's Hausmanns then and now. Certainly Engels should have realized that revolutions are not made in a heaven of ideas, they are usually made, at least in their final stages, in cities where the question of disposition of forces is crucial. Perhaps Engels' strategic neglect of working class topology was a product of the failure of the now classic revolutionary scenario of the Paris Commune played out a year before *The Housing Question* was published. More likely it was the result of a deeper categorical failure of Marxist understanding of the Enclosures that remains central to Marxism to this day. This is especially true of its "third worldist" variants that are frequently accepted by those in the frontline struggles against the New Enclosures, either as organizers of anti-IMF demos or guerrilla armies fighting for land. These forms of Marxism are now in deep crisis. At first sight the crisis of "third world" Marxism seems rooted in the collapse of its major socialist models, the Soviet Union and China, and has nothing to do with the understanding of the Enclosures both Old and New. First and foremost, therefore, the crisis appears as the end of military and economic aid that often had been provided by the socialist bloc as an aspect of "proletarian internationalism." Such a view is superficial.

"Third world" Marxists accept the notion of the progressivity of original accumulation. Consequently, even though they officially fight against the New Enclosures, they envision their party and state as carrying out their own Enclosures on their own people even more efficiently and "progressively" than the capitalists could do. They interpret communal ownership of land and the local market exchanges as being the marks of "petty bourgeois" characteristics they must extirpate. Their revolutionary action aims to nationalize land and wipe out local markets as well as kick out the IMF and the "comprador" ruling elite. Yet the first goal is an anathema to many of those people attracted by the struggle against the New Enclosures in the first place! The confusion thickens at victory where there is a tendency to create or continue the two "advanced" forms of land tenure — state plantations (Mozambique) or capitalist firms (Zimbabwe) — at the expense of communal possibilities and actualities. Inevitably the conditions for counterrevolution ripen while the impossibility of carrying out autarchic economic measures becomes clear, since the very structures that might have sustained autarchy and denied land to the "contras" have been destroyed by the revolutionary forces themselves.

As a consequence, low intensity counterrevolutionary warfare and high interest rates unravel the revolution. For it is relatively easy in the late twentieth century to practice the science of revolution and succeed. It is this ease that has made it imperative for capital, on the other side, to make sure that the consequences of winning will be catastrophe and despair. Hence the crisis of the third worldist left, which has its roots not only in the insidious demonic plans of the CIA, but also in the failure of Marx's own analysis of the Old Enclosures themselves.

In contrast, capital's most advanced public self-understanding of the New Enclosures, with the visible collapse of the socialist models and a crisis of revolutionary "third world" Marxism, is embodied in the slogan "the End of History." This phrase interprets the end of socialist states and parties as the annihilation of the driving contradiction of world history, and the triumph of the world market as the mark of a uniform planetary commodification called "Westernization" and "democracy." With no such "contradiction" there is no History of the grand narrative, of course. How seriously we should take this piece of State Department post-modernism is moot, but the scenario it suggests is simple. It returns the class struggle back to its pre-WWI situation and poses two choices to OECD workers: "liberalism" or "imperialism." The liberal moment accepts the "market mechanism" where we meet as different functions of the work process in a triage-like environment, so that upgrading our "survival skills" becomes the only goal in "life." The imperialist moment urges the internationalization of conquest and plunder whereby we reject competition by becoming accomplices of our immediate bosses in the direct exploitation of other proletarians, so that victory means a South African deal: better wages and a home of one's own ... protected by martial law, torture cells and a gun in the handbag. More probably a disgusting mix of the two would be more palatable!

THE GREENING OF THE DEAL

In the looming shadow of these bleak capitalist prospects and with the collapse of socialism, the "greens" have come forward with a global perspective calling on human aspirations transcending the market. From Earth First!'s "Think like a mountain" to Greenpeace's "Nuclear-free seas," the ecological movement seems to have been a major force in confronting the New Enclosures in the 1980s. "Green" militants have sabotaged deforestation, blown up power lines, aborted nuclear tests, and in general have played the "Luddites" of the New Enclosures, while "Green" parties in Europe attracted the support of many (who in a previous period would have joined the socialists or communists) by voicing political and ideological resistance to the grossest consequences of capitalist development. The "Greens" (along with their animal liberation allies) have brought some outlaw guts and angelic passion to the struggles of the last decade. But their class composition has limited their efforts up to now.

As we pointed out in *Strange Victories* (Midnight Notes, vol. 1 no. 1, 1979), the US anti-nuke movement in the 1970s — which is the political root of the contemporary ecological movement — had a limited class composition. It was based on the rural population living around the nuclear plants and "an additional factor": an intellectual labor force that had relocated in the rural areas around the plants after the 1960s. We also argued then that unless the anti-nuclear movement went beyond this rather limited class composition and brought the urban and industrial proletariat into the movement, the nuclear industry would not be defeated. Energy prices were the key to expanding the class composition of the movement and so it proved. The explosion of struggles against energy price hikes in the streets and highways of the US (as well as revolutions and insurrections in oil producing countries) in 1979–80 forced capital to stabilize energy prices. This sealed the doom of the US nuclear industry in this century at least.

The contemporary ecology movement, however, has not learned the secret of its predecessor's "strange victories." The peculiar dialectic between rioting petroleum junkies and antinuke angels in 1979–80 never developed into a truly proletarian movement that could have gone beyond merely managing the environmental consequences of capitalist accumulation. Ecologists in the Reagan period returned to the self-righteous ideology of "natural consciousness," morality of "good will" and a practice of "recycling" and "stewardship" of the 1970s. This movement has all the markings of Marx and Engels' petty producers' thought and manners writ large. Even the etymology of its name has echoes of the ancient Greek aristocrat's "aikos" or "hearth and home." But just as the word

"economy" surreptitiously introduces into the capitalist factory the rural patri-
archal relations of father-wife-child-slave, so too "ecology" presumes that the
earth is an "aikos" to be well managed instead of the terrain of global class struggle. For proletarians might be natives of the earth but we have no home here.

As a consequence of this political conservatism, the ecology movement
has missed an enormous historical opportunity to once again transcend its
rather limited class composition. For with the collapse of the post-WWII deal
in the US, there is finally a chance to break the tie that bound working class
wage increases in the past with the destruction of the commons. These wage
increases have been definitively denied, the deal is off, but capital is still operating as if it can use our *"lebensraum"* for its defecations. But workers are increasingly denying capital its "right to shit." For example, an important aspect
of the strike against International Paper in Jay, Maine, lies in the strikers'
support for an environmental ordinance that literally said to IP: if you demand
total control of the production process inside the plant, we demand total control of the reproduction process outside the plant. This type of action is at the
heart of a new possibility for a new ecology movement that would reject its angelic status and come to a proletarian earth. For if one generalized the Jay
workers' tactic into a struggle that denied capital the possibility of enclosing
and selectively destroying the natural commons gratis, a truly revolutionary
crisis would emerge.

Such a shift in the direction of the ecology movement would be one part of
a larger process which would transform the New Enclosures into a definitive oc-
casion of proletarian unification and capitalist catastrophe. In practice this means
the creation of individuals and organizations that can both think and act globally
and locally, which is exactly what the struggles around the New Enclosures do.
The root of this result is actualized in the struggles against the New Enclosures
that simultaneously re-appropriate and hold places from capital while opening
spaces for proletarian movement. This is why defensive localism, provincialism,
nationalism and racism appear so attractive to many in the working class at the
moment, for they seem to offer some protection against the most obvious sign of
the New Enclosures for many in North America and Europe: the arrival of the
"other" worker. But such a reaction is doomed, the more such places are sealed
off by "Whites Only" signs, the more constricted the spaces of proletarian action. There are those, on the contrary, especially in the Third World and the socialist countries, who now revel in the opening of proletarian space for movement
seeking to escape the most immediate consequences of the New Enclosures there,
wagelessness. But if they do not create places against capital at the termini of
their trajectory, they will find themselves, like the pirates of the Caribbean, continually displaced and eventually exhausted and exterminated.

The concrete task of reconstructing a new proletarian geometry is going on
in such places like New York, Boston, Zurich, Jay, Maine, Beijing and Lagos.
They find a place here in this issue.

THE LAST JUBILEE?

But can we end here with this dry hope for an abstract, almost paradoxical proletarian geometry? Have we too been infected by the post-modern anti-revolutionary malaise? This malaise is strange indeed, for with the definitive collapse of the era's three basic deals, a moment of classic revolutionary crisis opens. Yet, though at the instant of this initiation capital is most unstable, capital's fetishistic charm still seems potent. While all around us unprecedented revolutionary events unfold, positivists hail the end of revolution, the end of class struggle, the end of the Grand Proletarian Narrative or, implicitly and conversely, the total triumph of capital.

It is now time at midnight for other words and spells in the magic struggle of classes. In this paper we have reintroduced some old terms, "enclosure" and "commons." As we end let us recall another: "Jubilee." We might at first be thought slightly mad. After all, as our comrades are being hunted down, blown up, imprisoned and tortured around the globe, the very utterance of "jubilee" seems incongruous or even obscene. Is this the time for jubilation? But every struggle against enclosure and for the commons inevitably becomes a call of jubilee.

The term itself comes from the Old Testament but was revived in two central spots in the capitalist period. "Jubilee," in general, meant the abolition of slavery, the cancellation of all debt and a return of all lands to the common. It did occur periodically among ancient Mesopotamian peoples, including the Hebrews. But in the late eighteenth century the term was used in the English countryside to demand an end to enclosures while across the Atlantic African slaves used "jubilee" to demand liberation from slavery. This word thus linked the poles of trans-Atlantic struggle against capital in the pre-Marxian era. Can it do so again? Perhaps not, but the secret energies within the demand for Jubilee are far from spent. On the contrary, at this moment when the roof has been blown off all the covenants between classes, the demand to re-begin the story of humankind in common is the force that capital itself must depend upon to create a true world market. It is that force of jubilee that has led to this issue.

Down with the New Enclosures, Time for the Last Jubilee...!

---

[1] [Editor's Note: The essay first appeared as 'Introduction' to "The New Enclosures," *Midnight Notes*, 10, 1990. The present version omits introductory remarks to contributions to that volume but remains otherwise unchanged.]

2

Marx and Primitive Accumulation
The Continuous Character of Capital's "Enclosures"[1]

Massimo De Angelis

INTRODUCTION

In the last twenty years the neoliberal orthodoxy has become predominant in all major levels of government and shaped the policy recommendations of the major think tanks all around the world.

Countries have witnessed continuous massive attacks on those functions of the state, which were designed to compensate for the inadequacies and injustices of the market.

Cuts in social spending have taken of course many forms and shapes. This depended on what was the historical and socio-economic context in which they were implemented, either the "rich" countries of the North, the "poor" countries of the South or the "transitional" countries of the East. Yet, upon a cursory reading of the enormous literature on this subject, one is left with the strong sensation that there is something common between, say, the cut in unemployment benefits in Britain brought about by the need to balance the budget; the wave of privatisation in Poland, brought about by the need to dismantle state socialism; and the cuts in food subsidies in Tanzania, brought about by the need to repay foreign debt.

This paper suggests that a reinterpretation of Marx's theory of primitive accumulation may give us some important insights on the *common* social character of what *prima facie* appears to be different policies brought about by different circumstances.

According to one main traditional interpretation, Marx's concept of primitive accumulation indicates the historical process that gave birth to the preconditions of a capitalist mode of production. These preconditions refer mainly to the creation of a section of the population with no other means of livelihood but their labour power to be sold in a nascent labour market and to the accumulation of capital that may be used for nascent industries. In this conception, the adjective "primitive" corresponds to a clear-cut temporal dimension (the past), which becomes the condition for a capitalist future. Alternatively, the same concept of primitive accumulation has been interpreted as a continuous phenomenon within the capitalist mode of production, especially in connection to Marxist analyses describing the subordination of the South to the North of the world economy.

In this chapter I argue that Marx's theory of primitive accumulation may be seen to contain both an historical and a continuity argument, but in forms that depart from traditional interpretations. In the second section I briefly review the two classical approaches to primitive accumulation within the Marxist tradition. In section three I discuss Marx's definition of primitive accumulation and locate it within his broader analysis of the capitalist mode of production. This will lead to my highlighting of two major theoretical implications of Marx's idea of primitive accumulation, that is, the fact that it describes a forced *separation* between people and social means of production and that this separation can take many forms. In section four I briefly expand on the latter and survey some of the forms of primitive accumulation discussed by Marx. Finally, in section five, I return to the social meaning of primitive accumulation as identified in section three. By drawing from Marx' theoretical apparatus — mainly his analysis of the relation between subject and object, his theory of alienation, and his distinction between accumulation and primitive accumulation — I argue that primitive accumulation is necessarily present in "mature" capitalist systems and, given the conflicting nature of capitalist relations, assumes a "continuous" character. In the conclusion, I briefly discuss the political implications of this analysis.

To focus on Marx's theoretical discussion, I will abstract here from the debates around the role and meaning of "socialist primitive accumulations." Also, for the same reason I will not engage in the dissection of the meaning of the different nuances taken by the category studied when in the literature is referred to as either "original," "primitive" or "primary" accumulation. My use of "primitive accumulation" in this chapter is only a choice of convenience, as I believe this has been the most common use of the category (followed by "original" and then "primary"). Challenging this established custom should be the object of another paper.

2. A BRIEF REVIEW OF THE TRADITIONAL INTERPRETATIONS

The concept of primitive accumulation is one of those ideas that has entered the common vocabulary of Marx scholars, without having generated much controversy or theoretical debate.[2]

Within the literature it is possible to identify two main interpretative frameworks of primitive accumulation. The first one may be represented by Lenin's early study *The development of capitalism in Russia* (1899). This approach sees primitive accumulation mostly as the historical premise to the capitalist mode of production and therefore focuses on the process of separation between people and means of production in the moment of transition *between* modes of production. In his polemic against the populists (who believed that the absence of a developed market would prevent capitalist development in Russia) Lenin argued that the disappearance of the peasants and their expropriation along with that of their communities, were the conditions for the creation of the capitalist market in Russia. Lenin saw this process as inevitable and ultimately positive, although he often underlined the contradictions of this process. However, these contradictions do not include patterns of peasants' resistance against expropriation and how such resistance could have contributed to create outcomes contradicting the requirements of the development of Russian capitalism. As he did not foresee a peasant resistance, he did not foresee a Russian's "bloody legislation" (Marx 1867, p. 896) to meet that resistance.

Rosa Luxemburg's *The Accumulation of Capital* (1913) represents a different interpretation. Although she formally accepted the understanding of primitive accumulation as a one-time, one-place phenomenon leading to capitalism (for a critique, see Rosdolsky 1977, p. 279), her theoretical framework points towards a different interpretation. In Luxemburg's framework, Marx's expanded reproduction schemes are only a representation of the mathematical conditions for accumulation in the case in which there are only two classes. In reality, she contends, capitalist production must rely on third parties (peasants, small independent producers, etc.) to be commodity buyers. Thus the enforcement of exchange relations between capitalist and non-capitalist production becomes necessary to realise surplus value. However, this exchange relation clashes with the social relations of non-capitalist production. To overcome the resistance to capital that arises from this clash, capital must resort to military and political violence.

Here Luxemburg introduces a crucial thesis that, independently from the validity of her reasoning and interpretation of Marx's schemes, seems to me fundamental: the extra-economic prerequisite to capitalist production what we shall call primitive accumulation is an inherent and continuous element of modern societies and its range of action extends to the entire world. Consequently, Luxemburg is able to combine her theoretical analysis of accumulation with a political conjecture: once the whole world becomes capitalist, capitalist accumulation will have reached its historical end. Here class struggle enters the scene as a *deus ex machina* before the collapse is brought about by objective conditions. As in the case of Lenin, also for Luxemburg resistance and struggle are not *constitutive* elements of primitive accumulation, but only a possible, albeit important, by-product.

Lenin's and Luxemburg's two classic interpretations have left a mark on subsequent approaches. It is perhaps useful to label Lenin's interpretation as "historical primitive accumulation," to indicate an age, historically and temporally defined, describing the pattern of separation between people and means of production. Luxemburg's approach to primitive accumulation could be instead labelled as "inherent-continuous primitive accumulation," to indicate the fact that the characteristic extra-economic process of separation between people and means of production is a continuous and inherent process of capitalist production. Subsequent more modern interpretations seem to share the basic characteristics of these two approaches. For example, in his classic studies on the development of capitalism, Maurice Dobb uses the category of primitive accumulation to indicate a well-defined age of accumulation of property rights better known as the mercantile age:

> If any sense is to be made, therefore, of the notion of a "primitive accumulation" (in Marx's sense of the term) *prior in time* to the full flowering of capitalist production, this must be interpreted in the first place as an accumulation of capital *claims* of titles to existing assets which are accumulated primarily for speculative reasons; and secondly as accumulation in the hands of a class that, by virtue of its special position in society, is capable ultimately of transforming these hoarded titles to wealth into actual means of production. In other words, when one speaks of accumulation in an historical sense, one must be referring to the *ownership* of assets, and to a *transfer* of ownership, and not to the quantity of tangible instruments of production in existence. (Dobb 1963, p. 178)

According to Dobb, therefore, primitive accumulation is accumulation "in an historical sense." It is worth noticing that also Paul Sweezy, Dobb's main opponent in the famous debate on the transition from feudalism to capitalism published in *Science and Society* 1950–53, acknowledges Dobb's "excellent treatment of the essential problems of the period of original accumulation" (Sweezy 1950, p. 157). The now historic debate on "transition" (collected in Hilton 1978) and its later developments and transfigurations such as the Brenner debate on the pages of the journal *Past and Present* of the 1970s (collected in Aston and Philperin 1985) and later exchanges in *Science and Society* (Gottlieb 1984; Laibman 1984; Sweezy 1986; McLennon 1986) is characterised by a general common acceptance of this historical definition of primitive accumulation.

Different from Dobb's approach of primitive accumulation as an historically prior period, is the approach by Samir Amin, which is closer to the notion of inherent and continuous primitive accumulation that occurs through what Amin defines transfer of value within the world economy:

> Relations between the formations of the "developed" or advanced world (the centre), and those of the underdeveloped world (the periphery) are affected by transfers of value, and these constitute the essence of the problem of accumulation on a world scale. Whenever the capitalist mode

of production enters into relations with pre-capitalist modes of production, and subjects these to itself, transfers of value take place from the pre-capitalist to the capitalist formations, as a result of the mechanisms of *primitive accumulation*. These mechanisms do not belong only to the pre-history of capitalism; they are contemporary as well. It is these forms of primitive accumulation, modified but persistent, to the advantage of the centre, that form the domain of the theory of accumulation on a world scale. (Amin 1974, p. 3)

Another interpretation within this general framework may also include Waller-stein's (1979) notion of a world-system. The continuous character of primitive accumulation in these accounts stresses objective mechanisms of accumulation and circulation of capital. More recently David Harvey (2003) builds on Luxemburg's position, and argues that capital needs "accumulation by dispossession" in order to overcome crises of overproduction. In his view, "what accumulation by dispossession does is to release a set of assets (including labour power) at very low (and in some instances zero) cost. Overaccumulated capital can seize hold of such assets and immediately turn them to profitable use." (Harvey 2003, p. 149) In this way, capital will be benefiting from lower costs and will overcome the overaccumulation crisis until the next round of enclosures is required.

There is a theoretical weakness in Harvey's turning of the problematic of "enclosures" into one of "accumulation by dispossession." This term, although evocative of the horrors of ripping apart communities, expropriating land and other means of life, is ultimately theoretically weak, since it posits "dispossession" as a *means* of accumulation, rather than as what accumulation is all about. Indeed, in the context of accumulation of which *both* continuous (and spatialised) enclosures and market disciplinary processes are two constituent moments, separation of producers and means of production means, as we will discuss in more details later, that the "objective conditions of living labour appear as *separated, independent* values opposite living labour capacity as subjective being, which therefore appears to them only as a value of *another kind*" (Marx 1858, p. 461).

A careful examination of Marx's definition of primitive accumulation allows us to critically appraise the historical and continuous arguments and reformulating them politically. The crucial idea at the core of Marx's approach is the concept of *separation between producers and means of production* (in what follows I will mostly refer to this simply as *separation*). This concept, when inserted within the contrasting logic of boundless accumulation of capital and people struggles for freedom and dignity, not only helps us to describe the recurrent nature of "primitive accumulation," but also points at the central political issue of any alternative to capitalism: that of the *direct access* to means of existence.

3. MARX'S CONCEPT OF PRIMITIVE ACCUMULATION

3.1. The definition of primitive accumulation

In the eight chapters of Part Eight of Volume One of *Capital*, Marx discusses "the so-called Primitive Accumulation." For any given time-period, the process of accumulation presupposes of course that some pre-accumulated capital was thrown into the process of production. It seems therefore that capitalist production as a whole presupposes some "original" or "primitive" accumulation. Although he never uses the term, Adam Smith was the first to refer to this notion by claiming that "the accumulation of stock" is a precondition for the division of labour (Smith 1776, p. 277) and, consequently, for the improvement of the productive power of labour. Marx's approach to primitive accumulation appears from the start linked to the different theoretical meaning he gives to the category of capital. The notion of primitive accumulation is based on the notion of capital as class relation, rather than capital as "stock":

> The *capital-relation* presupposes a complete separation between the workers and the ownership of the conditions for the realisation of their labour (Marx 1867, p. 874, my emphasis).

Given the meaning of capital as class relation, it follows therefore that

> the process...which creates the *capital-relation* can be nothing other than the process which divorces the worker from the ownership of the conditions of his own labour; it is a process which operates two transformations, whereby the social means of subsistence and production are turned into capital, and the immediate producers are turned into wage-labourers (Marx 1867, p. 874, my emphasis).

Thus, the

> so-called primitive accumulation...is nothing else than the historical process of divorcing the producer from the means of production (Marx 1867, pp. 874–75).

We can also find indication of Marx's emphasis on class relations in the structure of this section of *Capital*. Marx dedicates two chapters of this section on the formation of the working class (Chs. 27 and 28) and three chapters on the formation of the bourgeoisie (Chs. 29, 30 and 31).

There are three central points that I believe are key in understanding Marx's approach to primitive accumulation. The first is that the *separation* of producers and means of production is a common character of *both* accumulation and primitive accumulation. The second is that this *separation* is a central category (if not *the* central category) of Marx's critique of political economy.

The third is that the difference between accumulation and primitive accumulation, not being a substantive one, is a difference in the conditions and forms in which this *separation* is implemented. In what follows I analyse these three aspects in sequence.

3.2. Separation and the secret of (primitive) accumulation

The idea of *separation* applies to both accumulation and primitive accumulation. Marx is precise on this. In Volume 3 of *Capital* he stresses that accumulation proper is nothing else than the primitive accumulation that he defined in Volume 1 in terms of the *separation* "raised to a higher power" (Marx 1894, p. 354). In the *Theories of Surplus Value* he is even more precise, writing that accumulation "reproduces the *separation* and the independent existence of material wealth as against labour on an ever increasing scale" (Marx 1971, p. 315, my emphasis), and therefore "merely presents as a *continuous process* what in *primitive accumulation* appears as a distinct historical process" (Marx 1971, p. 271; and pp. 311–12). Again, in the *Grundrisse* he states: "Once this *separation* is given, the production process can only produce it anew, reproduce it, and reproduce it on an expanded scale" (Marx 1858, p. 462, my emphasis).

3.3. The meaning and centrality of "separation" in Marx's theory

It is known that Marx's own method of investigation starts from "the laws of bourgeois economy...[as] a key to the understanding of the past" rather than from the "*real history of the relations of production*" (Marx 1858, pp. 460–61). Thus, understanding what Marx meant by *separation* in the context of capital's accumulation enables us to appreciate the meaning he gives to the "original" or primitive separation.

In the context of accumulation, separation of producers and means of production means essentially that the "objective conditions of living labour appear as *separated, independent* values opposite living labour capacity as subjective being, which therefore appears to them only as a value of *another kind*" (Marx 1858, p. 461). The separation of producers and means of production at the social level means the positing of living labour and conditions of production as *independent values* standing in opposition with each other:

> The objective conditions of living labour capacity are presupposed as having an existence independent of it, as the objectivity of a subject distinct from living labour capacity and standing independently over against it; the reproduction and *realization*, i.e. the expansion of these *objective conditions*, is therefore at the same time their own reproduction and new pro-

duction as the wealth of an alien subject indifferently and independently standing over against labour capacity. What is reproduced and produced anew is not only the *presence* of these objective conditions of living labour, *but also their presence as independent values, i.e. values belonging to an alien subject, confronting this living labour capacity* (Marx 1858, p. 462).

This *separation* therefore is a fundamental condition for Marx's theory of reification, of the transformation of subject into object. In other words, because of this *separation* "the objective conditions of labour attain a subjective existence *vis-à-vis* living labour capacity" (Marx 1858, p. 462). This meant that the means of production are subjected to the drive towards self-valorisation and self-expansion, and this, from the perspective of capital, is all that counts. On the other hand living labour, the "subjective being" *par excellence*, is turned into a thing among things, "it is merely a *value* of a particular use value *alongside* the conditions of its own realisation as *values* of another use value" (Marx 1858, p. 462). The specificity of this reified subject – living labour — is that

> [t]he material on which it works is *alien* material; the instrument is likewise an *alien* instrument; its labour appears as a mere accessory to their substance and hence objectifies itself in things not *belonging to it*. Indeed, living labour itself appears as *alien vis-à-vis* living labour capacity, whose labour it is, whose own life's expression it is, for it has been surrendered to capital in exchange for objectified labour, for the product of labour itself (Marx 1858, p. 462).

The idea of *separation* therefore strictly echoes Marx's analysis of alienated labour, as labour alienated from the object of production, the means of production, the product, and the other producers (Marx 1844). The opposition that we have seen is implicit in this definition, is of course a clashing opposition expressing a "specific relationship of production, a specific social relationship in which the owners of the conditions of production treat living labour-power as a *thing*" (Marx 1863–66, p. 989)[3]. These same owners are regarded only as "capital personified," in which capital is understood as having "one sole driving force, the drive to valorize itself, to create surplus-value, to make its constant part, the means of production, absorb the greatest possible amount of surplus labour" (Marx 1867, p. 342). The concept of *separation* enables us to clarify Marx's reference to capital accumulation as accumulation of social relations: "The capitalist process of production...seen as a total, connected process, i.e. a process of reproduction, produces not only commodities, not only surplus-value, but it also produces and reproduces the capital-relation itself; on the one hand the capitalist, on the other the wage-labourer" (Marx 1867, p. 724).

3.4. The distinction between accumulation and primitive accumulation

Having defined the common character of both accumulation *and* primitive accumulation, Marx is of course also eager to point out their distinctiveness. As opposed to accumulation proper, what "may be called primitive accumulation…is the historical basis, instead of the historical result, of specifically capitalist production" (Marx 1867, p. 775). While sharing the same principle — *separation* — the two concepts point at two different *conditions* of existence. The latter implies the *ex novo production* of the *separation*, while the latter implies the *reproduction* — on a greater scale — of the same *separation*:

> It is in fact this divorce between the conditions of labour on the one hand and the producers on the other that forms the concept of capital, as this arises with primitive accumulation…subsequently appearing as a constant process in the accumulation and concentration of capital, before it is finally expressed here as the centralization of capitals already existing in few hands, and the decapitalization of many (Marx 1894, pp. 354–5).

The key difference thus resides for Marx not so much in the timing of the occurrence of this separation — although a sequential element is naturally always present — rather in the *conditions and circumstances* in which this separation is enforced. In the *Grundrisse* for example, Marx stresses the distinction between the conditions of capital's arising (becoming), and the conditions of capital's existence (being). The former "disappear as real capital arises," while the latter do not appear as "conditions of its arising, but as results of its presence" (Marx 1858, pp. 460–1).

Marx is emphasising here a simple but crucial point: "Once developed historically, capital itself creates the conditions of its existence (not as conditions for its arising, but as results of its being)" (Marx 1858, p. 459), and therefore it drives to reproduce (at increasing scale) the separation between means of production and producers. However, the *ex novo* production of the separation implies social forces that are posited outside the realm of impersonal "pure" economic laws. The *ex novo* separation of means of production and producers corresponds to the *ex novo* creation of the *opposition* between the two, to the *ex novo* foundation of the specific alien character acquired by labour in capitalism.

This is the element of novelty, of "originality" that Marx seems to indicate when he stresses that while accumulation relies *primarily* on "the silent compulsion of economic relations [which] sets the seal on the domination of the capitalist over the worker," in the case of primitive accumulation the separation is imposed *primarily* through "[d]irect extra-economic force" (Marx 1867, pp. 899–900), such as the state (Marx 1867, p. 900), particular sections of social classes (Marx 1867, p. 879), etc. We can say therefore that primitive accumulation for Marx is a social process instigated by some social actor (the state, particular social classes, etc.) aimed at the people who have some form of direct access to the means of production. This social process often takes the form of a strategy that aims to separate them from the means of production.

The above discussion allows us to explicate two broad theoretical cornerstones towards a reformulation of Marx's theory of primitive accumulation. First, separation does not only indicate the rupture *between* modes of production in an epochal period of "transition." This implies that primitive accumulation cannot be confined to a distant past. In Marx's interpretation I am proposing there is nothing indicating that this separation may not occur any time, even within a "mature" capitalist mode of production, when the conditions for an *ex novo* separation are posited. I will discuss this issue in more details in section 5, while assessing the elements of continuity of Marx's theory of primitive accumulation within the capitalist mode of production.

Second, insisting on the role of *separation* in the definition of primitive accumulation and stressing that the distinction between accumulation and primitive accumulation is based on the conditions of implementation of this separation opens the way for investigating what are the different possible forms of primitive accumulation. This of course may lead to the formulation of a taxonomy of primitive accumulation that cannot be discussed here. In section 4 I instead discuss some of the variants of primitive accumulation proposed by Marx.

4. DIFFERENT FORMS OF PRIMITIVE ACCUMULATION IN MARX

It is well known that Marx's discussion of the process of land enclosure in England, was a mere *illustration* of primitive accumulation, an illustration specific to England.[4] Furthermore, even Marx's discussion of primitive accumulation in England takes us by default to distant lands, to the extent these areas are linked and subordinated to the process of accumulation in England.[5] A typical example is the slave trade. Between 1690 and 1721 new ports were created (as in Liverpool), while old ones gained new life as result of flourishing slave trade (as in Bristol). The number of transported slaves jumped from 27,500 in the seventeenth century to an estimate of between 40,000 and 100,000 in the XVIII Century (Linebaugh 1991, p. 46). Marx has no difficulty in pointing out that "Liverpool grew fat on the basis of the slave trade" and that indeed "this was its method of primitive accumulation" (Marx 1867, p. 924). However, this method of primitive accumulation did not entail a classic-Marxist model of transition applied to Africa from feudalism to capitalism. This model, that was common Marxist orthodoxy until not long ago, by emphasising the role played by land enclosures in the "transition" from feudal to a capitalist mode of production in England, has contributed to turn the concept of primitive accumulation into a corner-stone of a monumental building generally referred to as "stage theory."[6] Instead, the example of the slave trade shows that primitive accumulation may occur through the interaction between North and South, an international division of labour, the destruction of African communities, and enslavement. Marx was of course very well aware of all these forms. Therefore, in this case, the "historical process of separating the producers from the means of production" revealed characteristics and dimensions quite different from the stereotypical representation of land enclosure portraying the passage from "feudalism" to "capitalism" in Europe.

Here primitive accumulation is consistent with an understanding of the capitalist economy as *a* world economy, in a Braudelian sense (Braudel 1982), in which accumulation in one place may correspond to primitive accumulation in another place, in which the *ex novo* production of the separation can be the condition of the *reproduction* of the same separation in another interlinked place. At this junction, we can fully appreciate the insights provided by the interpretation we labelled the "continuous-inherent" primitive accumulation.

Marx refers to other forms of primitive accumulation. These are the ones obtained through the manipulation of money by the State. Marx regards public debt, international credit system and taxes, as fundamental means to further primitive accumulation. Public debt

> becomes one of the most powerful levers of primitive accumulation. As with the stroke of an enchanter's wand, it endows unproductive money with the power of creation and thus turns it into capital, without forcing it to expose itself to the troubles and risks inseparable from its employment in industry or even in usury (Marx 1867, p. 919).

Complementary to public debt is the modern fiscal system,

> whose pivot is formed by taxes on the most necessary means of subsistence (and therefore by increases in their prices), thus contains within itself the germ of automatic progression. Over-taxation is not an accidental occurrence, but rather a principle. In Holland, therefore, where this system was first inaugurated, the great patriot, De Witt, extolled it in his *Maxims* as the best system for making the wage-labourer submissive, frugal, industrious...and overburdened with work (Marx 1867, p. 921).

All the same, the international credit system that grows along national debt

> often conceals one of the sources of primitive accumulation in this or that people...A great deal of capital, which appears today in the United States without any birth-certificate, was yesterday, in England, the capitalised blood of children (Marx 1867, p. 920).

All these examples point at the fact that primitive accumulation for Marx does not assume only the form of direct land enclosure as in the process of English primitive accumulation, but it also occurs through other means. A brief survey of the current literature on the link between third World debt and widespread poverty reveals that the features of XVIII–XIX Centuries capitalism may well have a striking resemblance to those of XXI Century capitalism, once of course the different historical contexts are taken into consideration.

5. THE CONTINUOUS CHARACTER OF PRIMITIVE ACCUMULATION

5.1. Introduction

In a recent important study Michael Perelman (2000, ch. 2) supports the idea of the continuous character of primitive accumulation in Marx along three main lines of interpretation[7] and provide some textural evidence[8]. Also, Perelman points out that Marx wanted to de-emphasise the concept of primitive accumulation for a political and strategic, rather than theoretical, reason.

Excessive emphasis on primitive accumulation would have distracted the reader from the "silent compulsion of the market" (Perelman 2000, p. 31). The argument is that Marx wanted to stress the role of market forces, where market forces have replaced primitive accumulation as a disciplinary device enforcing the separation between labour and means of production. Although this interpretation may explain Marx's relatively less extended discussion of the category of primitive accumulation, it does not address the question of the extent to which Marx's theoretical framework is compatible with the continuous character of the primitive accumulation.

5.2. Continuity, class conflict and communism

The interpretation of Marx's analysis of primitive accumulation presented thus far has revealed two basic interconnected points: first, primitive accumulation is the *ex-novo* production of the separation between producers and means of production and therefore, in certain conditions, it represents a strategy. Second, this social process or strategy can take different forms. The historicity contained in the concept is revealed not so much by the fact that primitive accumulation occurs *before* the capitalist mode of production — although this is *also* the case — but that it is the *basis*, the presupposition, the basic precondition which is necessary *if* accumulation of capital must occur. It must be noted that this last definition is Marx's own and it is more general than the one adopted by the classical "historical interpretation," and therefore it includes it. This is because if primitive accumulation is defined in terms of the preconditions it satisfies for the accumulation of capital, its temporal dimension includes in principle both the period of the establishment of a capitalist mode of production *and* the preservation and expansion of the capitalist mode of production *any time the producers set themselves as an obstacle to the reproduction of their separation to the means of production*, separation understood in terms described before.

Another way to put it would be through Karl Polanyi's concept of "double movement" (Polanyi 1944). On one side there is the historical movement of the market, a movement that has no inherent limit and that therefore threatens society's very existence. On the other there is society's natural propensity to defend itself, and therefore to create institutions for its protection. In Polanyi's terms, the continuous element of Marx's primitive accumulation could be identified in those social processes or sets of strategies aimed at dismantling those institutions that protect society from the market. The crucial element of continuity in the reformulation of Marx's theory of primitive accumulation arises therefore once we acknowledge the *other* movement of society.

We have derived the strategic character of primitive accumulation from its definition: "the historical process of divorcing the producer from the means of production," while in the definition of accumulation this divorcing occurred at increasing scale. In Marx, this latter divorcing is clearly the result of the driving force of what we may call a main historical subject — albeit a depersonalised one — that is, capital, which Marx repeatedly defines in term of its endless drive for self-expansion, accumulation.[9] This endless drive for expansion is bound to clash against such limits as those posed by geographical areas unaffected by capitalist production or at its margin. Examples of expansion in geographical areas include for example the already cited slave trade mentioned by Marx, and Luxemburg's discussion may at least be seen as highlighting this insight within Marx's text.[10] However, Marx often refers to capital also as *reactive* vis-à-vis those social forces that pose a limit to accumulation. Especially, capital is seen as reacting against the effects of various struggles engaged by what Marx believed was the historical subject of social transformation *par excellence* — the working class.[11]

The clash of these two historical forces reveals the oppositional nature of the "present form of production relations" which "gives signs of its becoming — foreshadowing of the future" (Marx 1858, p. 461). We have seen that Marx defines the oppositional nature embedded in capitalist relation of production in terms of the separation between producers and means of production. Thus, the definition of primitive accumulation — of the *origin* of this *separation* — is linked to the heart of Marx's vision of a human society, as it mirrors a vision of its opposite: that the producers have *direct* access to the means of production (it goes without saying that the latter refers to a condition of *collective* production and not merely to an individual market strategy of survival which is alternative to wage labour). For Marx, direct access to the means of production can certainly acquire many forms, some of which can historically coexist also with forms of exploitation (see for some examples Marx 1867, pp. 170–71). However, they all show different degrees of the thing, which is with no doubt so central in Marx's thinking: producers' autonomy and self-determination in the organisation and administration of social labour. Thus, primitive accumulation defined in terms of *separation* (which is treated in the last section of Volume One of *Capital*) is only a mirrored image of Marx's leap into an hypothetical post-capitalist society (suggested in the first section of the same volume), in which he imagines "an *association* of free men, *working with the means of production held in common*, and expending their many different forms of labour-power in full self-awareness as one single social labour force" (Marx 1867, p. 171, my emphasis).

In a previous section I have indicated that the alienated character of labour results from the reproduction of the separation between producers and means of production within the accumulation process. The alienated character of labour is of course one of the main sources of inherent and continuous class conflict within Marx's theory of capitalism. Also, its transcendence is for Marx the main horizon along which he can envisage a post-capitalist society. Within Marx's theoretical and critical framework therefore, the divorcing embedded in the definition of primitive accumulation can be understood not only as origin of capital vis-à-vis pre-capitalist social relations, but also as a reassertion of capital's priorities vis-à-vis those social forces that run against this *separation*. Thus, pre-capitalist spaces of autonomy (the common land of the English yeomen; the commons of Africa targeted by the slave merchants) are not the only objects of primitive accumulation strategies. Objects of primitive accumulation also become any given balance of power among classes that constitutes a "rigidity" for furthering the capitalist process of accumulation, or that runs in the opposite direction.

Since for Marx working-class struggles are a continuous element of the capitalist relation of production, capital must continuously engage in strategies of primitive accumulation to recreate the "basis" of accumulation itself.

This element of continuity of primitive accumulation is not only consistent with Marx's empirical analysis describing the process of primitive accumulation, but seems also to be contained in his theoretical framework. This because accumulation is equal to primitive accumulation "to a higher degree," and "once capital exists, the capitalist mode of production itself evolves in such a way that it maintains and reproduces this *separation* on a constantly increasing scale *until the historical reversal takes place*" (Marx 1971, p. 271, my emphasis). Thus, the "historical reversal" is set as a *limit* to accumulation, and primitive accumulation is set as a challenge — from capital's perspective — to that "historical reversal." To the extent class conflict creates bottlenecks to the accumulation process in the direction of reducing the distance between producers and means of production, any strategy used to recuperate or reverse this movement of association is entitled with the categorisation — consistently with Marx's theory and definition — of primitive accumulation. Marx's text is quite clear on this. As cited earlier — I reproduce here for convenience — accumulation relies on "the silent compulsion of economic relations [which] sets the seal on the domination of the capitalist over the worker." In this case,

> [d]irect extra-economic force is still of course used, but only in exceptional cases. In the ordinary run of things, the worker can be left to the

"natural laws of production," i.e. it is possible to rely on his dependence on capital, which springs from the conditions of production themselves, and is guaranteed in perpetuity by them (Marx 1867, pp. 899–900).

Differently

during the historical genesis of capitalist production. The rising bourgeoisie needs the power of the state, and uses it to "regulate" wages, i.e. to force them into the limits suitable for making a profit, to lengthen the working day, and to keep the worker himself at his historical level of dependence. This is an essential aspect of so-called primitive accumulation (Marx 1867, pp. 899–900).

The key difference between "the ordinary run of things" and "primitive accumulation" therefore seems to be the existence of "a working class which by education, tradition and habit looks upon the requirements of that mode of production as self-evident natural laws" (ibid.). Therefore, insofar as the working class accepts capital's requirement as natural laws, accumulation does not need primitive accumulation. However, working class struggles represent precisely a rupture in that acceptance, a non-conformity to the laws of supply and demand, a refusal of subordination to the "ordinary run of things." When this happens, two interrelated phenomena follow in Marx's opinion.

First the ideological use of political economy to legitimise the "ordinary run of things," or the "natural laws of capitalist production":

as soon as the workers learn the secret of why it happens that the more they work, the more alien wealth they produce…as soon as, by setting up trade unions, etc., they try to organize planned co-operation between the employed and the unemployed in order to obviate or to weaken the ruinous effects of this natural law of capitalist production on their class, so soon does capital and its sycophant, political economy, cry out at the infringement of the "eternal" and so to speak "sacred" law of supply and demand (Marx 1867, p. 793).

To the extent we identify ideology as a form of social *power* (Bobbio 1990), then this ideological use of political economy at this juncture is in itself an extra-economic means to *re*-impose the "ordinary run of things."

Second, Marx of course emphasises other, more material "extra-economic means":

Every combination between employed and unemployed disturbs the "pure" action of this law. But on the other hand, as soon as…adverse circumstances prevent the creation of an industrial reserve army, and with it the absolute dependence of the working class upon the capitalist class, capital, along with its platitudinous Sancho Panza, rebels against the "sacred" law of supply and demand, and tries to make up for its inadequacies by forcible means (Marx 1867, p. 794).

It follows therefore that not only is "primitive accumulation… the historical basis, instead of the historical result, of specifically capitalist production" (Marx 1867, p. 775) but it also acquires a continuous character — depended on the inherent continuity of social conflict — within capitalist production. In the next two sections I provide two short illustrations of these elements of continuity extrapolated from Marx's text.

5.3. Illustration I: The continuity of primitive accumulation and the enclosures

The first example does not entail a "mature" capitalist mode of production, but serves as a better way to point out the conceptual relevance of class struggle for the definition of primitive accumulation in Marx. I take this example from an event that took place during the "classic" period of English land enclosure. On Sunday 1 April 1649 a small group of poor men collected on St. George's Hill just outside London and at the edge of the Windsor Great Forest, hunting ground of the king and the royalty. They started digging the land as a "symbolic assumption of ownership of the common lands" (Hill 1972, p. 110). Within ten days, their number grew to four or five thousand. One year later, "the colony had been forcibly dispersed, huts and furniture burnt, the Diggers chased away from the area" (Hill 1972, p. 113). This episode of English history could be consistently added to Marx's Chapter 28, entitled "Bloody Legislation against the Expropriated." Yet, while most of that chapter deals with Tudors' legislation aimed at criminalizing and repressing popular behaviour induced by the expropriation of land (vagrancy, begging, theft), this episode goes a step further, by making clear that primitive accumulation acquires meaning *vis-à-vis* patterns of resistance and struggle.

This episode entails the active and organised activity of a mass of urban and landless poor aimed at the direct re-appropriation of land for its transformation into common land. Paraphrasing Marx, it was an activity aimed at "*associating* the producer with the means of production." It is clear therefore that the force used by the authorities to disperse the Diggers, can be understood, consistently with Marx's theory, as an act of "primitive accumulation," because it reintroduces the separation between producers and means of production. Although Marx did not include this episode in his treatment of primitive accumulation, in Chapter 28 he does refer to a handful of cases in which struggles are counterpoised to state legislation, which either represents a "retreat" of capital vis-à-vis these struggles[12] or an attempt to contain them.[13]

5.4. Illustration II: The continuity of primitive accumulation and the "social barrier" against capital

Another example involves a "mature" capitalist production and takes us to Marx's description of the relation between absolute and relative surplus value in the case of the limit to the working day.

At the end of Chapter 10 of *Capital* on the working day, Marx points out how working class actions are responsible for erecting a "social barrier" on the extension of the working day.

> For "protection" against the serpent of their agonies, the workers have to put their heads together and, as a class, compel the passing of a law, an all-powerful social barrier by which they can be prevented from selling themselves and their families into slavery and death by voluntary contract with capital. In the place of the pompous catalogue of the "inalienable rights of man" there steps the modest Magna Carta of the legally limited working day, which at least makes clear "when the time which the worker sells is ended, and when his own begins" (Marx 1867, p. 416).

This "all-powerful social barrier" brought about by workers' struggles and which defines the extension of the working day, sets a limit to the extraction of absolute surplus value. The definition of a social barrier evokes the idea of a *social limit* beyond which capital cannot go in furthering the opposition of dead to living labour. In this sense, this social barrier is a form of "social common" because it sets a limit to the extension, the scale of the separation between producers and means of production.

It is by "putting their heads together...as a class," and enforcing a limit to the working day that the producers assert their human needs vis-à-vis the alienating system of production and close the gap that separates them from the means of production.[14]

At this point, capital introduces machinery,[15] that is "the most powerful weapon for suppressing strikes, those periodic revolts of the working class against the autocracy of capital" (Marx 1867, p. 562)[16]. The introduction of machinery *at this junction* represents an act of accumulation, of recreation of the separation at a greater scale beyond the limit posed by the "social barrier." By rationalising the working day, restructuring the work process and dismissing the work force, the introduction of machinery aims at bypassing that "social barrier" that was erected and therefore recreate the *separation* between forces of production and producers at a greater scale. In so doing it intensifies labour to the extent that "the denser hour of the 10-hour working day contains more labour, i.e. expended labour power, than the more porous hour of the 12-hour working day" (Marx 1867, p. 534). It goes without saying that any attempt to repeal the law that sets the extension of the working day would be instead an act of *ex novo* production of that separation, an act of primitive accumulation.

6. Conclusion

The interpretative framework here provided stressed the continuity of primitive accumulation and its fundamental persistence in mature capitalist economies. The foundation of this continuity is found once we recognise what Marx calls the "oppositional nature of the capitalist-relation." The result is, I believe, a picture of Marx's theory of primitive accumulation which gives us insights into the essential character of capitalist accumulation itself — the divorce between producers and means of production — and about the limits posed on capitalist accumulation by social struggles. Reformulating Marx's theory of primitive accumulation in this way contributes to rescue Marx's theory of capitalist mode of production from its political irrelevance at best and its instrumentality for capitalist oppression at worst. Indeed, to consider "primitive accumulation" as an historical phase rather than a recurrent strategy vis-à-vis the continuous character of struggles, has opened the way even for "revolutionaries" to welcome it and promote it as a necessary stage towards "socialism."

The emphasis here put on the basic conceptual similarity between those processes occurred in the period regarded by historians as the dawn of capitalist era and the age regarded by simple common sense as a mature capitalist system, did not mean to downplay the obvious remarkable differences. The modern forms of primitive accumulation occur in contexts quite different from the ones in which the English enclosure movement or the slave trade took place. Yet, to emphasise their common character allows us to interpret the new without forgetting the hard lessons of the old. Socio-economic rights and entitlements are in most cases the result of past battles. State institutions have developed and attempted to accommodate many of these rights and entitlements with the priorities of a capitalist system. The entitlements and rights guaranteed by the post-war welfare state for example, can be understood as the institutionalisation in particular *forms* of social commons. Together with high growth policies, the implementation of full employment policies and the institutionalisation of productivity deals, the welfare state was set to accommodate people's expectations after two world wars, the Soviet revolution, and a growing international union movement. Therefore, the global current neoliberal project, which in various ways targets the social commons created in the post war period set itself as a modern form of enclosure, dubbed by some as "new enclosures."[17]

Thus, the understanding of the continuous character of enclosures points to two crucial *political* questions. First, the fact that there is a common ground between different phenomenal forms of neoliberal polices, and that peoples of the North, East and South are facing possibly phenomenally different but substantially similar strategies of separations from the means of existence. Second, it allows us to identify the broad essential question that any discussion on alternatives within the growing global anti-capitalist movement must pose: the issue of the direct access of the means of existence, production and communication, the issue of *commons*.

NOTES

1 [Editor's Note: This is the revised version of an essay that first appeared in *The Commoner*, no. 2, 2001.

2 This is not the case for the *application* of this concept to historical descriptions of feudalism to capitalism. As I will briefly discuss later, this has generated much debate.

3 For a more detailed analysis of the connection between reification and commodity-fetishism in Marx's analysis, see De Angelis (1996).

4 In a letter to the editorial board of the *Otechestvenniye Zapitski* of November 1877, Marx clarifies how "[t]he chapter on primitive accumulation claims no more than to trace the path by which, in Western Europe, the capitalist economic order emerged from the womb of the feudal economic order. It therefore presents the historical movement which, by divorcing the producers from their means of production, converted the former into wage-labourers (proletarians in the modern sense of the word) and the owners of the latter into capitalists" (Marx 1878, p. 135).

5 The narrow geographical confinement often implicit in the traditional historical approach has of course been at the basis of some criticism. For example in his famous study on African underdevelopment, Walter Rodney (1972, p. 101) writes: "The ideological gulf is responsible for the fact that most bourgeois scholars write about phenomena such as the industrial revolution in England without once mentioning the European slave trade as a factor of primary accumulation of capital...But even Marxists (as prominent as Maurice Dobb and F.J. Hobsbawn) for many years concentrated an examining the evolution of capitalism out of feudalism inside Europe, with only marginal reference to the massive exploitation of Africans, Asians and American Indians."

6 According to the "stage theory" interpretation, Marx divides world history into stages, each of which has its own economic and social structure. The transition from an "inferior" to a "superior" stage must follow a logical path, and it is not possible to skip stages of development. This interpretation, which was dominant until not long ago, constitutes the basic framework of classic historical materialism. It is linked to the historical interpretation of primitive accumulation, in that a temporally clear-cut primitive accumula-

tion would create the conditions for the transition to the capitalist stage of world history. Unfortunately, Marx wrote against turning the English experience into a model for the universal history of social and economic development. For example, in the French edition of *Capital*, the last edited by Marx himself, Marx clearly limits his analysis of primitive accumulation to *Western* Europe (Smith 1995, p. 54). In a clear statement against universal stage theory, Marx's famous reply to Vera Zasulich is self-explicatory: "The 'historical inevitability' of a complete separation of…the producer from the means of production…is therefore *expressly* restricted to *the countries of Western Europe*" (Marx 1881, p. 124).

7 These are the following: first, the material in part 8 does not appear to be qualitatively different from what is found in the previous chapter entitled "the general theory of capitalist accumulation." Second, "When Marx's study of primitive accumulation finally reached the subject of Edward Gibbon Wakefield, Marx did not qualify his appreciation of the father of modern colonial theory by limiting its relevance to an earlier England. Instead, he insisted that Wakefield offered significant insights into the England where Marx lived and worked" (Perelman 2000, Ch. 2: 4). Third, "read in this light, Marx's letter to Mikhailovsky is also consistent with the idea that the importance of primitive accumulation was not what it taught about backward societies, but about the most advanced societies…Marx himself, referring to the institutions of Mexico, insisted that '[t]he nature of capital remains the same in its developed as in its underdeveloped forms' (Marx 1867, p. 400n)" (Perelman 2000, Ch. 2: 4).

8 For example, in relation to the discussion of the falling rate of profit, Marx's reference to "expropriating the final residue of direct producers who still have something left to expropriate" (Marx 1894: 348). This of course presupposes that the process of expropriation, of *ex-novo* separation between producers and means of production, is not completed within a mature capitalist society, one in which the rate of profit is subjected to the tendency to fall.

9 For a discussion of Marx's notion of boundlessness of accumulation see De Angelis (1995).

10 There are many other examples in referred to by radical scholars. Perelman (2000) cites household economy as a target of primitive accumulation, as well as the expropriation of other commons such as turning traditional holidays into working days. Federici (1992), Fortunati (1981) and Mies (1986) among others, refer to the expropriation of women's bodies, that is of sexual and reproductive powers of women, for the accumulation of labour power that suits capital's valorisation requirements. Federici (1988) refers

to the witch-hunt terror in the sixteenth and seventeenth centuries that opened the way for these state attempts to control demographic rates and the reproduction of labour power.

11 Here enters Marx's broader approach in which the class struggle plays a central role (Cleaver 1979; Caffentzis 1995; De Angelis 1995).

12 "The barbarous laws against combinations of workers collapsed in 1825 in the face of the threatening attitude of the proletariat" (Marx 1867, p. 903).

13 "During the very first storms of the revolution, the French bourgeoisie dared to take away from the workers the right of association they had just acquired" (Marx 1867, p. 903).

14 This separation, as we have seen, is realised by the degree in which dead labour commands living labour, that is "the means of production utilize the worker, so that work appears only as an instrument which enables a specific *quantum of value*, i.e. a specific mass of objectified labour through the agency of living labour. *Capital* utilizes the *worker*; the *worker* does not utilize *capital*, and only *articles which utilize the worker* and hence possess *independence*, a consciousness and a will of their own in the capitalist, are *capital*"(Marx 1863–1866, p. 1008).

Because of the separation between means of production and the direct producers, "the motion and the activity of the instrument of labour asserts its independence *vis-à-vis* the worker. The instrument of labour now becomes an industrial form of perpetual motion. It would go on producing for ever, if it did not come up against certain natural limits in the shape of the weak bodies and the strong wills of its human assistants" (Marx 1867, p. 526).

15 "As soon as the gradual upsurge of working-class revolt... made impossible once and for all to increase the production of surplus-value by prolonging the working day, capital threw itself with all its might, and in full awareness of the situation, into the production of relative surplus-value, by speeding up the development of the machinery system" (Marx 1867, pp. 533–4).

16 Marx argues that machinery "does not just act as a superior competitor to the worker, always on the point of making him superfluous. It is a power inimical to him, and capital proclaims this fact loudly and deliberately, as well as making use of it.... It would be possible to write a whole history of the inventions made since 1830 for the sole purpose of providing capital with weapons against working class revolt" (Marx 1867, pp. 562–3).

17 See for example, Federici (1992) and the contribution of Midnight Notes to this volume. See also Caffentzis (1995).

REFERENCES

Amin, S. (1974), *Accumulation on a World Scale. A critique of the theory of Underdevelopment*. New York: Monthly Review Press.

Aston, T.H. and C. Philpin (eds) (1985), *The Brenner Debate: Agrarian Class Structure and Economic Development in Early Modern Europe*. Cambridge: Cambridge University Press.

Bobbio, N. (1990). "Politica," in N. Bobbio, N. Matteucci, G. Pasquino. *Dizionario di Politica*. Torino: Utet.

Braudel, F. (1992), *Civilization and Capitalism*. 15th–18th Century. London: Fontana.

Caffentzis, G. (1995), "The Fundamental Implications of the Debt Crisis for Social Reproduction in Africa," in M. Dalla Costa and G. F. Dalla Costa (eds), *Paying The Price. Women and the Politics of International Economic Strategy*. London: Zed Books.

De Angelis, M. (1995), "Beyond the Technological and the Social Paradigms: A Political Reading of Abstract Labour as the Substance of Value," in *Capital and Class*, no. 57.

De Angelis, M. (1996), "Social Relations, Commodity-Fetishism and Marx's Critique of Political Economy," in *Review of Radical Political Economics*, vol. 28 no. 4.

Dobb, M. (1963), *Studies in the Development of Capitalism*. London, Routledge.

Federici, S. (1988), "The Great Witch Hunt of the Sixteenth Century," in *The Maine Scholar*, 1.

Federici, S. (1992), "The Debt Crisis, Africa and the New Enclosures," in *Midnight Notes*.

Gottlieb, R. S. (1984), "Feudalism and Historical Materialism: a Critique and a Synthesis," in *Science and Society*, vol. 48, no. 1.

Harvey, D. (2003), *The New Imperialism*, Oxford: Oxford University Press.

Hill, Ch. (1972), *The World Turned Upside-Down. Radical Ideas During the English Revolution*. London: Penguin.

Hilton, R. (ed) (1978), *The Transition from Feudalism to Capitalism*. London: Verso.

Laibman D. (1984), "Modes of Production and Theories of Transition," in *Science and Society*, vol. 48, no. 3.

Lenin, V. I. [1899] (1960), "The Development of Capitalism in Russia," in *Collected Works*, Volume 3. London: Lawrence & Wishart.

Linebaugh, P. (1991), *The London Hanged. Crime and Civil Society in the Eighteenth Century*. London: Penguin.

Luxemburg, R. [1913] (1963), *The Accumulation of Capital*. London: Routledge.

Marx, K. [1844] (1975), *Economic and Philosophical Manuscript*, in *Early Writings*. New York: Vintage Book.

Marx, K. [1858] (1974), *Grundrisse*. New York: Penguin.

Marx, K. [1867] (1976), *Capital*. Volume 1. New York: Penguin Books.

Marx, K. [1863–1866] (1976). "Results of the Immediate Process of Production," in *Capital*, Volume 1. New York: Penguin Books.

Marx, K. [1878] (1983), A Letter to the Editorial Board of *Otechestvennye Zapiski*, in T. Shanin, *Late Marx and the Russian Road*, New York: Monthly Review Press.

Marx, K. [1881] (1983), Reply to Vera Zasulich, in T. Shanin, *Late Marx and the Russian Road*, New York: Monthly Review Press.

Marx, K. [1894] (1981), *Capital*, Volume 3. New York: Penguin Books.

Marx, K. (1971), *Theories of Surplus Value*, Volume 3. Moscow: Progress Publisher.

McLennon, G. (1986), "Marxist Theory and Historical Research: Between the Hard and Soft Options." in *Science and Society*, vol. 50, no. 1.

Mies, M. (1986), *Patriarchy and Accumulation on a World Scale*. London: Zed Books.

Perelman, M. (2000), *The Invention of Capitalism. Classical Political Economy and the Secret History of Primitive Accumulation*. Durham, NC: Duke University Press.

Polanyi, K. (1944), *The Great Transformation. The Political and Economic Origins of our Time*. Boston: Beacon Press.

Rodney, W. (1972), *How Europe Underdeveloped Africa*. London: Bogle-L'Overture Publications.

Rosdolsky, R. (1977), *The Making of Marx's "Capital."* London: Pluto Press.

Smith, A. [1776] (1976), *An Inquiry into the Nature and Causes of the Wealth of Nations*. New York: Oxford University Press.

Smith, C. (1995), *Marx at the Millennium*. London: Pluto Press.

Sweezy, P. (1950), "The Transition from Feudalism to Capitalism," in *Science and Society*, vol. 14, no. 2.

Sweezy, P. (1986), "Feudalism to Capitalism Revisited," in *Science and Society*, vol. 50, no. 1.

Wallerstein, I. (1979), *The Capitalist World-Economy*. Cambridge: Cambridge University Press.

3

The Permanence of Primitive Accumulation
Commodity Fetishism and Social Constitution

Werner Bonefeld[1]

INTRODUCTION

Over the last decade there has been an increase in the trafficking of women and children, prostitution and slavery. New markets have emerged in human organs and babies. The proprietors of labour power are confronted not only with new forms of exploitation (see Caffentzis, 2003). They are also transformed into a saleable resource to be operated on and sold, with babies being produced for export (Federici, 1997). Some commentators have suggested that we witness the re-emergence of conditions of primitive accumulation (see, amongst others, Dalla Costa, 1995a, 1995b). These works show clearly that Marx's insight according to which "a great deal of capital, which appears today in the United States without certificate of birth, was yesterday, in England, the capitalist blood of children" (Marx, 1983, p. 707), remains a powerful judgement of contemporary conditions.

This chapter argues that primitive accumulation describes not just the period of transition that led to the emergence of capitalism. Primitive accumulation is, in fact, the foundation of capitalist social relations. Its systematic content is constitutive of capitalist social relations. It is the premise and presupposition of capitalistically organised social relations. Capitalist social relations rest on the divorce of the mass of the population from the means of production. This divorce was the result of primitive accumulation and it is the historical presupposition and constitutive basis of capitalist social relations. At issue is thus the transformation of capitalism's historical presupposition into the constitutive premise of its existence.

PRIMITIVE ACCUMULATION AND CAPITAL

Within the Marxist tradition, primitive accumulation is usually seen as a phase that belongs firmly to the pre-history of capitalism. Capitalism developed out of primitive accumulation and once capitalism had been established, the history of primitive accumulation — a history of blood and fire where sheep replaced humans during the clearing of estates — is seen to be just that: history. Primitive accumulation, then, is seen as a period of historical transition towards capitalist social relations. The time specific systematic character of primitive accumulation refers to the "clearing of the estates," that is, the separation of labour from the means of production and the natural conditions of labour.

Marxist writing on imperialism, especially Rosa Luxemburg (1963), implicitly acknowledged that "capitalism proper" depends for its own expanded reproduction on subjugation of new populations to capitalist exchange relations. Luxemburg, while not denying the conventional view that primitive accumulation is a distinct period at the dawn of capitalism, accepted nevertheless the coincidence of constituted capitalist relations with conditions of primitive accumulation. The contradictory logic of capitalist accumulation necessitates the opening of new markets and new populations to capitalist reproduction. In this view, then, primitive accumulation derives from the contradictory logic of capitalist accumulation and its crisis-ridden process of reproduction. This made it possible for Luxemburg to accept the view that primitive accumulation marks the period of transition to capitalism and to argue, at least by implication, that primitive accumulation is a feature of the crisis-ridden character of capitalist accumulation. The contradictory character of capitalist accumulation seeks — the always temporary — resolution by forcing conditions of primitive accumulation upon non-capitalist social relations, gaining new markets and integrating new workers into the capital relation. Primitive accumulation would thus be a permanent feature of capitalist accumulation but it would be so only as an effect of the contradictions of capitalist accumulation, resulting from it. Its character as a specific historical period is thus preserved: capitalist accumulation takes the form of imperialism, or imperialist forms of accumulation, and imperialism enforces transition to capitalism onto new populations. Samir Amin, writing in the 1970s, focuses this well: the mechanisms of primitive accumulation "do not belong only to the prehistory of capitalism; they are contemporary as well. It is these forms of primitive accumulation, modified but persistent, to the advantage of the centre, that form the domain of the theory of accumulation on a world scale" (Amin, 1974, p. 3). Primitive accumulation appears here as a continuous-inherent feature of capitalist accumulation. However, it is so only as something that derives from the crisis-ridden character of capitalist accumulation in the form of imperialist means of crisis-resolution. It is not constitutive of "capital's logic" but merely results from it.

The understanding of primitive accumulation as a mere period of transition, be it as capitalism's pre-history or as the imperialist effect of capitalist accumulation, fails to see that the divorce of labour from her means of production is not just the historical premise of capitalist social relations. It is also, and importantly so, the condition and presupposition of the capitalist social relations. As Marx (1973, p. 515) put it, *"the exchange of labour for labour — seemingly the condition of the workers' property — rests on the foundation of the workers' propertylessness."* Capitalist social relations are founded on the separation of labour from the means of production. This is the one historical pre-condition of capitalist social relations, a precondition that is constitutive of capitalist social relations. In distinction to Massimo de Angelis' argument, primitive accumulation is permanent not because of its apparent strategic importance to the enforcement of market rule on (new) populations nor because it is a weapon employed by capital to decompose society's natural desire to protect itself from such rule. The division of society into, on the one hand, the objective power of capital that as an active though depersonalised subject makes use of certain weapons and strategies, and on the other the naturalised life world of a human suspect that seeks to protect itself from capital's colonising logic, makes little sense (cf. Bonefeld, 2002). There is only one world. This also says that it make no sense to argue that contemporary forms of primitive accumulation comprise just an "imperialist effect" of capitalist accumulation. The capitalistically organised form of social relations rests on the permanent reproduction of the systematic content of primitive accumulation, that is, the separation of labour from her means. The originality of primitive accumulation is not that it gave "birth" to capitalism. Rather its originality is entailed in its social contents, that is, the forceful separation of labour from her means — the condition sine qua non of capitalist social relations. Capital is the form assumed by this separation. The following section focuses on this issue.

PRIMITIVE ACCUMULATION AND SOCIAL CONSTITUTION

Marx's critique of political economy makes clear that "capital" is not a "thing" and he argues that the standpoint of capital and wage labour is the same.[2] Capital is not a thing because it is a definite social relationship and the standpoint of capital and wage labour is the same because both are perverted social forms.[3] For Marx, each "form," even the most simple form, like, for example, the commodity, "is already an inversion and causes relations between people to appear as attributes of things" (Marx, 1972, p. 508) or, more emphatically, each form is a "perverted form" (Marx, 1962, p. 90).[4] The most developed perversion, the constituted fetish of capitalist society, is the relationship of capital to itself, of a thing to itself (see Marx, 1972, p. 515). The extreme expression of this perversion is interest-bearing capital: the "most externalised and most fetish-like form" of capital (Marx, 1966, p. 391). And the "wage" — the defining characteristic of wage labour? *"Labour — wages, or price of labour"* is an expression that "is just as irrational as a yellow logarithm" (ibid., p. 818). What, then, needs to be explained is not the relation between capital and wage labour in its direct and immediate sense but rather the social constitution upon which this relationship is founded and through which it subsists. In other words, what needs to be explained is why human social purposeful practice takes the form of relations between things. Hence, Marx's question, "why does this content [human social productive practice] assume that form [the form of capital]" (Marx, 1962, p. 95).5 This question raises the issue of the social constitution of value as an apparently self-moving thing, or as a seemingly automatic subject. The critical dimension of this insight is this: "it is not the *unity* of living and active humanity with the natural, inorganic conditions of their metabolic exchange with nature, and hence their appropriation of nature, which requires explanation or is the result of historic process, but rather the *separation* between these inorganic conditions of human existence and this active existence, a separation which is completely posited only in the relation of wage labour and capital" (Marx, 1973, p. 489). The class antagonism between capital and labour rests on and subsists through the separation of human social practice from its means, a separation that appears to invest these means with independent power over the very human social practice form which it springs.

Commodity exchange and "money" pre-date capitalist production. For money, however, to be "transformed into capital, the prerequisites for capitalist production must exist" (Marx, 1972, p. 272). The first historical presupposition is the separation of labour from her conditions and "therefore the existence of the means of labour as capital" (ibid.). For Marx, this separation comprises a world's history. "Commodity and money are transformed into capital because the worker... is compelled to sell his labour itself (to sell directly his labour power) as a commodity to the owner of the objective conditions of labour. This separation is the prerequisite for the relationship of capital and wage labour in the same way as it is the prerequisite for the transformation of money (or of the commodity by which it is represented) into capital" (ibid., p. 89). The perverted existence of human purposeful activity as an activity that appears to derive from the things themselves is based on this separation. Separation is the constitutive presupposition of capitalist social relations (see Krahl, 1971, p. 223). In sum, the separation of labour from her conditions is the precondition of their existence as capital and — importantly — it "is the foundation of [capitalist] production...[and] is given in capitalist production" (Marx, 1972, p. 272). There can be no capitalist accumulation, nor can there be capital or wage labour, without the continued reproduction of the divorce of social labour from her means.

Separation means that the conditions of work confront labour "as alien capital" (Marx, 1972, p. 422) because the conditions of "production are lost to [the labourer] and have assumed the shape of alien property" (ibid.). The divorce, then, of human purposeful practice from her conditions and their transformation into an independent force, i.e. capital, transforms the product of labour into a commodity and makes the commodity appear as "a product of capital" (Marx, 1966, p. 880). This entails "the materialisation of the social features of production and the personification of the material foundations of production" (ibid.). Thus, the capitalist and wage-labourer "are as such merely embodiments, personifications of capital and wage-labour; definite social characteristics stamped upon individuals by the process of social production" (ibid.). In this way, primitive accumulation appears suspended (*aufgehoben*) in the commodity form. Yet, however suspended, it is the constitutive condition of capitalist social relations as relations between things. The presuppositions of capital, "which originally appeared as conditions of its becoming — and hence could not spring from its *action as capital* — now appear as results of its own realization, reality, as *posited by it* — *not as conditions of its arising, but as results of its presence*" (Marx, 1973, p. 460). In short, primitive accumulation is not just an historical epoch which predates capitalist social relations and from which capital emerged. It entails, fundamentally, the constitutive presupposition through which the class antagonism between capital and labour subsists — primitive accumulation is the "foundation of capitalist reproduction" (Marx, 1983, p. 585) and therefore the foundation of wage labour. That is, the presupposition of capital — separation — transforms into the result of its presence.

Primitive accumulation is the centrifugal point around which resolves the specific capitalist mode of existence of labour power, the determination of human purposeful activity in the form of a labouring commodity.[6] While capitalist production and exchange relations subsist through the commodity form, primitive accumulation is the secrete history of the determination of human purposeful practice in the form of a wage-labouring commodity. The commodity form subsists through this determination, presupposes it and, through its form, denies it in the name of abstract equality and freedom. This insight is focused in Marx's critique of fetishism: "The sum total of the labour of all these private individuals and private groups makes up the aggregate of social labour. Since the producers do not come into social contact which each other until they exchange their products, the specific social character of each producer's labour does not show itself except in the act of exchange. In other words, the labour of the individual asserts itself as a part of the labour of society, only by means of the relations which the act of exchange establishes directly between the products, and indirectly, through them, between producers. To the latter, therefore, the relations connecting the labour of one individual with that of the rest appear, not as direct social relations between individuals at work, but as what they really are, material relations between persons and social relations between things" (Marx, 1983, pp. 77–8). Thus, capital is a perverted form of social cooperation. Social cooperation subsists in and through the perverted form of commodity relations where human beings produce through their own social labour a reality that increasingly enslaves them to things.

The commodity form posits the totality of bourgeois social relations and as such a totality posits the basis of the productive practice of all individuals as alienated individuals. The commodity form includes not only the activity of each individual it is, also, *independent* of *this connection from the individual*. The divorce, then, of labour from its conditions entails not only the complete independence of the individuals form one another but, also, their complete dependence on the seemingly impersonal relations established by the commodity form. Thus, the independence of the individual is an "illusion, and so more accurately called indifference" (Marx, 1973, p. 162). Their independence is that of atomised market individuals that are "free to collide with one another and to engage in exchange within this freedom" (ibid., pp. 163–64). The separation of human activity from its conditions is thus not only the real generation process of capital but, also, once constituted, the "real" process of the commodity form. That is to say, the "logic of separation" (cf. Negri, 1991) is the secrete foundation of the commodity form. The historical pre-condition of primitive accumulation transforms into the constitutive presupposition of capitalist accumulation, its premise and result of its reproduction. In short, and paraphrasing Marx's treatment of the commodity, the process of the disappearance of primitive accumulation in accumulation proper "must, therefore, appear at the same time as a process of the disappearance of its disappearance, i.e. as a reproduction process" (Marx, 1987, p. 98). The logic of separation is thus the "real process of capital" (Marx, 1972, p. 422). Indeed, as Marx argues, capital is "the separation of the conditions of production from the labourer" (ibid.).

The "logic of separation" entails that the individual capitalist has constantly to expand "his capital, in order to preserve it, but extend it he cannot, except by means of progressive accumulation" (Marx, 1983, p. 555). The risk is bankruptcy. Thus, mediated through competition, personified capital is spurred into action. "Fanatically bent on making value expand itself, [the personified capitalist] ruthlessly forces the human race to produce for production's sake," increasing "the mass of human beings exploited by him" (ibid.). The positing of the results of human labour as a force over and above the social individual, including both the capitalist and the wage labourer, and the "fanatic" bent to make workers work for the sake of work, is founded on the separation of labour from its means. "The means of production become capital only in so far as they have become separated from labourer and confront labour as an independent power" (Marx, 1963, p. 408). In short, the freedom of labour from her conditions and their transformation into private property entails the capitalist property right to preserve abstract wealth through the "sacrifice of 'human machines' on the pyramids of accumulation" (Gambino, 1996, p. 55). The law of private property entails that "labour capacity has appropriated for itself only the subjective conditions of necessary labour — the means of subsistence for actively producing labour capacity, i.e. for its reproduction as mere labour capacity separated from the conditions of its realization — and it has posited these conditions themselves as *things, values,* which confront it in an alien, commanding personification" (Marx, 1973, pp. 452–53).

Capital is not a thing in-itself that, endowed with its own objective logic, exchanges itself with itself and that, by doing so, generates profit. Rather, it is a social relationship between labour and the conditions of labour which are "rendered independent in relation" to labour (ibid, 422). "The loss of the conditions of labour by the workers is expressed in the fact that these conditions of labour become independent as capital or as things at the disposal of the capitalist" (ibid, p. 271). This loss appears as original in primitive accumulation because it is the origin of the loss of the conditions of labour. This loss delineates the systematic content of separation. That is to say, separation "forms [*bildet*] the conception [*Begriff*] of capital" (Marx, 1966, p. 246). The separation of labour from its conditions and the concentration of these in the hands of "non-workers" (Marx, 1978, p. 116) posits capital as a perverted form of human social practice where the "process of production has mastery over man, instead of being controlled by him" (Marx, 1983, p. 85). The class struggle, then, that freed master from serf and serf from master is constitutive of the relation between capital and labour. Primitive accumulation persists — within the capital relation, as its constitutive pre-positing action.[7] This "action" lies at the heart of capital's reproduction: the pre-positing action of the separation of labour from her means is not the historical result of capital but its presupposition, a presupposition which renders capital a social production relation in and through the divorce of labour's social productive power from her conditions.

The systematic character of primitive accumulation is, then, suspended (*aufgehoben*) in the constituted relations of capital. The separation is not the result of capital but its genesis and it is now posited as the presupposition of capital. It no longer "figures" as the condition of its historical emergence but, rather, as the constitutive presupposition of its fanatic bent on reproducing human relations as relations between commodity owners, and that is, as social categories of capitalist reproduction. In short, the separation "begins with primitive accumulation, appears as a permanent process in the accumulation and concentration of capital, and expresses itself finally as centralisation of existing capitals in a few hands and a deprivation of many of their capital (to which expropriation is now changed)" (Marx, 1966, p. 246).

The terror of separation, of capitalism's original beginning, weights like a nightmare on the social practice of human purposeful activity. The commodification of human productive power in the form of wage labour means that human social practice confronts its conditions as alien conditions, as conditions of exploitation, and as conditions which appear, and so exist contradictorily, as relations between things.

Man is confronted by things, labour is confronted by its own materialised conditions as alien, independent, self-contained subjects, personifications, in short, as *someone else's property* and, in this form, as "employers" and "commanders" of labour itself, which they appropriate instead of being appropriated by it. The fact that value — whether it exists as money or as commodities — and in the further development the conditions of labour confront the worker as the *property of other people*, as independent properties, means simply that they confront him as the *property* of the non-worker or, at any rate, that, as a capitalist, he confronts them [the conditions of labour] not as a worker but as the *owner* of value, etc., as the *subject* in which these things possess their own will, belong to themselves and are personified as independent forces (Marx, 1972, pp. 475–76).

Capital presupposes labour as wage labour and wage labour presupposes capital as capital. Each is the precondition of the other.

> Every pre-condition of the social reproduction process is at the same time its result, and every one of its results appears simultaneously as its pre-condition. All the *production relations* within which the process moves are therefore just as much its products as they are its conditions. The more one examines its nature as it really is, [the more one sees] that in the last form it becomes increasingly consolidated, so that independently of the process these conditions appear to determine it, and their own relations appear to those competing in the process as objective conditions, objective forces, aspects of things, the more so as in the capitalist process, every element, even the simplest, the commodity for example, is already an inversion and causes relations between people to appear as attributes of things and as relations of people to the social attributes of things (Marx, 1972, pp. 507–08).

The perverted form of value presents, in other words, the mode of existence of human purposeful activity in the form of impersonal relations, conferring on the human being the indignity of an existence [*Dasein*] as a personification of things. Thus, concerning the capital-labour relation, "the workers produces himself as labour capacity, as well as the capital confronting him." At the same time, "the capitalist reproduces himself as capital as well as the living labour capacity confronting him" (Marx, 1973, p. 458). "Each reproduces itself, by reproducing the other, its negation. The capitalist produces labour as alien; labour produces the product as alien" (ibid.).

Once the logic of separation is taken for granted, i.e. once its constitutive presupposition is merely assumed as an historical past or indeed functionalised as a mere weapon of capital, the logic of separation can be understood merely in terms of the constitut*ed* fetish of capital as the subject that structures or decomposes the actions of human agents. Orthodox accounts feed on this separation between (capitalist) structure and (human) agency.[8] The dogmatic character of orthodox thought lies precisely in its acceptance of the separation of "genesis" from "existence" (cf. Horkheimer, 1985, p. 246). This does, however, not mean that orthodox approaches cannot provide an analysis of value.

But they can do so only in terms of labour as a human agency, and in terms of value as embodied labour. This theory of value merely shows that "the development of social labour produces either a process of accumulation of value or a complex norm of distribution" (Negri, 1992, p. 70). In this view, the perverted existence of human relations as relations between things is assumed to be true in practice and the driving force of capitalist development becomes to be seen to be capital itself as a self-constituted objective subject. Such analytical offerings merely confirm that "myth" is not a condition merely of former times but, rather, that it continuous to exercise its domination over thought itself. Hence Marx's insistence on demystification: Neither "nations" nor "history" nor, one might add, capital have made war. "History does nothing, does not 'possess vast wealth,' does not 'fight battles'! It is Man, rather, the real, living Man who does all that, who does possess and fight, it is not 'history' that uses Man as a means to pursue its ends, as if it were a person apart. History is nothing but the activity of Man pursuing its ends" (Marx and Engels, 1980, p. 98). Marx's critique of fetishism is fundamentally a critique of unreflected presuppositions: instead of hypothesising capital as an objective and thus irresistible objective subject and instead of deriving human social practice from the assumed structural properties of this subject, it shows the necessity of capitalist forms in the light of their social constitution. That is to say, all theoretical mysteries find their rational resolution in the comprehension of human social practice. In short, and as Marcuse reports, "the constitution of the world occurs behind the backs of the individuals, yet it is their work" (1988, p. 151).

Without an understanding of the social constitution of the perverted world of capital, there could be no critique of capital without, at the same time, espousing it as as performing a useful economic function. This, then, would lead to the view of capital as "the subject" that embodies the logic of an abstract market structure whose empirical reality is mediated by class struggle and other social forces (Jessop, 1991). Against this theoretical rationalisation of capital as an extra-human but nevertheless subjective force, it is only on the basis of an understanding of "separation" that a critique of capital can be supplied: this critique breaks into the understanding of capitalist exploitation and accumulation as a constituted form and "unhinges this constitution and marks the singularity and the dynamics of the antagonism which the law of labour comprehends" (Negri, 1992, p. 70). The capital relation is the historical product of labour's alienation from her condition: Capital is "the form assumed by the conditions of labour" (Marx, 1972, p. 492) and "labour becomes productive only by producing its opposite," i.e. capital (Marx, 1973, p. 305). It is the labourer who "constantly produces material, objective wealth, but in the form of capital, of an alien power that dominates and exploits [the labourer]: and the capitalist as constantly produces labour-power, but in the form of a subjective source of wealth, separated from the objects in and by which it can alone be realised; in short he produces the labourer, but as a wage-labourer. This incessant reproduction, this perpetuation of the labourer, is the sine qua non of capitalist production" (ibid., pp. 535–36). Thus, the contention that capitalist accumulation is not just based on the results of primitive accumulation but, rather, that primitive accumulation is the constitutive presupposition of the class antagonism between capital and labour. As Marx put it, capitalist "accumulation merely presents as a *continuous process* what in *primitive accumulation*, appears as a distinct historical process, as the process of the emergence of capital" (Marx, 1972 p. 272; see also Marx, 1983, p. 688). There would be no capitalist accumulation without the reproduction of labour as "object-less *free workers*" (Marx, 1973, p. 507). The social constitution of capitalist property rights is the divorce of labour from her means, object-less labour "under the command of capital" (ibid., p. 508).

The presupposition of capitalist social reproduction is the freedom of labour from her condition; this presupposition informs and in-forms the real movement of capitalist social relations. Capital, "fanatically bent on making value expand itself" (ibid., p. 555) can do no other than to intensify the division of labour so as to increase its productive power. There is no doubt that "the subdivision of labour is the assassination of a people" (Urquhart, quoted in Marx, 1983, p. 343); yet it merely consolidates the "original" separation of labour from its conditions through further and further fragmentations of the social labour process, dismembering Man [*Mensch*] (cf. Marx, 1977, p. 155). Still, however much social labour is fragmented, divided and subdivided, human cooperation remains "the fundamental form of the capitalist mode of production" (Marx, 1983, p. 317). This cooperation exists against itself in the commodity-form that integrates the "assassination of a people" with the respectful forms of equal and free exchange relations.

Labour "is and remains the presupposition" of capital (Marx, 1973, p. 399). Capital cannot liberate itself from labour; it depends on the imposition of necessary labour, the constituent side of surplus labour, upon the world's working classes. It has to posit necessary labour at the same time as which it has to reduce necessary labour to the utmost in order to increase surplus value. This reduction develops labour's productive power and, at the same time, the real possibility of the realm of freedom.[9] The circumstance that less and less socially necessary labour time is required to produce, for want of a better expression, the necessities of life, limits the realm of necessity and so allows the blossoming of what Marx characterised as the realm of freedom. Within capitalist society, this contradiction can be contained only through force (*Gewalt*), including not only the destruction of productive capacities, unemployment, worsening conditions, and widespread poverty, but also the destruction of human life through war, ecological disaster, famine, the burning of land, poisoning of water, devastation of communities, the usage of the human body as a container that can be dissected for profit, for example organ sale, etc.

The existence of Man as a degraded, exploited, debased, forsaken and enslaved being, indicates that capitalist production is not production for humans

— it is production through humans, sacrificing human beings on the altar of money in an effort to secure the accumulation of capital for the sake of accumulation. In other words, the value form represents not just an abstraction from the real social individual. It is an abstraction that is "true in practice" (cf. Marx, 1973, p. 105). The universal reduction of all specific human social practice to the one, some abstract form of labour, from the battlefield to the cloning laboratory, is now no longer satisfied with the appropriation qua exploitation of an excessive number of working hours. It is now also in the process of transforming the individual owner of redundant or, in any case, superfluous labour-power into a bodily thing that can be hired out or dissected into saleable parts (cf. Dalla Costa, in this volume). The "logic of separation," which as Marx insists, is constitutive of capital, "begins with primitive accumulation, appears as a permanent process in the accumulation and concentration of capital, and expresses itself finally as centralisation of existing capitals in a few hands and a deprivation of many of their capital (to which expropriation is now changed)" (Marx, 1966, p. 246). It now passes through labour as a carrier of human capital — development as capitalist freedom where humanity, paraphrasing Dalla Costa, is "turned topsy turvy, vivisectioned, and made a commodity" (Dalla Costa, 1995b, p. 12). Marx's notion of the doubly free wage labourer appears to have been transformed. The doubly free wage labourer has indeed become, at least for a growing part of humanity, more than just a labouring commodity. It has also become a carrier of body substances that, like any other commodity, can be sold on the market at prevailing prices.

CONCLUSION

Primitive accumulation is a constantly reproduced accumulation, be it in terms of the renewed separation of new populations from the means of production and subsistence, or in terms of the reproduction of the wage relation in the "established" relations of capital. The understanding of separation as the constitutive condition of capitalist social relations has formidable political consequences.

"The society of the free and equal" (cf. Agnoli, 2000) or the "mode of production of associated producers" (cf. Godelier, 2000), can not be achieved through a politics on behalf of the working class. Theory on behalf of the working class leads to the acceptance of programs and tickets whose common basis is the everyday religion of bourgeois society: commodity fetishism. A politics on behalf of the working class affirms what needs to be negated. Or, as Marx (1983, p. 477) saw it, "to be a productive labourer is... not a piece of luck, but a misfortune." How can this misfortune be overcome? The emancipation of the working class can only be achieved by the working class itself. Yet, *pace* Lebowitz's (2003) authoritarian, and in any way redundant but no less dangerous idea of socialism as the liberation of the working class from capital and government on its behalf by the workers' state, the working class can emancipate itself only by abolishing its own wage-labouring existence. And it can do so only on the condition that it transcends its class character by abolishing all classes, and therewith all forms of coercion, domination, exploitation that are characteristic of class society. That is to say, all who live from their labour and the sale of their labour power "find themselves directly opposed to the form in which, hitherto, the individuals, of which society consists, have given themselves collective expression, that is, the State; in order, therefore, to assert themselves as individuals, they must overthrow the state" (Marx, and Engels 1962, p. 77). The emancipation of the working class entails thus the struggle for the realisation of the human subject as a self-determining democratic subject. Marx called this transcendence of the working class by one name: communism. Emancipation means human emancipation. Communism entails the end of class, a classless society — a commune of subjects or, as Marcuse (2000) put it, an association of communist individuals. The emancipation of the working class then means that the human subject "recognises and organises his 'forces propres' as social forces and thus no longer separates social forces from himself in the form of political forces" and material forces (Marx, 1964, p. 370).

Marx saw this new form of society anticipated in the

> community of revolutionary proletarians, who extend their own control over the conditions of their own existence and those of all members of society. It is as individuals that the individuals participate in it. It is exactly this combination of individuals (assuming the advanced stage of modern productive forces, of course) which puts the conditions of the free development and movement of individuals under their control — conditions which were previously abandoned to chance and had won an independent existence over and against the separate individuals precisely because of their separation as individuals (Marx and Engels, 1962, p. 74).

Paraphrasing Adorno (1975, p. 44), full-employment makes sense in a society where labour is no longer the measure of all things. That is, it makes sense in a society where the measure of all things is the satisfaction of human needs, and where equality is no longer an equality before money but, rather, an equality of individual human needs. For humans to enter into relationship with one another, not as separated individuals whose social existence is made manifest behind their backs through the commodity form, but as social individuals, as human dignitaries who are in control of their social conditions, the basic prerequisite of this struggle for the democratic commune is the transformation of the means of production into means of emancipation.

Struggle for the democratic self-organisation of society — the transport of the means of production into means of emancipation — entails the politicisation of social relations. Discussion of this issue is beyond the remit of this chapter, but see the contributions to Part III. Suffice to say that such politicisation does entail social conflict, which might force bourgeois society into making material concessions in an attempt to divide and rule; better still, it might succeed in transforming the means of production into the common property of the communist individuals, or it might bring to power "well-meaning dictators... genuinely anxious to restore" law and order (Hayek in praise of Pinochet, cited in Cristi, 1998, p. 168). There is no certainty.

NOTES

1 The chapter builds on an earlier version that first appeared in English in *The Commoner*, issue no. 2, 2001. See also Bonefeld (1988).

2 See Marx (1966, Ch. 48).

3 See Marx (1966, p. 880; 1972, p. 491).

4 In the English translation the German *verrückte Form*, is translated as "absurd form" (Marx, 1983, p. 80). The translation is "absurd." In German, "verrückt" has two meanings: verrückt (mad) and ver-rückt (displaced). Thus, the notion of "perverted forms" means that these forms are both mad and displaced. In the following "perversion" or "perverted" will be used in this double sense. For discussion, see Backhaus (1992, 2005).

5 I am quoting from the German edition of *Capital*. The English edition omits this all-important sentence.

6 On this see Negt and Kluge (1981).

7 On this see Psychopedis (1992).

8 For a critique, see Clarke (1980).

9 "In fact, the realm of freedom actually begins only where labour which is determined by necessity and mundane considerations ceases; thus in the very nature of things it lies beyond the sphere of actual material production.... Freedom in this field can only consist in socialised Man [*Mensch*], the associated producers, rationally regulating their interchange with Nature, bringing it under their common control, instead of being ruled by the blind forces of Nature.... But it nonetheless still remains a realm of necessity. Beyond it begins that development of human energy which is an end in itself, the true realm of freedom, which, however, can blossom forth only with this realm of necessity as its basis" (Marx, 1966, p. 820). See the exchange between Wildcat and Holloway for a useful exchange on this issue (Wildcat, 1999).

REFERENCES

Adorno, T. (1975), *Gesellschaftstheorie und Kulturkritik*, Suhrkamp, Frankfurt.

Agnoli, J. (2000), "The Market, the State and the End of History," in Bonefeld, W. and K. Psychopedis (eds) *The Politics of Change*, Plagrave, London.

Amin, S. (1974), *Accumulation on a World Scale. A critique of the theory of Underdevelopment*, Monthly Review Press, New York.

Backhaus, H.G. (1992), "Between Philosophy and Science: Marxian Social Economy as Critical Theory," in Bonefeld, W., R. Gunn and K. Psychopedis (eds) *Open Marxism*, Pluto, London.

Backhaus, H.G. (2005), "Some Aspects of Marx's Concept of Critique in the Context of his Economic-Philosophical Theory," in Bonefeld, W. and K. Psychopedis (eds) *Human Dignity: Social Autonomy and the Critique of Capitalism*, Ashgate, Aldershot.

Bonefeld, W. (1988), "Class Struggle and the Permanence of Primitive Accumulation," *Common Sense* no. 8.

Bonefeld, W. (2002), "Labour, Capital and Primitive Accumulation: Class and Constitution," forthcoming in Dinerstein, A. and M. Neary (eds) *The Labour Debate*, Ashgate, Aldershot.

Caffentzis, G. (1995), "The Fundamental Implications of the Debt Crisis for Social Reproduction in Africa," in Dalla Costa, M. and G.F. Dalla Costa (eds) *Paying the Price*, Zed Books, London.

Caffentzis, G. (2003), "The End of Work or the Renaissance of Slavery?," in Bonefeld, W. (ed) *Revolutionary Writing*, Autonomedia, New York.

Clarke, S. (1980), "Althusserian Marxism," in ibid. et.al., *One Dimensional Marxism*, Alison & Busby, London.

Cristi, R. (1998), *Authoritarian Liberalism*, University of Wales Press, Cardiff.

Dalla Costa, M. (1995a), "Development and Reproduction," *Common Sense* no. 17, reprinted in Bonefeld, W. (ed) *Revolutionary Writing*, Autonomedia, New York, 2003.

Dalla Costa, M. (1995b), "Capitalism and Reproduction," in Bonefeld, W. etal. (eds) *Open Marxism: Emancipating Marx*, Pluto, London, also available in this volume.

Federici, S. (1997), "Reproduction and Feminist Struggle in the New International Division of Labour," in Dalla Costa, M. and G.F. Dalla Costa (eds) *Women, Development and Labour Reproduction*, African World Press, Lawrenceville.

Gambino, F. (1996), "A Critique of Fordism and the Regulation School," *Common Sense* no. 19, reprinted in W. Bonefeld (ed) *Revolutionary Writing*, Autonomedia, New York, 2003.

Godelier, M. (2000), "The Disappearance of the 'Socialist System': Failure or Confirmation of Marx's View on the Transition from One Form of Production and Society to Another?," in Bonefeld, W. and K. Psychopedis (eds), *The Politics of Change*, Palgrave, London.

Horkheimer, M. (1985), *Zur Kritik der instrumentellen Vernunft*, Fischer, Frankfurt.

Jessop, B. (1991), "Polar Bears and Class Struggle," in Bonefeld, W. and J. Holloway (eds) *Post-Fordism and Social Form*, Macmillan, London.

Krahl, J. (1971), *Konstitution und Klassenkampf*, Verlag Neue Kritik, Frankfurt, 4th ed. 1985.

Lebowitz, M. (2003), *Beyond Capital*, Palgrave, London.

Luxemburg, R. (1963), *The Accumulation of Capital*, Routldege, London.

Marcuse, H. (1988), "Philosophy and Critical Theory," in ibid. *Negations*, Free Association Press, London.

Marcuse, H. (2000), *Reason and Revolution*, Routledge, London.

Marx, K. (1962), *Das Kapital*, vol. I, MEW 23, Dietz Verlag, Berlin.

Marx, K. (1963), *Theories of Surplus Value Part I*, Lawrence & Wishart, London.

Marx, K. (1964), *Zur Judenfrage*, in MEW 1, Dietz, Berlin.

Marx, K. (1966), *Capital Vol. III*, Lawrence & Wishart, London.

Marx, K. (1972), *Theories of Surplus Value Part III*, Lawrence & Wishart, London.

Marx, K. (1973), *Grundrisse*, Penguin, Harmondsworth.

Marx, K. (1975), "Contribution to Critique of Hegel's Philosophy of Law. Introduction," *Collected Works*, vol. 3, Lawrence & Wishart, London.

Marx, K. (1977), *Das Elend der Philosophy*, MEW 4, Dietz, Berlin.

Marx, K. (1978), *Capital*, Vol. II, Penguin, Harmondsworth.

Marx, K. (1983), *Capital*, Vol. I, Lawrence & Wishart, London.

Marx, K. (1987), *From the Preparatory Materials (Urtext)*, *Collected Works*, vol. 29, Lawrence and Wishart, London.

Marx, K. and F. Engels (1962), *Die deutsche Ideology*, MEW 3, Dietz, Berlin.

Marx, K. and F. Engels (1980), *Die heilige Familie*, MEW 2, Dietz, Berlin.

Negri, A. (1991), *Marx Beyond Marx*, Autonomedia, New York.

Negri, A. (1992), "Interpretation of the Class Situation Today," in Bonefeld, W., Gunn, R. and K. Psychopedis (eds) *Open Marxism: Theory and Practice*, Pluto Press, London.

Negt, O. and A. Kluge (1981), *Geschiche und Eigensinn*, Verlag 2001, Frankfurt.

Psychopedis, K. (1992), "Dialectical Theory," in Bonefeld, W., Gunn, R. and K. Psychopedis (eds) *Open Marxism: Dialectics and History*, Pluto Press, London.

Wildcat and J. Holloway (1999), "Wildcat (Germany) reads John Holloway — A Debate on Marxism and the Politics of Dignity," *Common Sense*, no. 24.

4

Primitive Accumulation in Marxism
Historical or Trans-historical
Separation From Means of Production?[1]

Paul Zarembka

The Commoner for September 2001 is devoted to "Enclosures," i.e., the process of separation of laborers from any means of production so that they become free wage-laborers for the purposes of capitalist exploitation. This process is not a natural development, but rather the result of violent confrontations. It is a process not just having happened in the past, but is continuing to this day. That awareness is lacking in many discussions of social development, some even purporting to be Marxist recognizing the importance of class struggle. *The Commoner* is, therefore, to be commended for driving home the continuing importance of the issue.

Nevertheless, the set of articles also includes a basic theoretical mistake, the mistake of presenting "primitive accumulation" as if the concept is applicable for all times of capitalist development rather than just the process of initial transition from the feudal to the capitalist mode of production. In this commentary, we review the usage of primitive accumulation centering the collection, and compare that usage to Marx's own, clear statements. We suggest that accumulation of capital proper, without need for an adjective "primitive," includes force and violence in achieving capitalist aims of separation of laborers from their means of production; there is no need to invoke "primitive" to recognize this fact. The work of Rosa Luxemburg is consistent with our perspective. Lenin is partly responsible for distortion when he focused accumulation of capital on more production[2], but he followed upon a certain ambiguity within Marx himself, a problem to which Luxemburg's work called attention (see Zarembka, 2000). Throughout this paper, "historical" refers specifically to the original transition from feudalism to capitalism. "Trans-historical" includes this transition, but also the capitalist mode of production proper (although not to other modes of production) as it operates on a continuing basis, suggesting usage independent of historical context.

I. The Problem: Primitive Accumulation as Trans-historical

Most of the articles in the special issue of *The Commoner* are quite clear in what they want the reader to understand. Michael Perelman's lead article is a reprint of much of the introduction and first chapter of his book *The Invention of Capitalism: Classical Political Economy and the Secret History of Primitive Accumulation*. The material reprinted in *The Commoner* does not actually address Marx's understanding of primitive accumulation, so we will go to the book's second chapter, "The Theory of Primitive Accumulation," for Perelman's perspective. Given that it is well-known that Marx's concept of primitive accumulation includes and highlights force and violence in separating laborers from means of production, the only issue being addressed now is whether the concept is applicable to the modern world as well as to the world before the nineteenth century, or is only applicable regarding the transition from feudalism to capitalism.

Perelman is at first uncomfortable that Marx, even late in life, "seemed to take an almost Smithian position, diminishing the importance of primitive accumulation by relegating it to a distant past" (Perelman, 2000, p. 27). But he then says (pp. 28–29) that the material on primitive accumulation in Volume 1 "does not appear to be qualitatively different" from Marx's discussion of accumulation proper, suggesting Marx's willingness to include force and violence for the latter. He goes on later to cite a passage from Volume 1 that "accumulation of capital is...multiplication of the proletariat" and claims flat out that this is about primitive accumulation (p. 36), neglecting to notice that this passage appears in the first section of Marx's chapter "The General Law of Capitalist Accumulation" which says nothing at this point about primitive accumulation. A passage nine pages later (Marx, 1867, p. 585, cited below) specifically describes primitive accumulation as an historical issue.

For Perelman, the explanation for Marx's downgrading of the continuing importance of separation from means of production is that such a focus would have tended to undermine another message: the brutality of market forces themselves. Still, Perelman claims a passage from Marx purporting to show that Marx considered separation, understood as "primitive accumulation," to obtain even after the constitution of the capitalist mode of production. Quoting a passage in Volume 3 referring to "expropriating the final residue of direct producers who still have something left to expropriate," Perelman says that the passage is important because "it indicates that Marx realized the ongoing nature of primitive accumulation [sic]" (p. 31). However, the antecedent to Marx's passage concerning whom is being expropriated seems to be "expropriation of minor capitalists" (Marx, 1894, p. 241 — this being the Progress edition and corresponding to the German text; the Vintage translation used by Perelman may include peasants), and, in any case, the paragraph from which the citation is drawn concerns falling profits and accumulation proper, not primitive accumulation. Perelman goes on to provide his own examples of separation from means of production continuing in the present, and labels these as examples of primitive accumulation. The labeling permits him to conclude that "primitive accumulation remains a key concept for understanding capitalism — and not just the particular phase of capitalism associated with the transition from feudalism, but capitalism proper. Primitive accumulation is a process that continues to this day." (p. 37) To conclude, Perelman simply takes separation as synonymous with primitive accumulation, without recognizing the possibility that accumulation proper could, in its own conception, include separation within capitalist development.

The article by De Angelis (2001) develops an argument that "primitive accumulation is necessarily present in mature capitalist systems and, given the conflicting nature of capitalist relations, assumes a continuous character" (p. 2). De Angelis proposes that the "core of Marx's approach is the concept of *separation between producers and means of production*" and that the "difference between accumulation and primitive accumulation, not being a substantive one, is a difference in the conditions and forms in which this *separation* is implemented" (pp. 5 and 6, italics in original). He suggests that primitive accumulation is *ex novo* separation, while accumulation proper is separation "on a greater scale" (p. 8). Exactly what "a greater scale" for separation is to mean remains rather unclear, although an example De Angelis cites may help. When labor organizes to create a barrier to capital being able to extend the length of the working day, capital responds by introducing machinery as an counter element against the working class:

> The introduction of machinery *at this juncture* represents an act of accumulation, of re-creation of the separation at a greater scale beyond the limit posed by the "social barrier." By rationalizing the working day, restructuring the work process and dismissing the work force, the introduction of machinery aims at bypassing that "social barrier" that was erected and therefore re-creates the *separation* between forces of production and producers at a greater scale. In so doing it intensifies labour to the extent that "the denser hour of the 10-hour working day contains more labour, i.e. expended labour power, than the more porous hour of the 12-hour working day" [citing Marx's Volume 1]. It goes without saying that any attempt to repeal the law that sets the extension of the working day would be instead an act of *ex novo* production of that separation, an act of primitive accumulation. (p. 18, italics in original)

As best as we can understand, forcing *more* work hours (repealing working-day laws) is additional separation (primitive accumulation), while *more intense* hours of work (in this case, through the introduction of facilitating machinery) is greater separation (accumulation proper). In any case, historical time does not seem to be involved in the distinction.

Bonefeld's (2001) article in the special issue of *The Commoner* cites De Angelis' work as background (p. 2, fn. 2). Regarding primitive accumulation he asserts its incorporation into accumulation proper:

> primitive accumulation describes not just the period of transition that led to the emergence of capitalism....[Rather,] primitive accumulation is a constantly reproduced accumulation, be it in terms of the renewed separation of new populations from the means of production and subsistence, or in terms of the reproduction of the wage relation in the "established" relations of capital. The former seeks to bring new workers under the command of capital and the latter to contain them as an exploitable human resource — the so-called human factor of production.... Capitalist accumulation itself rests on the continuously reproduced divorce of labor [from means of production]. (pp. 1–3)

And throughout Bonefeld's article no distinction between accumulation proper and primitive accumulation is even attempted (De Angelis at least tries to draw some distinction), suggesting the question whether we should bother at all with any concept of primitive accumulation. Bonefeld goes on to use and re-interpret Luxemburg's (1913) *Accumulation of Capital*, inappropriately we argue. He says that, in Luxemburg's view, "*primitive accumulation* derives from the contradictory logic of capitalist accumulation and its crisis. This made it possible for Luxemburg to accept the view that primitive accumulation marks the period of transition to capitalism and to argue, at least by implication, that *primitive accumulation* is a feature of the crisis-ridden character of capitalist accumulation" (p. 2, italics added). Bonefeld's characterizaiton would be perfectly correct, except that, at the italized instances, Luxemburg would have used "separation of laborers from means of production" (note: the third instance in his passage of "primitive accumulation" is an historical reference and thus correct).

Luxemburg herself is absolutely clear that primitive accumulation is historical:

> At the time of primitive accumulation, i.e. at the end of the Middle Ages, when the history of capitalism in Europe began, and right into the nineteenth century, dispossessing the peasants in England and on the Continent was the most striking weapon in the large-scale transformation of means of production and labor power into capital. Yet capital in power performs the same task even today, and on an even more important scale — by modern colonial policy.... With that we have passed beyond the stage of primitive accumulation; this process is still going on. (Luxemburg, 1951, pp. 369–70)

In other words, Luxemburg — even while recognizing exactly what the whole issue of *The Commoner* draws attention to: dispossession — reserves primitive accumulation for the original rise of the capitalist mode of production. Otherwise, she writes in the spirit of *The Commoner*: "Accumulation, with its spasmodic expansion, can no more wait for, and be content with, a natural internal disintegration of non-capitalist formations and their transition to commodity economy, than it can wait for, and be content with, the natural increase of the working population. Force is the only solution open to capital." (pp. 370–71). Indeed, we can utilize Luxemburg's understanding of accumulation of capital proper as inclusive of separation/dispossession, with all the blood, sweat and tears it entails, and at the same time not give up on primitive accumulation as being historical.

De Angelis and Bonefeld are quite correct to emphasize separation from means of production. But never do they cite a place in Marx where Marx himself refers to primitive accumulation other than in the historical process of movement from feudalism to capitalism. And they avoid certain passages in Marx where he is quite clear for his own context for usage of primitive accumulation. Thus, neither one cites the first paragraph of Marx's "The So-called Primitive Accumulation" in which Marx notes that accumulation of capital presupposes surplus-value and surplus-value presupposes capitalist production and, therefore, everything "seems to turn in a vicious circle, out of which we can only get by supposing a primitive accumulation (previous accumulation of Adam Smith) preceding capitalistic accumulation; an accumulation not the result of the capitalistic mode of production, but its starting point" (Marx, 1867, p. 667). Primitive accumulation, says Marx, "appears as primitive, because it forms the pre-historic stage of capital and of the mode of production corresponding with it" (p. 668). In order to sustain their argument De Angelis and Bonefeld would have to confront these well-known passages. But they would also have to deal satisfactorily with many other similar, less well-known passages, such as:

> primitive accumulation... is the historic basis, instead of the historic result of specifically capitalist production. How it itself originates, we need not here inquire as yet. It is enough that it forms the starting-point. (1867, p. 585)

> It is this same severance of the conditions of production, on the one hand, from the producers, on the other, that forms the conception of capital. It begins with primitive accumulation, appears as a permanent process in the accumulation and concentration of capital, and expresses itself finally as centralization of existing capitals... (1894, p. 246 — this passage is cited by Bonefeld, p. 7, and also by Perelman, 2000, p. 31, neither recognizing that the passage only says that separation appears in both primitive accumulation and accumulation proper).

> Accumulation merely presents as a *continuous process* what in *primitive accumulation* appears as a distinct historical process, as the process of the emer-

gence of capital and as a transition from one mode of production to another (1910, p. 272, italics in original — this passage is cited by De Angelis, p. 6 and by Bonefeld, p. 10, but both cut out "as a transition from one mode of production to another"!).

It is this separation which constitutes the concept of capital and of *primitive* accumulation, which then appears as a continual process in the accumulation of capital and here finally takes the form of the centralization of already existing capitals... (1910, pp. 311–12, italics in original).

The primitive accumulation of capital...This historical act is the historical genesis of capital, the *historical* process of separation... (1910, pp. 314–15, italics in original).

De Angelis and Bonefeld skirt the problem by arguing that the essence of accumulation of capital, as well as of primitive accumulation, is separation from means of production. At one level, they are to be commended, for it is rare to understand accumulation of capital itself as separation. But, on the other hand, their position is reductionist. A stronger theoretical position is to stay with Marx's definition of primitive accumulation, and to probe more deeply the concept of accumulation of capital as used by Marx. Elsewhere, we have argued that there is an ambiguity in Marx concerning accumulation proper which needs to be directly understood as such. One can then go on to appreciate Luxemburg's work in a new and more appreciative light (see Zarembka, 2000).

The two articles in the middle of the special issue, by the Midnight Notes Collective (2001), and "Debt Crisis, Africa and the New Enclosures," by Silvia Federici, are both reprints from a 1990 issue of *Midnight Notes*. They do not really sustain the theoretical arguments of the other three papers, except by their presence in the middle. The article by the Collective starts with a quote from Marx which clearly refers to the transition from feudalism to capitalism. Later, the article notes that "original" or "primitive accumulation" in Marx refers to the transition to capitalism from feudalism. Nowhere is applicability of the concept primitive accumulation to today's world specifically discussed. The Collective does claim that the 1980s had seen the largest enclosures in world history,[3] a very important insight and illustrating the persistence of enclosures since the late 1400s. But this claim is not the same as saying that primitive accumulation, insofar as the concept is correctly understood, obtains in the modern world.

Federici's article does not deal with primitive accumulation, focusing rather on the extent to which Africa has *not* had consummation of the separation from means of production: "to this day at least 60 percent of the African population lives by subsistence farming, done mostly by women. Even when urbanized, many Africans expect to draw some support from the village, as the place where one may get food when on strike or unemployed, where one thinks of returning in old age, where, if one has nothing to live on, one may get some unused land to cultivate from a local chief or a plate of soup from neighbors and kin." (p. 2) Such demonstration of incomplete separation remains very important.

II. THE SOLUTION: SEPARATION INCLUDED WITHIN ACCUMULATION OF CAPITAL PROPER

This author and all those in the special issue of *The Commoner* share a same concern: it is of utmost importance to recognize the *continuing* role of separation of laborers from their means of production. *The Commoner*'s collection — especially Perelman, De Angelis, and Bonefeld — centers understanding of that separation in both accumulation of capital proper as well as primitive accumulation. Fine, and it represents an important step forward from some kind of economistic reading of accumulation of capital.

But then why did Marx bother at all with primitive accumulation? There seem to be three possible answers: 1) "primitive accumulation" is separation whenever it occurs, while accumulation of capital proper includes this separation and expands it to *also* include something else rather unclearly specified, 2) "primitive accumulation" is reserved for the *historical* separation in the rise of capitalism, while accumulation proper centers on separation after the establishment of capitalism, or 3) like "2" "primitive accumulation" is historical separation only, and, like "1," accumulation proper is separation and also "something else." From Marx"s texts and theoretical necessity, the first alternative ought to be eliminated; "primitive accumulation" should be used to highlight an essential component for understanding specifically the transition from feudalism to capitalism. It mandates our need to understand that transition and not take it for granted, merely because history happened that way. "In the history of primitive accumulation, all revolutions are epoch-making that act as levers for the capitalist class in course of formation" (Marx, 1867, p. 669).

The third alternative is rather too vague, not only in the collection we have examined but more generally. Still, that "something" could be considered. In any case, we posit that an unwillingness to confront an ambiguity in Marx regarding the meaning of accumulation of capital is at the root of broadening the concept of primitive accumulation to become something trans-historical. We should note, in any case, that there are others who recognize the problem at least in part. For example, Frank (1978, particularly Chapter 7) distinguishes "primary accumulation" from the primitive, with "primary" referring only to modern capitalist undermining of non-capitalist forms of production. Primitive accumulation thus retains Marx's usage as the "original" separation of labor from means of production in the initial transition to capitalist mode of production, principally in Europe. In spite of this advance in clarity, accumulation of capital proper otherwise retains its ambiguity in Frank's work.

Seeing accumulation of capital as inclusive of enclosures, of separation from means of production, opens new vistas for a Marxist understanding. For, "extra-economic" factors are forefronted and an economistic understanding of capital-ism becomes impossible.

NOTES

1 [Editor's Note: Paul's essay appeared first in *The Commoner*, "Debate on Prim-itive Accumulation," at www.commoner.org.uk. This is a revised version.]

2 "New and important in the highest degree is Marx"s analysis of the *accumula-tion of capital*, i.e. the transformation of a part of surplus value into capital, and its use, not for satisfying the personal needs or whims of the capitalist, but for new production" (Lenin, 1915, pp. 63–64). Parallel to his delimita-tion of accumulation of capital proper from including forceful separation, Lenin refers to "primitive accumulation": "From the accumulation of capi-tal under capitalism we should distinguish what is known as primitive ac-cumulation: the forcible divorcement of the worker from the means of production, the driving of the peasants off the land, the stealing of commu-nal land, the system of colonies and national debts, protective tariffs, and the like. 'Primitive accumulation' creates the 'free' proletarian at one pole, and the owner of money, the capitalist, at the other" (p. 64).

Given that accumulation of capital proper is not to include separation, we can surmise that Lenin would agree with *The Commoner*'s trans-histori-cal usage of "primitive accumulation" to refer to any time period.

3 "In the biggest diaspora of the century, on every continent millions are being uprooted from their land, their jobs, their homes through wars, famines, plagues, and the IMF ordered devaluations (the four knights of the modern apocalypse) and scattered to the corners of the globe" (p. 2). One example they cite (pp. 2–3): "In China, the transition to a "free market economy" has led to the displacement of one hundred million from their communally operated lands. Their urban counterparts are facing the loss of guaranteed jobs in factories and offices and the prospect of emigrating from one city to another to look for a wage. The 'iron rice bowl' is to be smashed while a similar scenario is developing in the Soviet Union and Eastern Europe."

REFERENCES

Bonefeld, W. (2001), "The Permanence of Primitive Accumulation: Commodity Fetishism and Social Constitution," *The Commoner*, No. 2, at www.com-moner.org.uk, revised version reprinted in this volume.

De Angelis, M. (2001), "Marx and Primitive Accumulation: The Continuous Character of Capital's 'Enclosures'," *The Commoner*, No. 2, at www.com-moner.org.uk, revised version reprinted in this volume.

Federici, S. (2001), "Debt Crisis, Africa and the New Enclosures," *The Commoner*, No. 2, at www.commoner.org.uk.

Frank, A. G. (1978), *World Accumulation, 1492–1789*, Monthly Review, New York.

Lenin, V.I. (1915), "Karl Marx: A Brief Biographical Sketch with an Exposition of Marxism," *Collected Works*, Volume 21, Progress Publishers, Moscow, 1964.

Luxemburg, R. (1913), *The Accumulation of Capital*, translated by Agnes Schwarzschild, Monthly Review Press, New York, and Routledge & Kegan Paul, London, 1951.

Marx, K. (1867), *Capital*, Volume 1, Progress Publishers, Moscow, 1954, and Lawrence and Wishart, London. Also, translated by Ben Fowkes, Vintage Books, New York, 1977.

Marx, K. (1894), *Capital*, Volume 3, edited by Frederick Engels, Progress Publishers, Moscow, 1959, Lawrence and Wishart, London, 1974.

Marx, K. (1910), *Theories of Surplus Value: Part III*, Progress Publishers, Moscow, 1971.

Midnight Notes Collective, 2001, "The New Enclosures," Midnight Notes Collective, *The Commoner*, No. 2, at www.commoner.org.uk, revised version reprinted in this volume.

Perelman, M. (2000), *The Invention of Capitalism: Classical Political Economy and the Secret History of Primitive Accumulation*, Duke University Press, Durham and London.

Zarembka, P. (2000), "Accumulation of Capital, Its Definition: A Century after Lenin and Luxemburg," *Value, Capitalist Dynamics and Money, Research in Political Economy*, Vol. 18, edited by P. Zarembka, JAI/Elsevier, Amsterdam.

5

History and Social Constitution
Primitive Accumulation is not Primitive[1]

Werner Bonefeld

PROLOGUE

Paul Zarembka (2002) focuses well on the conceptual difficulties that "primitive accumulation" presents. He argues that primitive accumulation is epoch-making but denies its epochal character by insisting that it refers merely to the period of transition from feudalism to capitalism. He insists that the accumulation of capital entails violence and continued processes of dispossession but argues that this should be seen in abstraction from primitive accumulation. Marx, he insists, offered clear statements and, then, says that there are ambiguities in Marx's thought. He commends the arguments on the permanence of primitive accumulation for showing that separation is the constitutive presupposition and result of the accumulation of capital, but charges that the argument is reductionist.

This charge appears to derive from what he sees as "the basic theoretical mistake" of "presenting 'primitive accumulation' as if the concept is applicable for all times of capitalist development rather than just the process of initial transition." He argues, with relish, that I "never cite a place in Marx where Marx himself refers to 'primitive accumulation' other than in the historical process of movement from feudalism to capitalism." He criticises my argument for its lack of differentiation. As he sees it, there is not even an attempt at distinguishing between accumulation proper and primitive accumulation. I agree with him that separation is the essence of both but disagree that no distinction between them is drawn. Whether Marx really never referred to primitive accumulation other than in terms of transition, is of little interest in my view. If he really did not, than clearly he should have.

THE PAST IN THE PRESENT

Concerning the significance of primitive accumulation, Paul Zarembka states that "a stronger theoretical position is to stay with Marx's definition of 'primitive accumulation,' and to probe more deeply the concept of 'accumulation of capital' as used by Marx." Paul Zarembka's argument is schematic: primitive accumulation is time-defined as the period of transition that gave rise to capitalist accumulation, and the concept is thus peculiar to a specific era. Primitive accumulation brought about capitalism. Once capitalism is there, primitive accumulation has finished and its conceptual relevance vanishes. Marx's insight that the history of past generations weights like a nightmare on the living, is thus dismissed. If primitive accumulation really is an history-making epoch — an epoch that brought about the establishment of capitalist social relations (!) — one would expect that capitalism is "marked" by the pains of its origin. That is, the understanding of the systematic character of primitive accumulation does indeed probe the concept of accumulation of capital. It exposes its origin, reveals the social basis of its conceptuality, and shows the logic of separation at work within its established form (cf. Negt and Kluge, 1981).

Even if one were to accept that primitive accumulation refers only to the pre-history of capitalism, problems arise. When did primitive accumulation end and when did capitalism begin? For England, Marx indicated that the period of primitive accumulation lasted about 350 years, coming to an end about 1850. And in Germany or in Russia? Is the era of primitive accumulation still continuing in North Korea, and when did it come to a close in South Korea? The question of transition was of great concern to the Russian left: could Russia "leap" directly into socialism or should there have to be a bourgeois revolution first. In his *State and Revolution*, Lenin provided the magic resolution, stating that the new proletarian state of the Bolsheviki was to be a bourgeois state without the bourgeoisie. The question of transition had already been raised in the correspondence between Vera Zasulich and Karl Marx, the former asking whether Russia could leap directly from feudalism to socialism and the latter writing several drafts, finally offering a most conditional, and that is, prohibitive "yes" (see Godelier, 2000). When did primitive accumulation come to a conclusion in Russia? Did it conclude after the forceful industrialisation which under Stalin amounted to a form of primitive accumulation, as Dyer-Witheford (1999) argues, or was Yeltsin the modern Russian version of Elizabeth I, the Queen of primitive accumulation in England?

Primitive accumulation is extremely difficult to "time." It occurred in different countries at different times, and is still occurring now. It was not a one historical event but a series of events, divided by space and time, and form. England was the classical form, but not the only form, of primitive accumulation (cf. de Angelis, in this volume). The difficulty of offering a time-specific delineation of primitive accumulation does not invalidate the understanding that it belongs, as an independent historical form of social relations, to the pre-history of capital-ism. However, it remains a matter of debate when this pre-history was concluded and when new forms of enforced separation emanate from capitalist accumula-tion itself. The answer to this, interesting though it might be, is academic. Much more important than the precise timing of the end of the one and the beginning of the other, is the understanding of its constitutive character. The divorce of labour from her means forms or constitutes the concept of capital. The original separation of labour from her means is a time-specific event of transition. At the same time, this separation is constitutive of capitalist social relations and prim-itive accumulation is therefore also a concept that brings to the fore the system-atic character of separation upon which capitalism rests. It reveals the constitutive content of capitalistically constituted social relations. Once capital-ist social relations are established, the significance of primitive accumulation changes from historical presupposition to constitutive premise and result of cap-italist reproduction. Capitalist accumulation rests on the "logic of separation" and has permanently to reproduce this constitutive separation of labour from her means in order to posit itself as "capital accumulation." The historical gen-esis of capitalist social relations transforms thus into its existing concept: its gen-esis becomes its existence. Capitalist accumulation carries its original beginning within itself, as the secrete determination of its concept: what first appeared as the constitutive historical presupposition of capital is now the result "of its pres-ence" (Marx, 1973, p. 460).

The difficulties of timing apart, Zarembka's reproach appears to based on misconceptions concerning the meaning of primitive accumulation. This might be because by the sort of language difficulties that Backhaus (1992) detects in relation to Marx's critique of political economy. My previous chapter talked about the permanence of primitive accumulation in the following terms: social constitution, presupposition, constitutive separation, constitutive pre-positing action, etc. Most importantly, I argue that primitive accumulation is suspended (*aufgehoben*) in capitalist accumulation as its secrete history of constitution. These terms draw attention to the critique of political economy as a theory of social constitution. This leads me to a few

SEMANTIC CLARIFICATIONS

In the German original, Marx does not speak of "primitive" accumulation. This term is offered in the English translation and, I suppose, it is as close to the Ger-man original as that is possible. Yet, it is inaccurate. The German text says "*ur-sprünglich*." This term can also be translated as "original," "initial," "unspoiled," as well as "beginning," "first manifestation," and "springing to life." Its meaning does not connote "causality," where, say, an historical event is seen to have "caused" the formation of a distinct mode of social relations. However, primitive accumulation is primitive only from the standpoint of the established relations of capitalist accumulation, which conceal their genesis and hide their social constitution in the doubly free labourer. More then causality, the term *"Ursprung"* refers to a beginning which is not the result of that which comes afterwards but, instead, its historical presupposition, and therefore also its constitutive precondition and basis. Primitive accumulation is the constitutive condition of capitalist social relations. The constitution of capital in and through object-less labour appears to vanish in the law of capitalist accumulation proper. Yet, however much the established relations of capital conceal their social constitution, capital cannot be without the permanently reproduced divorce of human social practice from its means. The sharp distinction that Zarembka draws between "primitive accumulation" and "accumulation proper" is schematic. It does not reveal the social constitution of capital. Instead he divorces the established relations of accumulation from their constitutive presupposition in the divorce of labour from her means. Marx's notion that capital "is the separation of the conditions of production from the labourer" (1972, p. 422) and that this separation "forms (*bildet*) the conception (*Begriff*) of capital" (Marx, 1966, p. 246), not only conceives of capital as separation but, also, sees it as the constitutive force of capital. Social constitution is historical constitution.

What is to be understood by "permanent" in this context? In Latin, *"per"* means through, way; and *"manere"* means to remain, to be continuous; permanent then connotes a lasting character, something which is maintained through time. Regarding primitive accumulation, permanence means that the constitutive principle of capitalist social relations in-forms its dynamic and movement. Permanence, then, means a constantly re-constituted process of separation where nothing remains in the way it was and where at the same time, nothing changes. Adorno (1975) concept of "dynamic within stasis" focuses this well: capitalism is a dynamic, ever developing and changing configuration of social relations, where everything that is solid melts, at the same time as which the "law" of development remains unchanged: restless exploitation of object-less labour on the altar of profit. That is to say, the freedom of labour from its conditions entails the capitalist property right to preserve abstract wealth through the "sacrifice of 'human machines' on the pyramids of accumulation" (Gambino, 1996, p. 55). The law of capitalism can thus be summarised as follows: the law is what remains in disappearance. Whatever the specific and changing historical forms of capitalism, it rests on and develops by force of "the logic of separation."

Capital is not constituted once and for all. It has continuously to return to its *Ursprung*: on the one hand, labour is reproduced on an expanded scale as free labour and, on the other, the concentration of the means of production in fewer and fewer hands. Capital achieves this permanent return to its *Ursprung* with no cost: it is the outcome of the accumulation of capital. That is to say, primitive accumulation is the secrete history of capitalist social relations. Primitive accumulation, I argued, is the first presupposition of capital and the commodity form is the first presupposition of the principle of capital, where the separation of the producers from their means forms the basis of their existence as mere personifications of things. The critical issue here is the precise meaning of "suspended" (*aufgehoben*).

"Suspended" is usually used as the English translation of the German term "*aufgehoben*" or "*Aufhebung*." "*Aufhebung*" is a term that is most difficult to translate into English, and "suspended" does not carry the full meaning of this typically many-sided German term. The understanding that primitive accumulation is "suspended" in capitalist accumulation appears to have caused some confusion, leading to the charge that my account collapses two distinct concepts into one, and that I therefore do not distinguish between primitive accumulation and accumulation proper. I accept that I used an inappropriate term. The German term should have been used throughout to give full meaning to the argument that primitive accumulation is suspended — *aufgehoben* — in the commodity form as its "subterranean condition, constitutive presupposition, and historical basis."

In Hegelian language, *Aufhebung* connotes a dialectical process of determinate negation. That is, the determination of a term negates it at the same time as which the so negated term transforms into a new term. In this process, the negated term loses its independent existence and it does so at the same time as which its essence is maintained in the new term — the new term is informed by the negated term. The circumstance that the essence of the negated term is maintained in the new term, does therefore mean that the essence of the old term is also the essence of the new term. *Aufhebung* has more than just different meanings; they are also contradictory. The concept entails all these different and contradictory meanings. *Aufheben* has three main meanings: "to lift up" or "to raise"; "to make invalid" or "to cancel/eliminate"; and "to keep" or "to maintain." In our context, *Aufhebung* means that the historic form of primitive accumulation is raised to a new level where its original form and independent existence is eliminated (or cancelled) at the same time as its substance or essence (*Wesenshaftigkeit*) is maintained, putting it on to a new footing, transforming it into a new form and informing its existence. In other words, the notion that the essence of primitive accumulation is *aufgehoben* in accumulation proper means that the principle of primitive accumulation, that is separation, is raised to a new level, eliminating the history of primitive accumulation as a specific epoch. At the same time its essential character is maintained in the new form, that is, the historical presupposition of capitalism transforms into its constitutive presupposition: separation. In short, my argument that primitive accumulation is suspended in accumulation proper does not equate primitive accumulation with accumulation proper, as Zarembka asserts. Rather, it shows that the principle of primitive accumulation, that is separation, is the constitutive presupposition of capitalist accumulation and that this principle constitutes the essence of capitalist social relations. Primitive accumulation is not the result of capital, but its presupposition; and once it is *aufgehoben*, it transforms from historical presupposition into the constitutive presupposition of capitalistically constituted social relations. The historical presupposition of primitive accumulation inverts thus into the premise and precondition of capitalist accumulation. The result of primitive accumulation, that is the separation of labour from its means, has to be posed continuously in capitalist accumulation as its result. The divorce of labour from her means is now the result of capitalism's existence.

In short, capital cannot liberate itself from the results of primitive accumulation — they are constitutive of its form, in-form its concept, and have to be reconstituted continuously in the process of accumulation proper. Its genesis in primitive accumulation informs its existence in and through the logic of separation. This leads me to:

SOME CONCEPTUAL CONSIDERATIONS

I suggested that the conventional restriction of primitive accumulation to a time-specific historic period of transition from Feudalism to Capitalism contradicts characterisation of primitive accumulation as epoch-making. If primitive accumulation is indeed merely an "historic thing in itself," the notion of primitive accumulation as an epoch would mean that its meaning is also contained within itself. History, once made, would thus appear to be cancelled in the present which itself assumes the dubious quality as a self-constituted thing. Is history really bunk?

Primitive accumulation, Marx writes, "is written into the annals of mankind in letters of blood and fire" (Marx, 1983, p. 669). Have these letters of blood and fire been expunged from the modern world — have the annals of mankind been cleansed of the barbarism of its inception? If so, how can one comprehend the social constitution of "the logic of separation" upon which capital rests and which it has to reproduced on an expanding scale? There are, then, two sides to the primitive accumulation of capital. On the one hand, primitive accumulation is the historical epoch that precedes capital and from which capitalist social relations developed. In this dimension it is a time-specific historical event that delineates the transition towards capitalist social relations. On the other hand, primitive accumulation is defined by its systematic content of separation. This is the so-called "logic of separation." This logic "begins with primitive accumulation, appears as a permanent process in the accumulation and concentration of capital, and expresses itself finally as centralisation of existing capitals in a few hands and a deprivation of many of their capital (to which expropriation has now changed)" (Marx, 1966, p. 246). This systematic character of primitive accumulation, or its social content, does not comprise a specific chronological time frame — from feudalism via primitive accumula-

tion to capitalist relations of accumulation — but is rather a process of continuously re-constituted new "beginnings" (cf. Bonefeld and Gunn, 1991). It posits
the principle of capital: the separation of labour from the means of production.
This principle is the presupposition, precondition, and premise of capitalist social relations, as well as the result of their reproduction. "Capitalist production,
therefore, under its aspects of a continuous connected process, of a process of
reproduction, produces not only commodities, not only surplus-value, but it
also produces and reproduces the capitalist relation; on the one side the capitalist, on the other the wage-labourer" (Marx, 1983, p. 542) Further, "this incessant reproduction, this perpetuation of the labourer, is the sine quá non of
capitalist production" (ibid., p. 536). In short, "[c]apitalist production, therefore, of itself reproduces the separation between labour-power and the means
of labour" (ibid., p. 541). The constitutive presupposition of capital is the divorce of labour from the means of production, and this presupposition is posited
in the accumulation of capital as its result. That is to say, the separation of "genesis" from "existence" is uncritical. I used the term *aufgehoben* earlier to indicate this inversion between the historical presupposition of separation and its
transformation into the constitutive presupposition of capital. The "logic of separation" is capital's historical presupposition and the premise and the result of
its reproduction. Capital can not liberate itself from its constitutive presupposition; it has to posit it in order to maintain itself as "the form assumed by the
conditions of labour" (Marx, 1972, p. 492).

Primitive accumulation focuses the dissolution of the *ursprüngliche* unity between labour and the means of labour (historical presupposition) and forms
(*bildet*) the concept of capital (constitutive presupposition and premise of capital and result of capitalist reproduction). Marx emphasised this when he argued
that "it is not the unity of living and active humanity with the natural, inorganic
conditions of their metabolic exchange with nature, and hence their appropriation of nature, which requires explanation or is the result of historic process,
but the separation between these inorganic conditions of human existence and
this active existence, a separation which is completely posited only in the relation of wage labour and capital" (Marx, 1973, p. 489). It is completely posited
because the presupposition of primitive accumulation, i.e. separation, is *aufgehoben* in the social constitution of capitalist accumulation. It figures now no
longer as its historical genesis but as the premise and result of its existence as accumulation proper.

The capital relation pre-supposes the complete separation between the
labourers and the means by which they can realise their labour. As soon as
capitalist production stands on its own legs, it not only maintains this separation, but reproduces it on a continually expanding scale [hence perma-
nent]. The process, therefore, that creates the capital relation, can be none
other than the one which separates the labourer from possession of his

means of labour; a process that transforms, on the one hand, the social means of subsistence and production into capital, on the other, the immediate producers into wage-labourers [hence the systematic meaning of primitive accumulation]. The so-called primitive accumulation, therefore, is nothing else than the historical process of divorcing the producer from the means of production [primitive accumulation as time-specific]. It appears as "primitive" ["*ursprünglich*"], because it is the pre-history of capital and it forms [*bildet*] its mode of production [constitutive presupposition] (Marx, 1983, p. 668; adapted from the German original: Marx, 1979, p. 742).

In sum, capitalist "accumulation merely presents as a *continuous process*, what in *primitive accumulation*, appears as a distinct historical process, as the process of the emergence of capital" and following Zarembka's proper referencing, "as a transition from one mode of production to another" (Marx, 1972, p. 272). Despite the addition, the quotation still says that accumulation presents as a continuous process what in primitive accumulation appears as a distinct historical process; it is the historical basis of capital, is *aufgehoben* in the form of capital and thus forms and informs its concept. And finally, the universal reduction of all specific human social practice to the one, some abstract form of labour, from the battlefield to the cloning laboratory (cf. Dalla Costa, in this volume), is indeed characteristic of a form of social relations based on the separation of labour from its means. "The separation of labour from its product, of subjective labour-power from the objective conditions of labour, was therefore the real foundation in fact, and the starting-point of capitalist production. But that which at first was but a starting point, becomes, by the mere continuity of the process, by simple reproduction, the peculiar result, constantly renewed and perpetuated, of capitalist production" (Marx, 1983, p. 535). Further, "it may be called primitive accumulation, because it is the historic basis, instead of the historic result of specifically capitalist production.... [I]t forms the starting point. But all methods of raising the social productive power of labour that are developed on this basis, are at the same time methods for the increased production of surplus value or surplus-product, which in its turn is the formative element of accumulation" (Marx, 1983, p. 585), which is to say, the systematic force of primitive accumulation does indeed weight like a nightmare on the brain of the living. The violence of capital's original beginning is the formative element of the "civilised" forms of equality, liberty, freedom, and utility. These forms mystify the real content of bourgeois "equality" as an equality in the inequality of property. They are the constituted forms of the original violence — violence as civilised normality (cf. Benjamin, 1965). In sum, "the tradition of the oppressed teaches us that the "state of emergency" in which we live, is not the exception but the rule. We must attain to a conception of history that is in keeping with this insight" (ibid., p. 84).

Luxemburg's dictum "socialism or barbarism" recognises that the "civilised forms" of capitalist accumulation have a barbaric content. Barbarism is not an aberration of capitalism. Rather, the violence of its beginning is suspended in its constituted form. Just as the primitive accumulation of capital, Auschwitz has been written into the annals of human history. The difference between primitive accumulation and Auschwitz should not be overlooked. Primitive accumulation has been written into the annals of human history with blood and tears, but also with the hope in the power of the Enlightenment to lead human kind to maturity, as Kant saw it. Auschwitz has been written into the annals of human history with industrialised slaughter, transforming the bourgeois notion of rationality into delusion (cf. Postone, 1986, Bonefeld, 2005). Barbarism amounts to a form of primitive accumulation within the established relations of capital. It posits the concept of capital that hidden in the pleasant form of abstract equality, reveals this same equality as an equality of death.

POSTSCRIPT

Marx's critique of political economy is more than just an explanation of the accumulation of capital and the violence of separation that its genesis entailed — that too; it is also, and importantly so, a critique of the fetishism of capital as a self-constituted thing. This fetishism, as Marx's critique makes clear, has a real existence. The "relations connecting the labour of one individual with that of the rest appear, not as direct social relations between individuals at work, but as what they *really* are, material relations between persons and social relations between things" (Marx, 1983, p. 78, emphasis WB). The critique of fetishism does not deny the reality of fetishism. Rather, its critique reveals its reality. It shows the social constitution of a perverted world, and that is, it brings to the fore the social constitution of a social world in which human beings produce, through their own labour, a reality which increasingly enslaves them. In short, "[a]ll emancipation is the restoration of the human world and of human relationships to Man [*Mensch*] himself" (Marx).

NOTE

1 The is a revised version of an essay that originally appeared in *The Commoner,* "Debate on Primitive Accumulation," at: www.commoner.org.uk.

REFERENCES

Adorno, T. (1975), "Über Statik und Dynamik als soziologische Kategorien," in ibid., *Gesellschaftstheorie und Kulturkritik*, Suhrkamp, Frankfurt.

Backhaus, H.G. (1992), "Between Philosophy and Science: Marxian Social Economy as Critical Theory," in Bonefeld, W., Gunn, R., and K. Psychopedis (eds) *Open Marxism, vol. I: Dialectics and History*, Pluto, London.

Benjamin, W. (1965), *Zur Kritik der Gewalt und andere Aufsätze*, Suhrkamp, Frankfurt.

Bonefeld, W. (2005), "Nationalism and Anti-Semitism in Anti-Globalisation Perspecticve," in Bonefeld, W. and K. Psychopedis (eds) *Human Dignity: Social Autonomy and the Critique of Capitalism*, Ashgate, Aldershot.

Bonefeld, W. and R. Gunn (1991) "La constitution et sa signification: Réflexions sur l'épistémologie, la forme et la pratique sociale," *Futur antérieur*, no. 8.

Dyer-Witheford, N. (1999), *Cyper-Marx*, University of Illinois Press, Chicago.

Godelier, M. (2000), "The Disappearance of the 'Socialist System': Failure or Confirmation of Marx's View on the Transition from One Form of Production and Society to Another?," in Bonefeld, W. and K. Psychopedis (eds) *The Politics of Change: Globalization, Ideology and Critique*, Palgrave, London.

Marx, K. (1966), *Capital*, vol. III, Lawrence & Wishart, London.

Marx, K. (1972), *Theories of Surplus Value*, Part III, Lawrence & Wishart, London.

Marx, K. (1973), *Grundrisse*, Penguin, London.

Marx, K. (1979), *Das Kapital*, vol. I, MEW 23, Dietz, Berlin.

Marx, K. (1983), *Capital*, vol. I, Lawrence & Wishart, London.

Negt, O. and A. Kluge (1981), *Geschichte und Eigensinn*, Verlag 2001, Frankfurt.

Postone, M. (1986), "Anti-Semitism and National Socialism," in Rabinbach, A. and J. Zipes (eds) *Germans and Jews since the Holocaust*, Holmes & Meier, New York.

Zarembka, P. (2002), "Primitive Accumulation in Marxism, Historical or Transhistorical Separation from the Means of Production," *The Commoner*, March, revised version reprinted in this volume.

6

Capitalism and Reproduction[1]

Mariarosa Dalla Costa[2]

The sphere of reproduction today reveals all the original sins of the capitalist mode of production. Reproduction must be viewed, of course, from a planetary perspective, with special attention being paid to the changes that are taking place in wide sectors of the lower social strata in advanced capitalism as well as in an increasing proportion of the Third World population. We live in a planetary economy, and capitalist accumulation still draws its life-blood for its continuous valorization from waged as well as unwaged labour, the latter consisting first of all of the labour involved in social reproduction (Dalla Costa and James, 1972), in the advanced as well as the Third World countries.

We find that social "misery" or "unhappiness" which Marx (Marx, 1975, p. 286) considered to be the "goal of the political economy" has largely been realized everywhere. But, setting aside the question of happiness for the time being — though certainly not to encourage the myth of its impossibility — let me stress how incredible it now seems, Marxist analysis apart, to claim that capitalist development in some way brings a generalised well-being to the planet.

Social reproduction today is more beset and overwhelmed than ever by the laws of capitalist accumulation: the continual and progressive *expropriation* (from the "primitive" expropriation of the land as a means of production, which dates from the16th–18th centuries in England, to the expropriation, then as now, of all the individual and collective rights that ensure subsistence); the continual *division* of society into *conflictual hierarchies* (of class, sex, race, and nationality, which pit the free waged worker against the unfree unwaged worker, against the unemployed worker, and the slave labourer); the constant production of *inequality and uncertainty* (with the woman as reproducer facing an even more uncertain fate in comparison to any waged worker and, if she is also member of a discriminated race or nation, she suffers yet deeper discrimination); the continual *polarisation* of the production of *wealth* (which is more and more concentrated) and the production of *poverty* (which is increasingly widespread).

As Marx writes in *Capital* (1976, p.799):

> Finally, the law which always holds the relative surplus production or industrial reserve army in equilibrium with the extent and energy of accumulation rivets the worker to capital more firmly than the wedges of Hephaestus held Prometheus to the rock. It makes an accumulation of misery a necessary condition, corresponding to the accumulation of wealth. Accumulation of wealth at one pole is, therefore, at the same time accumulation of misery, the torment of labour, slavery, ignorance, brutalization and moral degradation at the opposite pole, i.e. on the side of the class that produces its own product as capital.

This is true, not only for the population overwhelmed by the Industrial Revolution of the nineteenth century. It is even more accurate today, now that capital's accumulation passes, for example, through factory, plantation, dam, mine, and even carpet weaving workshops where it is by no means rare for children to be working in conditions of slavery.

Indeed, capitalist accumulation spreads through the world by extracting labour for production and reproduction in conditions of stratification which end in the reestablishment of slavery. According to a recent estimate, slavery is the condition in which over 200 million persons are working in the world today (*The Economist*, January 6 1990).

Those macro-processes and operations which economic forces, supported by political power, unfolded during the period of primitive accumulation in Europe with the aim of destroying the individual's value in relationship to his/her community in order to turn him/her into an isolated and valueless individual, a mere container for labour-power which s/he is obliged to sell to survive, continue to mark human reproduction on a planetary scale. The indifference shown by capital towards the possibility of labour-power's reproduction in the first phase of its history was only very partially, and today increasingly precariously, redeemed centuries later by the creation of the Welfare State. Currently, the task being set by the directives of the major financial agencies, the International Monetary Fund and the World Bank, is to re-draw the boundaries of welfare and economic policies as a whole (Dalla Costa and Dalla Costa, 1995) in both the advanced and the developing countries. (The economic, social welfare and social insurance measures recently introduced in Italy correspond precisely to the various "structural adjustment" plans being applied in many Third World countries.) The result is that increasingly large sectors of world population are destined to extinction because they are believed to be redundant or inappropriate to the valorization requirements of capital.

Just as at the end of the 1400s, when the bloody legislation against the expropriated (Marx, 1976, ch. 28) led to the mass hanging, torturing, branding, and chaining of the poor, so today the surplus or inadequately disciplined population of the planet is exterminated through death by cold and hunger in eastern Europe and various countries of the advanced West ("more coffins less cradles in Russia" — *La Repubblica*, February 16, 1994); death by hunger and epidemic in Africa, Latin America and elsewhere; death caused by formally declared war, by genocide authorized directly or indirectly, by military and police repression. The other variant of extinction is an individual or collective decision for suicide because there is no possibility to survive. (It is significant that, according to the Italian press reports in 1993–94, many cases of suicide in Italy are due to unemployment or to the fact that the only work on offer is to join a criminal gang, while, in India, the "tribal people" in the Narmada valley have declared a readiness to die by drowning if work continues on a dam which will destroy their habitat and, hence, the basis of their survival and cultural identity).[3]

The most recent and monstrous twist to this campaign of extinction comes from the extreme example of resistance offered by those who sell parts of their body, useless container for a labour-power that is no longer saleable. (In Italy, where the sale of organs is banned, press and TV reports in 1993–94 mentioned instances in which people said explicitly that they were willing to break the ban in exchange for money or a job.) For those impoverished and expropriated by capitalist expansion in the Third World, however, this is already a common way for obtaining money. Press reports mention criminal organisations that traffic in organs and supply perfectly legal terminals such as clinics. This trade flourishes thanks to kidnapping, often of women and children, and false adoption. An enquiry was recently opened at the European Parliament on the issue (*La Repubblica*, September 16, 1993), and various women's networks are trying to throw light on and block these crimes. But this is where capitalist development, founded on the negation of the individual's value, celebrates its triumph; the individual owner of redundant or, in any case, superfluous labour-power is literally cut to pieces in order to re-build the bodies of those who can pay for the right to live to the criminal or non-criminal sectors of capital which profit from it.

During the era of primitive accumulation, when the free waged worker was being shaped in England, the law still authorized slavery (Marx, 1976, ch. 28), treating the vagabonds, created by the feudal lords' violent and illegal expropriation of the land, as "voluntary" perpetrators of the crime of vagabondage and ordaining that, if anyone should refuse to work, he would be "condemned as a slave to the person who denounced him as an idler" (Marx, 1976, p.897). But, if this reduction of the poor to slavery remained on a relatively limited scale in England, not that much later, capital launched slavery on a much vaster scale, emptying Africa of the equivalent of Europe's population at that time through the slave trade to the Americas and the Caribbean.

But slavery, far from disappearing, has remained as one of capitalism's unmentioned, concealed constants. The poverty imposed on a large part of the planet by the major financial agencies chains entire families to work in conditions of slavery so that they can pay their creditors; workers are made to work in conditions of slavery in livestock farms, plantations and mines; children are made to work in conditions of slavery in carpet work-shops; women are kidnapped or fooled into working in the sex industry. But these are only some examples. It is significant that the problem of slavery was raised by the Non-Government Organisations at their Forum in Vienna on June 10–12 that preceded the UN's World Conference on Human Rights on June 14–25, 1993.

Again, in the period of primitive accumulation, with the birth of free waged labour after the great expropriations, there was the greatest case of sexual genocide in history, the great witch-hunts, which, with a series of other measures directed expressly against women, contributed in a fundamental way to forging the unfree, non-waged woman worker in the production and reproduction of labour-power (Federici, 1988). Deprived of the trades and means of production and subsistence typical of the previous economy, and largely excluded from craft-work or access to the new jobs that manufacturing was offering, the woman was essentially faced by two options for survival: marriage or prostitution. Even for women who had found some form of work external to the home, prostitution at that time was also a way of supplementing low family income or the low wages paid to women. Over and above the various regimes and meanings it has gone through in different eras and social contexts, it is interesting that, in that period, prostitution first became a trade exercised by women at the mass level, whence one can say that during the manufacturing period the individual proletarian woman was born fundamentally to be a prostitute (Fortunati, 1981; 1984, p.209).

From this insoluble contradiction in the woman's condition as an unwaged worker in a wage economy (Dalla Costa and James, 1972) sprouted the conditions for mass prostitution in that period — and also the conditions on which the same phenomenon is based today, but on a vaster scale, in order to generate profits for one of the most flourishing industries at the world level, the sex industry. This led the World Coalition against Trafficking in Women to present the first World Convention against Sexual Exploitation in Brussels (May 1993). The women in the Coalition also agreed to work for the UN's adoption of the convention and its ratification by the national governments.

Internationally, in fact, the sexual exploitation of women by organised crime is increasingly alarming. In Italy, these organisations have already brought many women from Africa and Eastern Europe to work as prostitutes. The tricks used to cover up exploitation by prostitution — for example, wife sales by catalogue or "sexual tourism" in exotic destinations — are legion and well-known. According to the Coalition's charges, various countries already accept forms of "sexual tourism" as a planned component in national income. Thanks to individual women and NGOs, studies of the direct government responsibility in forcing women to serve as prostitutes for soldiers during World War II have also begun.

Woman's condition in capitalism is born with violence (just as the free waged worker is born with violence); it is forged on the witches' pyres, and it is maintained with violence (Dalla Costa, 1978). Within the current context of the population's reproduction, the woman continues to suffer violence as the subject of poverty at the world level (since her unpaid responsibility for the home makes her the weak contracting party in the external labour market), but because of her lack of economic resources, she also suffers a further violence of being sucked increasingly into organised prostitution. The warlike visage that development increasingly assumes simply worsens woman's condition still further and magnifies the practice and mentality of violence against women.[4] A paradigmatic case is the war rape exercised as ethnic rape in the war in ex-Yugoslavia.

I have mentioned only some of the social macro-operations which allowed the capitalist system to "take off" during the period of primitive accumulation. But just as important were a series of other operations (Marx, 1976, chs. 26–33) left unmentioned here for the sake of brevity, but which could also be illustrated today as aspects of the continual re-foundation on a world scale of the class relationship on which capitalist development rests: the perpetuation of the stratification of workers in society based on the separation and counterposition imposed through the sexual division of labour.

All the considerations are designed to lead to one fundamental thesis: capitalist development *has always been unsustainable* because of its *human impact*. To understand the point, all one needs to do is to take the viewpoint of those who have been and continue to be killed by it. A presupposition of capitalism's birth was the sacrifice of a large part of humanity, mass exterminations, the production of hunger and misery, slavery, violence and terror. Its continuation requires the same presuppositions. Particularly from the *woman's* viewpoint, capitalist development has always been unsustainable because it places her in an *unsustainable contradiction*, by being an unwaged worker in a wage economy and, hence, for that reason, denied the right to an autonomous existence. And if we look at the subsistence economies — continually besieged, undermined and overwhelmed by capitalist development — we see that capitalist development continually deprives women of the land and water which for them are fundamental means of production and subsistence in sustaining the entire community.

The expropriation of land leaped to the world's attention in January, 1994 with the revolt of the indigenous people of Chiapas in Mexico. The media could hardly avoid reporting it because of the crucial role played by Mexico's alignment with the Western powers through the agreement for the North American Free Trade Area. The perversity of producing wealth by expropriation and the production of misery was there for all to see. But it is also significant that the dramatic consequences of expropriation of the land led those involved in drawing up the *Women's Action Agenda 21* in Miami in November, 1991 to make a forceful appeal for women to be guaranteed land and access to food. At the same time, the process of capitalist expansion—in this case, with the Green Revolution — led many people to practice the selective abortion of female foetuses and girl-child infanticide in some areas of the Third World (Shiva, 1990): from sexual genocide to preventive annihilation.

The question of unsustainable development has become topical fairly recently with the emergence of evidence for various environmental disasters and forms of harm inflicted on the ecosystem. The Earth, the water running in its veins, and the air surrounding it have come to be seen as an ecosystem, a living organism of which humans are a part-humans who depend for their life on the life and equilibrium of the ecosystem — as against an idea of Nature as the "other" of Humanity — a Nature to be dominated and whose elements are to be appropriated as though they were potential commodities waiting in a warehouse. After five centuries of expropriation and domination, the Earth is returning to the limelight. In the past it was sectioned, fenced in, and denied to the free producers. Now, it is itself being expropriated of its reproductive powers — turned topsy-turvy, vivisectioned, and made a commodity. But these extreme operations (like the "banking" and patenting of the genetic codes of living species) belong to a single process whose logic of exploitation and domination has brought the planet to such devastation in human and environmental terms as to provoke disquieting questions as to the future possibilities and modalities of human reproduction.

Environmental destruction is united with the destruction wreaked on an increasingly large proportion of humanity. The destruction wreaked on humans is necessary for the perpetuation of capitalist development today, just as it was at its origins. To stop subscribing to this general destruction, and hence to approach the problem of "sustainable development," means, above all, to take into account the struggles that are moving against capitalist development in the metropolises and the rural areas. It also means finding the ways, and defining the practices to set capitalist development behind us by elaborating a different approach to knowledge.

But in interpreting and taking into account the various anti-capitalist struggles and movements, a global vision must be maintained of the many sections of society rebelling in various forms and contexts throughout the planet. To give priority to some and ignore others would mean adopting the same logic of separation and counterposition which is the soul of capitalist development. The cancellation and annihilation of a part of humanity cannot be given as a foregone conclusion. In the metropolises and the advanced capitalist countries in general, many no longer have the waged job which, in their context, is the source of subsistence. At the same time, the welfare measures representing the complex of individual and collective rights that contribute to ensuring survival are being cut back. Human reproduction has already reached its limits: the woman's reproductive energy is increasingly dried out like a spring whose water has been used for too much land, and water, says Vandana Shiva (1990), does not multiply.

Reproduction is crushed by the general intensification of labour, by the over-extension of the working day, amidst cuts in resources whereby the lack of waged work, too, becomes a stress-laden search for work and/or illegal employment, added to the laborious work of reproduction. I have no space to give a more extensive description of the complex phenomena that have led to the drastic reduction in the birth-rate in the advanced countries, particularly in Italy (fertility rate 1.26, population growth zero). But it should also be remembered that women's refusal to function as machines for reproducing labour-power, demanding instead to reproduce themselves and others as social individuals, has represented a major moment of women's resistance and struggle (Dalla Costa and James, 1972). The contradiction in women's condition — whereby women are at a disadvantage in searching for financial autonomy through waged work outside the home, since they also remain primarily responsible for labour-power's production and reproduction — has exploded in all its unsustainability: women in the advanced countries have fewer and fewer children. In general, humanity in the advanced countries is less and less desirous of reproducing itself.

But women's great refusal in countries like Italy at the same time demands an answer to the overall question we are discussing: it demands a *new type of development* in which human reproduction is not built on an *unsustainable sacrifice by women*, as part of a conception and structure of life which is nothing but labour time within an *intolerable sexual hierarchy*. The "wage" struggle, in both its direct and indirect aspects, does not concern solely "advanced" areas as something distinct from "rural" ones, for there are very few situations in which survival rests solely on the land. To sustain the community, the wage economy is most often interwoven with resources typical of a subsistence economy, whose overall conditions are continually under pressure from the political and economic decisions of the major financial agencies such as the IMF and the World Bank (Dalla Costa and Dalla Costa, 1995). Today, it would thus be a fatal error not to defend the wage level and guarantees for the income — in money, goods and services — that it is working humanity's right to demand, since the wealth and power of capitalist society has been accumulated on the basis of five centuries of its labour. At the same time, land, water and forests must remain available for those whose subsistence comes from them, and to whom capitalist expropriation offer only extinction. As different sectors of mankind seek and demand a different kind of development, the strength to demand it grows to the extent that no one accepts their own extinction or the extinction of others.

The question of human reproduction posed by women's rejection of procreation is now turning into the demand for another type of development and seeks completely new horizons. The concept of welfare is not enough. The demand is now for happiness. The demand is for a formulation of development that opens up the satisfaction of the basic needs on whose suppression capitalism was born and has grown. One of those needs is for time as against a life consisting solely of labour, another is the need for physical life/sexuality (above all, with one's own and other people's bodies, with the body as a whole, not just the functions that make it more productive) as against the body as a mere container for labour-power or a machine for reproducing labour-power. Yet another need is the need for sociality/collectivity (not just with other men and women, but with the various living beings with which can now only be encountered after a laborious journey out of the city) as against the separation/isolation of individuals in the body of society and living nature as a whole. And still another need is for public space (not just the public parks and squares or the few other areas permitted to the collectivity) as against the enclosure, privatisation, and continual restriction of available space. Then there is the desire to find a relationship with the totality of the Earth as a public space as well as the need for play, indeterminacy, discovery, amazement, contemplation, emotion....

Obviously, the above has no pretence to "defining" fundamental needs, but it registers some whose systematic frustration by this mode of production has certainly not served human happiness. But I think one must have the courage to pose happiness as a problem. This requires the reanalysis of the notion of development, in order to think again "in the grand manner," and to reject the fear that raising the question of happiness may appear as too daring or as something too subjective. Rigoberta Menchu (Burgos, 1991) tells how the mothers in her community teach their girls from the start that the life facing them will be a life of immense toil and suffering. But she also wondered why, and the why reflects very precise, capitalist reasons: "We started to reflect on the roots of the problem, and we came to the conclusion that its roots lay in possession of the land. We did not have the best land, the landowners did. And every time we clear new land, they try to take it from us or to steal it in some way" (Burgos, 1991, p.144). Rigoberta has raised the problem of how to change this state of affairs; she has not cultivated the myth of human unhappiness. And the Christian teaching she has used alongside the Mayan traditions, has offered various lessons, including that of the Old Testament's Judith.

In my view, it is no coincidence that, in these last 20 years, the women's question, the question of the indigenous populations,[5] and the question of the Earth have assumed growing importance, for they are linked by an especially close synergy. The path towards a different kind of development cannot ignore them. There is much knowledge still in civilisations that have not died but have managed to conceal themselves, and their secrets have been maintained thanks to their resistance to the will to annihilate them. The Earth encloses so many powers, especially its power to reproduce itself and humanity as one of its parts. These powers have been discovered, preserved and enhanced more by women's knowledge than male science. It is crucial, then, that this other knowledge — of women, of indigenous populations and of the Earth, whose "passiveness" is capable of regenerating life (Shiva, 1990) — should find a way of emerging and being heard. This knowledge appears now as a decisive force that can lift the increasingly deadly siege capitalist development imposes on human reproduction.

NOTES

1 Translated from Italian by Julian Bees.

2 This essay was first presented as a paper at the seminar, Women's Unpaid Labour and the World System, organised by the Japan Foundation, April 8 1994, Tokyo, as part of the Foundation's "European Women's Study Tour for Environmental Issues." It has since been published in many languages, and was first published in English in *Open Marxism*, vol. III, edited by W. Bonefeld, R. Gunn etal., Pluto Press, London, 1995.

3 The protest over the Narmada dam has received extensive coverage in international publications and the international media. For a critical interpretation of the proliferation of dams in the world, see Shiva (1990).

4 Currently, there is a wide-ranging debate on the issue. Michel's essay (1987) remains a good reference-point.

5 As was stressed by the Working Group on Indigenous Peoples at the NGO Forum in Vienna (June 10–12, 1993), these peoples have worked especially hard during the last two decades to get their voice heard, to make progress on questions concerning them (the question of land, above all), to obtain greater respect for and a formalisation of their rights in written form. Significant stages in the process have been the Kari Oca Declaration, the Land Charter of the Indigenous Peoples, and the Convention of the International Labour Organisation on Indigenous and Tribal Peoples (ILO Conv. No. 169). This growing liaison and promotion of their demands was a major factor in the speedy expressions of solidarity from the North American indigenous populations during the rebellion of the indigenous people of Chiapas.

REFERENCES

Burgos, E. (1990), *Mi chiamo Rigoberta Menchù*, Florence, Giunti.

Dalla Costa, M. and James S. (1972), *The Power of Women and the Subversion of the Community*, London, Falling Wall Press.

Dalla Costa, G.F. (1978), *Un lavoro d'amore. La violenza fisica componente essenziale del "trattamento" maschile nei confronti delle donne*, Rome, Edizioni delle Donne.

Dalla Costa, M. and Dalla Costa, G.F. (eds) (1995), *Paying the Price*, London, Zed Books.

Federici, S. and Fortunati, L. (1984), *Il grande Calibano. Storia del corpo sociale ribelle nella prima fase del capitale*, Milan, Franco Angeli.

Federici, S. (1988), "The Great Witch-Hunt," in *The Maine Scholar*, Vol.1, No.1.

Fortunati, L. (1981), *L'arcano della riproduzione. Casalinghe, prostitue, operai e capitale*, Venice, Marsilio.

Fortunati, L. (1984), *Sesso come valore d'uso per il valore*, in Fortunati L., Federici S., *Il grande Calibano. Storia del corpo sociale ribelle nella prima fase del capitale*, Milan, Franco Angeli.

Marx, K. (1975), *Economic and Philosophical Manuscripts (1844)*, in *Early Writings*, London, Penguin.

Marx, K. (1976), *Capital. A Critique of Political Economy*. Volume One, London, Penguin.

Michel, A. (1987), "La donna a repentaglio nel sistema di guerra," in *Bozze*, No.2, April–March.

Shiva, V. (1990), *Staying alive: Women, Ecology and Survival in India*, London, Zed Books.

Women's Action Agenda 21 (1991), in *World Women's Congress for a Healthy Planet*, Official Report, 8–12 November 1991, Miami, Florida, USA, United Nations, New York, N.Y.

PART II

SUBVERSION IN EVERYDAY LIFE
MOVEMENTS, CURRENTS & CLASS STRUGGLE

7

Dancing Amidst the Flames
Imagination and Self-Organization in a Minor Key

Stevphen Shukaitis

In the autobiography of James Carr, one-time Black Panther and cofounder of the "Wolf Pack" with George Jackson in Soledad Prison, it is related that upon hearing the song "Dancin in the Streets" by Martha and the Vandellas, he knew that his political philosophy had changed. He wanted to overcome the duality between Martha and the Vandellas and the ruthless ends-justifies-the-means militancy of Sergei Nechayev: to find a way to "make the revolution a dance in the street."[1] During the mid-1960s in Chicago there emerged a crossover between the militant syndicalist labor organizing of the Industrial Workers of the World (IWW) and Surrealist inspired flights of fancy, embodied and circulated in publications such as the *Rebel Worker*. But rather than the somber and austere images of labor struggle that one often finds, this section of the IWW embraced youth revolt, free jazz and artistic experimentation, and rock 'n' roll in their pursuit of developing "critical theory at its Bugs Bunniest Best" and "dialectics in the spirit of the Incredible Hulk." Taking their inspiration from the growing tides of political unrest expressed increasingly through forms of pop culture they would come to write about the political potential for developing social struggle drawing from these social energies, arguing in pamphlets like *Mods, Rockers, and Revolution* that songs like "Dancin in the Streets" show that the yearning for freedom and refusal to submit to bureaucratic pressures are not just the desires of small bands of militants but rather "almost *instinctive* attitudes of most of our fellow workers."[2] From this they would conclude that their task was not to "bring" awareness of the problems of capitalism, racism, and social injustice to people who for the most part were already quite aware of them. Rather, taking more inspiration from Lennon than Lenin, they sought to connect the multitude of forms of rebellion and discontent that already existed involving all sorts of social subjects whose actions were not often assumed to have a political character:

Long live the Incredible Hulk, wildcat strikes, the Nat Turner Insurrection, high-school dropouts, draft-dodgers, deserters, delinquents, saboteurs, and all those soul-brothers, wild-eyed dreamers, real and imaginary heroes of defiance and rebellion who pool their collective resources in the exquisite, material transformation of the world according to desire![3]

But how are these moments and revolts and insubordination, bridged tenuously through the semiotic scaffolding of this pop song, connected? While such a question could easily raise the concern that such is a mere coincidence, it is illustrative of a larger process of the politics of minor composition—a politics based on using whatever materials are available in the social milieu to formulate new relations, forms of self-organization, and embodiments of the radical imagination. Indeed, everywhere that Martha and the Vandellas played in the late 1960s they seemed to be accompanied by the occurrence of a riot—people "dancing amidst the flames."[4] While touring they were constantly questioned by the press if their music was a call to riot and if they were the leaders of militant movements in the United States. Music here can be seen as constituting a key part of daily life rather than a distraction from it, as crystallizing and bringing together social energies and political passions through a tune that one could easily claim is "just a party song." Through the circulation of particular musical compositions people found a means to organize and articulate their desires for escaping from the daily grind of the workday, to develop a critique in culture (rather than of culture) of the dystopian nature of work that people sought to escape from.[5] A form of political composition materializes around the form of an artistic composition, articulated through the distributed workings of an emergent social imaginary—another incarnation of the carnivalesque energies that have "displayed a power and ability to challenge traditional hierarchies unseen for centuries."[6] It is through these kinds of circulations, connections, and relays that the revolution of everyday life is fermented and realized—that is, it is embodied and evolves through a constantly morphing everyday life of revolution.

THE POLITICS OF MINOR COMPOSITION

Make do with what you have
Take what you can get
Pay no mind to us
We're just a minor threat
— Minor Threat

Insurgencies are the incubators of new ideas and knowledges: places where hopes and energies that there could exist other forms of social arrangements different from that what exists today, that there are alternatives, are cultivated. It is not, as it sometimes assumed, that there is an unbridgeable chasm between such forms of cultural politics and what might more commonly be understood as class issues (organizing around directly economic issues, work conditions, etc).[7] They are not merely symbolic struggles or superstructural issues, but a key part of how people order, understand, orient, and change their lives. Collective capacities and compositions are built up not only through the more obvious and visible forms of political organizing, but also through a myriad of channels and interactions unfolding across and through all spheres of social life.

Social and political ideas are circulated in ways that are both enunciated publicly and coded in ways that are not readily obvious to the gaze of existing political authorities. Through these infrapolitics of resistance, woven through the hidden transcripts of everyday life, songs, stories, and social interactions come to congeal and coalesce radical political desires.[8] It is this usage of cultural symbolism, as embodied in the example of the Martha and the Vandellas song, that expresses a doubly articulated seen and unseen aesthetics of organization — the continual morphing of the radical imagination — the importance of which is not necessarily the content of the composition itself but rather the energies in sets in motion for its listeners.[9] Rather than affirming an identity posited and defended through political organizing, there operates a form of politics which draws from existing social energies and ideas in circulation while using them to other means, to introduce new meanings and relations by circulating them to other uses and creating "chain links of singularities all oriented toward their self-production and multiplication"[10] — the politics of minor composition.[11]

The history of the IWW is formed by a discontinuous series of minor compositions formed around ebbs and flows of social resistance. Historically, with their organizing work rooted deeply in the culture and practices of migrant laborers, train hoppers, hoboes, bohemians, and traveling populations, the IWW used humor, irreverence, and wit, often adapting popular songs and religious hymns to rework with anticapitalist motifs.[12] Songs such as "The Preacher and the Slave" and "Dump the Boss Off Your Back," while most commonly associated with the better known IWW songwriters and re-workers such as T-Bone Slim and Joe Hill, have been in continuous circulation since the initial publication of the *Little Red Song Book* in 1904. And this process of constant circulation has continually expanded itself as new organizing campaigns and events of collective significance are added to this evolving history and reservoir of shared knowledge and experience. Through the medium of song the earliest IWW campaigns connect to the most recent, tracing a tenuous but unbroken line from T-Bone Slim to current musicians who are working within and expanding the tradition of labor song writing such as David Rovics, the various members of the Riot Folk collective, Shannon Murray, and New York-based hip hop group Kontrast, as well as the work of various artists who have explored the legacy of the IWW through comic art.[13]

101

Thus the particulars of events, campaigns, and actions become enmeshed within the evolving collective assemblage of minor cultural politics. It is not that the various individual concerns and interests become subsumed within a collective homogenous general interest (for the sake of the movement and so forth), but rather than individual intrigues are connected to other concerns; each connection and concern, "thus becomes all the more necessary, indispensable, magnified, because a whole other story is vibrating within it."[14] This dynamic can also be noted in the on going development of countercultural politics and organizing associated with punk rock[15] and forms of collective authorship that have been employed from Dada to the shared names of Karen Eliot, Monty Cantsin, and Luther Blissett.[16] In other words it is not a process of forming a new collective subject that will act towards achieving certain political goals (the punk community will do this or that), but rather that it operates as an assemblage for developing and articulating ideas through intensive forms of social relations created through the emergence and continuation of a dispersed and fluid community — for instance in relations to various concerns about war, poverty, ecology, gender, gentrification, and any other host of issues. In other words, there "isn't a subject; *there are only collective assemblages of enunciation.*"[17] The self-organization of the punk community, which at face value is often seen to only reflect a kind of youthful nihilism of no political content, is in many ways directly political through how the use of music and artistic expressions, the intensive usage of language, becomes an integral part of formulating non-alienating and often post-capitalist social relations in the present and connecting these emerging relations to what is more commonly recognized as politics.[18]

It is this form of politics based not upon projecting an already agreed upon political solution or calling upon an existing social subject (the people, the workers), but rather developing a mode of collective, continual and intensive engagement with the social world that embodies the politics of minor composition. It is a mode that rather than relying upon notions of already understood subjective positions works from within particular sets of identities, relations, and flows of power to develop continually open and renewing intersubjective positions to organize from. These processes of minor composition are articulated through forms of collective enunciation. For instance, in the mid 1960s, the UK Diggers, a British group of radicals inspired by the 17th-century radicals who they took the name from, put forth a conception of politics they argued was not based on representing the people but rather on electing them, that is to find a form of concerted political action through which subjective position of the people is created.[19] The politics of minor composition is concerned with developing a form of politics not based upon fixed identities, a consequent emphasis on the social relations formed with political organizing, and the intensive mode of engagement through which these emerge. The politics of minor composition are formed around particular situations and convergences of social forces intensively engaged with and complicated: "The particular thus becomes the site of innovation (not identity) as minorities rework their territory and multiply their borders.[20] It is this form of engagement, a constantly open and intensive engagement self-organized through redirecting the social energies of everyday life, which comprises the processes of minor composition.

One example can be found in the working of the Starbucks Workers Campaign, an effort of the New York City IWW that has been operating for the past two years. While the main demands advanced by the organizing campaign and unionization drives (increased pay, guaranteed hours and full-time positions, the end of understaffing, and various workplace health and safety issues) are not particularly striking themselves, what is more interesting is the methods that have been employed in the organizing, particularly the use of humor, irreverence, and an engagement with cultural politics growing out of the IWW tradition of employing these, a politics of class as a mode of creating and elaborating difference.[21] The campaign is also significant in that it is trying to develop ways to organize in retail chain stores, an area that due to high turn over and the often short-term nature of employment in such locations has not been an area of focus for the larger and better established in the United States (or for the most part elsewhere to a large degree). Also it is notable that the Starbucks Workers campaign is not seeking to become the bargaining representative for all Starbucks workers (to become the major, or representative form), but to participate in and organize protests and actions focusing on the collective demands enunciated through their organizing. The campaign, which has began to spread throughout the US and to the UK, has also attracted the attention of the business press, such as the *Wall Street Journal*.[22]

The operation of a company like Starbucks, much like the workings of any corporation in the highly mediated post-fordist economy, is increasingly dependent on the forms of symbolic labor and communication involved in creating the image and corporate persona.[23] Starbucks' operations, as one can see by looking through any of the company's literature and the way that it presents itself, is largely based upon creating an image and experience of the coffee drinking experience — one that appeals to its customers as somehow embodying a sort of "Italian café excursion," including finely ground and roasted coffees and wistfully referring to its employees as baristas.[24] Starbucks needs to create and maintain its image as an appealing company, but one that is different from what might expect from a large company that has become ubiquitous in the suburban landscape. This is done through the cultivation of imagery that portrays the company as placing high importance on ecological sustainability, treating its workers well, and buying into what might be described as generally progressive political values. This is accomplished through the well placed usage of Fair Trade coffees, support of tsunami relief efforts, forming a Citizen's Healthcare Working Group, general layout and design of the store, and carrying coffees from around the world evoking a "exotic" multicultural appeal. Starbucks has also began to release albums by various well-known artists (Elvis Costello, Ben

Harper, etc) specifically designed for release at its stores, which have taken measures to integrate listening to various genres and styles (jazz, folk, rock) as part of the coffee-drinking experience that Starbucks vigorously hawks.[25]

When campaigns like the Starbucks Workers union drive questions the image that Starbucks has built up for itself about being a different kind of company with an overall progressive agenda, one that respects and cares for its workers, and provokes the company to take measures to try and undercut the union organizing drive, it becomes increasingly difficult to maintain this image. In a sense then when the Starbucks Workers Campaign find ways to intervene and disrupt the symbolic labor and processes integral to the continued recreation of the Starbucks image that is so important to their operations, they are developing ways to directly intervene in the workings of Starbucks, even if it is occurring not directly inside the what one might usually think as of the labor process. A perfect example of this is the joint picket action staged between the Starbucks Workers campaign and the Billionaires for Bush in August 2005,[26] although for the purposes of the demonstration it was necessary to make it appear as if they were opposing forces. At different points during the day a group of campily dressed as *Great Gatsby*-esque billionaires appear at Starbucks situated on 1st Avenue and 8th Street and in Manhattan and proceeded to thank customers within the stores for "keeping the bucks within Starbucks" and to praise the company for its union-busting efforts. They then proceeded to present a mock award of the "Better Billionaires Business Bureau Award for Outstanding Unfair Labor Practices" (which regrettably was declined as management decided to call the regional manager to ask for advice of how to deal with this unforeseen set of circumstances).

When the Starbucks Workers and various allies arrived there resulted a mock confrontation, with the IWW picket line marching back and forth next to the line of Billionaires pretending that they were defending their cherished enterprise from the devious actions of the dastardly pro-union forces and their attempts to enforce rigidities in the labor market, thus potentially lowering the profits of Starbucks. One of the Billionaires obtained a pamphlet that the IWW was passing out and brought it inside the store, reading out loud with dramatic indignation the "absurd" demands of the workers for things like livable wages, a decent number of hours, bathroom breaks, and "similar claptrap that you might often hear the indentured class complain about."[27] Brandishing forth signs with slogans humorously twisting well known slogans such as "Think Globally, Oppress Locally" and "Let Them Work for Beans" the two allegedly-opposing sides proceeded to chant and glare at each other, trying desperately to stop from laughing at the humor and surrealness of the situation. The chants used by the Billionaires included "Sarah Bender [IWW member fired for her union organizing], don't defend her / Get in there and work the blender!" and "Starbucks workers, get a clue / Living wages aren't for you!" This serves to create new ways of articulating the demands of the campaign, but not simply through stating them: the Billionaires take what is often the logic and claims that they are arguing against and by ostensibly embracing and celebrating them, push them forward in a way that reveals their absurdity. Similar tactics have been employed by the media stunt the Yes Men as well as those involved in the London based Laboratory for Insurrectionary Imagination who in 2004 organized a "March for Capitalism" during the European Social Forum and a "Police Victory Party" during May Day this year.

The humor, play, and tactical frivolity are here not something that is external to the organizing, but rather are a part of it. The mock confrontation with the Billionaires for Bush as part of what otherwise might be a rather standard picketing and protest becomes a space where intensive forms of social engagement occurs as a integral part of the developing the collective self of the organizing campaign as well as an intervention within the symbolic labor process that Starbucks requires to maintain its image and profit margins. These forms of tactical absurdity have played a large role in the workings of the global justice movement, from the Clandestine Insurgent Revolutionary Clown Army to the fairy dances of the pink bloc, and also have a long history behind them.[28]

This is not to say that a process of a minor engagement and use of pop culture motifs is purely a positive thing. For every time that the energies of a pop culture motif can be used in another way, diverted to other ends, there are attempts to use this subversion against itself, to recuperate it back into the spectacle as the Situationists would say. As Brian Holmes argues, the social imaginary functions "simultaneously as a seductive capture device for popular culture, and as a productive discipline for mid-ranking symbolic analysts... to stimulate our interest, attention, passions—that is, to exercise the contemporary function of control, through the modulations of subjective energies."[29] These symbolic analysts, or the "creative class" of marketers and all those involved in various cultural fields, maintain a fluid relation (often borrowing from and bringing into its own operations) those who are attempting to subvert its functioning. Thus one should not look to these various attempts of cultural subversion, minor engagement, and self-organization as cases to be emulated and reused as is. Rather through understanding the process of composition of social relations and connections that emerges through and as a part of them the most valuable lessons are learned.

This turn toward cultural politics as a means to create common positions to organize and work from, positions that while formerly based around the community and constant contact of the bounded workplace and interactions within it, have become less available as people are engaged in part time, short term, and variable patterns of work where such longer term relationships and contact no longer exist — or at least not in the same form it did before. These concerns and conditions have been addressed increasingly over the past few years throughout Europe, organized around the issue of precarious existence, or the forms of non-standard and variable jobs that have emerged as a result of neoliberal restructuring and roll back of the various gains of social democracy over the past 60 years. This motif, originated by the Milan-based labor organizing and media activist group the Chainworkers, has spread quickly across the continent, particularly through the increasingly large EuroMayDay demonstrations held each year on May 1st which have taken up the concerns of precarious workers as a key area of focus. In particular this focus on precarious workers has spread effectively through the creation of seductive and creative imagery to embody the organizing process that it emerges out of. A particularly striking instance of this is the creation of a new saint, San Precario, to represent the needs and demands (housing, transportation, communication) of the precariously employed. By using the motif of the saint the Chainworkers have created an image which draws from the social energies of Catholicism in Italy while finding ways to enunciate their social demands, arguing for a new form of flexible security, or flexicurity, for those adrift in today's world.[30]

This tactic has also been used by projects such as Yo Mango. Yo Mango, which is colloquial Spanish for "I steal" plays on the name of the trendy fashion company Mango, to coordinate organized shoplifting actions replete with singing, dancing, and other forms of planned absurdity. Similarly in New Zealand the "Supersize My Pay" campaign playfully uses the McDonald's phrase as a motif for its demands around higher wages, the end of the youth rate pay scale, and attempts to organize those working in chainstores and precarious jobs such as Starbucks, Wellington, Burger King, and related call centers. The use of digital and communication technologies have also been used to create various forms of technopranks ranging from the creation of a mock website for various international financial institutions to the creation of political video games such as the "McDonald's Videogame" and "Tamatipico Your Virtual Flexworker," all of which exist along the more commonly expected uses of such technologies for communication and organizing in the electronic factory of struggle.[31] As examples of a general process of minor composition the energies of pop culture phraseology and imagery are used to expand the workings of what Cornelius Castoriadis calls the social imaginary, or the endless process of social self-creation enacted through a multitude of symbolic forms and channels. The actions of the social imaginary, which are developed here not at a society wide level but through various organizing campaigns that attempt to proliferate and spread anti-capitalist ideas through their operations, create what Castoriadis describes as figures of the thinkable, or frames in which forms of social interaction and relations become possible. The workings and expansion of the social imaginary, through these intensively engaged minor compositions, operate across three determinations: intention (the goals of the movements), affect (the social bonds and relations formed through them), and representation (the development and deployment of symbols used in these processes) as part of the "unlimited... representational flux and representational spontaneity without any assignable end" that is the work of the shared imaginary of resistance.[32] Thus there exists a constantly shifting relationship between the workings of the social imaginary, forms of self-organization, and the intensive relations and interactions that both express and develop through these compositions.

Often it is through subtle moments, movements and gestures that the formation and reformulation of the social imaginary can shift in unexpected minor directions, pushing social energies and relations in different directions. The social imaginary is not usually expressed in specifically theoretical terms, but in forms of collective understandings found between people in everyday life—embodied in images, stories, and myth making: it is how people imagine their social existence and how they understand and relate to each other. In the words, it is "that common understanding that makes possible common practices and a widely shared sense of legitimacy."[33] These shared imaginaries and understandings may be the result of what might seem like insignificant acts, but ones that nonetheless change the definition of the situation and the relation of those involved in it in substantial ways. Such gestures obviously do not mean the same for all those who witness them.[34]

To give a particular example of this form of social movement, one can look to yet another example of this phenomenon in the organizing of the IWW, one that I observed when I was in Sydney for the May Day protests in 2005. Upon arriving in the designated in the park where the march was announced to begin, it seemed at first glance to be shaping up as quite an uninspiring event. Despite all of the larger, more mainstream liberal and social democratic trade unions urging their members to come out for the march (easy enough since May Day happened to fall on a Sunday), the number of people was quite small. Protest marshals were busy scurrying about handing out information sheets indicating the march route and the order that the unions involved were to march, making sure that everyone has been neatly coded and arranged by their easily identifiable union affiliation (what color is your t-shirt, comrade?). Spots at the end were arranged for the less well politically connected groups involved and those unaffiliated from the ranks of recognized political formations. The planned trade route amounted to walking a not so large circle through Sydney's financial district, which given the day of the week meant that it would be a march seen and heard by virtually no one. Self-marginalization seemed not to be an unfortunate side effect of the situation, but rather was seemingly built into the very planning and framework that had been created.

As the event kicked off this initial impression was not dispelled. It was opened by a clichéd older bearded male who sang various songs about solidarity, the dignity of the working class, and other such motifs all trapped within an imaginary and aesthetic framework that seemed to have not moved since the 1920s. This was followed by a seemingly endless array of speakers who droned on about fighting the proposed cuts to various social welfare programs and changes in labor legislation. One topic for the speakers was the introduction of "Voluntary Student Unionism," a proposed change in legislation which would alter the framework of student support and funding across Australia and which was also the target of a national day of action that had occurred several days before.[35] If one thinks about rallies and actions as manifestations of the creative potentiality and possibilities of creating a new world out of the fabric of the present, this event seemed more like extending the mundanity of the present into an infinite future, focusing only upon maintaining the meager gains that had been won by previous organizing rather than putting forth anything new or inspiring.

Thankfully it was not all that bad. Members of the Sydney IWW had rigged up speakers and a sound system contained within a plastic garbage can on wheels, replete with a backing rhythm composed of various pieces of kitchenware and buckets. As the procession trickled on to the street the make shift sound system was used to play songs like "9 to 5" by Dolly Parton and "We Gotta Get Out of This Place" by The Animals. Contrasted to the somewhat uninspiring surrounding milieu, the rag tag drumming, improvised dancing, and off key singing along with the songs gave forth a feeling of joyous celebration and exuberance that seemed to be lacking elsewhere. Various individuals who did not seem to give the march any notice looked up and smiled when greeted by the admittedly amateurish but striking gaggle of singing, dancing people. Perhaps they recognized the songs in question and connected to the idea that indeed working 9 to 5 ain't no way to make a living and that we have to get out of this place — connected to in a way that for all the good intentions invoking the dignity of labor and solidarity just didn't seem possible.

But whatever one may speculate about how this was received by those watching the events, it certainly did create an affectively richer composition of relations for those involved. At one point during the dancing and merry making "Darth Vader's Theme" from *Star Wars* was played, leading to a heated debate about whether the Rebel Alliance in the film represented a progressive force trying to overthrow an empire, or rather embodied a reactionary attempt to reinstall a previously existing monarchy. The arguments about the politics of the film mingled freely in conversation with the experiences of several IWW members about their attempts to organize various parts of the crew involved during the filming of the latest installments of the series. These debates continued during the march and spilled over through many beers during the after party. Each of these moments of taking an element from the realm of pop culture, whether a song, movie, or anything else, to other ends, could be argued to take up and extend the Situationist idea of detournement, where combinations of social elements and practices are diverted to new ends, to create situations where the unleashing and realization of collective social energies can bring about a new world and social relations. It is not that a song like "Working 9 to 5" or "Dancin in the Streets," anymore than *Star Wars* or camped up imagery of wealth and disdain, are in themselves revolutionary, but rather that they are used in these situations to vibrate with new intensities and meanings. And, it is this vibration and social resonance, around which the workings of the social imaginary are constantly renewed and self-organized, that embodies the process of minor composition.

The everyday life of revolution, spreading out through songs, stories, snickers, rants, and mocking laughs, spares no sacred cows. Cycles of struggle multiply and form spirals not only through forms of politics usually recognized as such, but through all the facets of everyday life. Scrawled on the city walls, whispered in hush tones, related over a drink—the flow of ideas and the desire for liberation move according to the needs of the social terrain, constantly changing and reforming. Oh, a sigh for the poor tyrants, how their power crumbles when no one takes it seriously anymore, when everybody laughs as them. As the absurdity of spectacle and spectacle of absurdity, it reveals in full clarity the absurdity of the world around us—from the workings of capital and its state, to the lesser bunglings of union bureaucrats and other minions of the old world. This contains the wonderful, ambivalent paradox of minor politics: they do not seek to put themselves forward as a set model and plan for a new world, but yet in their joy contain the very seeds to build a new world. Organizing to undermine the state, capitalism, and all forms of social domination does not mean that one is faced with a choice between the joys of dancing and reveling and the serious work of class struggle. Far from it. Indeed, if one wants to be a revolutionary, perhaps it is the dancing that one should take more seriously.

NOTES

A version of this paper was presented at the Vilnius Interdisciplinary Lab for Media Arts in Lithuania on May 24, 2006. The author wishes to thank those who provided useful and interesting comments, in particular Gediminas and Nomeda Urbonas, Martin Parker, Stefano Harney, Ben Shepard, Dave Eden, David Graeber, Werner Bonefeld, and Jack Bratich.

1 Carr, James (2002) *Bad: The Autobiography of James Carr*. Oakland: AK Press, 214.

2 *Dancin' in the Streets: Anarchists, IWWs, Surrealists, Situationists & Provos in the 1960s* (2005) Ed. Franklin Rosemont and Charles Radcliffe. Chicago: Charles H. Kerr Publishing Company, 131. *Rebel Worker* had a sister publication in the UK called *Heatwave*.

3 Ibid., 434.

4 Smith, Suzanne (2001) *Dancing in the Street: Motown and the Cultural Politics of Detroit*. Harvard University Press. See also Martha Reeves and Mark Bego (1994) *Dancing in the Street: Confessions of a Motown Diva*. New York: Hyperion Books.

5 Lafargue, Paul (1989 [1883]]) *The Right to Be Lazy*. Chicago: Charles H. Kerr Publishing Company; Rhodes, Carl (forthcoming) "Outside the Gates of Eden: Utopia and Work in Rock Music," *Group and Organization Management*.

6 Kohl, Paul (1993) "Looking Through a Glass Onion: Rock and Roll as Modern Manifestation of Carnival," *Journal of Popular Culture*, 27(1), 146.

7 After 1968 it was common for figures such as Mario Tronti to declare that there was a movement from the era of the grand politics of class struggle and

communism to an age of small politics. As Ida Dominijanni observes, while figures such as Tronti tended to overlook that which was subversive and radical about this transition, not necessarily in relation to a conception of class politics that had been lost, but in themselves, figures such as Antonio Negri often made just the opposite mistake. That is, in celebrating the subversive character of these new minor forms of politics and struggle tended to overlook the way in which they inherited and took on many of the same problems and troubles with had plague the "old" politics. Ida Dominijanni (2006) "Heiresses at Twilight. The End of Politics and the Politics of Difference," *the commoner* Number 11.

8 Scott, James C. (1990) *Domination and the Arts of Resistance: Hidden Transcripts.* New Haven, CT: Yale University Press; Kelley, Robin D.G. (2002) *Freedom Dreams: The Black Radical Imagination.* Boston: Beacon Press. Also see Grossberg, Lawrence (1992) *We Gotta Get Out of This Place: Popular Conservatism and Postmodern Culture.* London: Routledge.

9 Linstead, Stephen and Heather Hopfl (2004) *The Aesthetics of Organization*, London: Sage. Nissley; Buchanan, Ian (1997) "Deleuze and Pop Music," *Australian Humanities Review*.

10 Negri, Toni and Felix Guattari (1990) *Communists Like Us.* Trans. Michael Ryan. New York: Semiotext(e), 109–110.

11 The concept of minor composition takes its cue from Deleuze and Guattari's notion of a minor literature and Nick Thoburn's expansion of this idea into a minor politics. Deleuze and Guattari develop the concept of a minor literature through their analysis of the work of Franz Kafka. Although this work is focused specifically on writing of Kafka it is oriented to drawing out the processes and dynamics that they find embodied in his writing. This process is not something particular to Kafka as a master author (as that would contradict their entire line of argument) or the particular media form in which he worked. In other words they are interested in how Kafka uses the German language to strange and unforeseen ends, how he uses German to become a stranger within the language itself and attaches himself to lines of flight and draw paths of escape characterized by a strange joy. A minor literature, which for Deleuze and Guattari emerges not from the existence of a distinct minor language but rather how a minority constructs within a major language, has three main characteristics: 1) its language is affected by a high degree of deterritorialization 2) everything within a minor literature is political, the concerns of the individual connect immediately to other individual concerns; the social environment no longer exists as a mere background against which these dynamics emerge 3) everything takes on a collective value; exists as a form of collective enunciation. Deleuze, Gilles, and Felix Guattari (1986) *Kafka: Towards a Minor Literature.* Trans. Dana Polen. Minneapolis: University of Minnesota Press.

12 For more on the history of the IWW see Kornbluh, Joyce (1998) *Rebel Voices:*

An IWW Anthology. Chicago: Charles H. Kerr Publishing Company; Renshaw, Patrick (1999) *The Wobblies: The Story of the IWW and Syndicalism in the United States.* Chicago: Ivan R. Dee, Publisher; and Bird, Stewart, Dan Georgakas, and Deborah Shaffer (1985) *Solidarity Forever: An Oral History of the IWW.* Chicago: Lake View Press.

13 Buhle, Paul (2004) *Wobblies! A Graphic History of the Industrial Workers of the World.* New York: Verso. For more on the artists mentioned, see David Rovics (www.davidrovics.com), members of the Riot Folk collective (www.riotfolk.org), Shannon Murray (www.shannonmurray. com), and Kontrast (www.myspace.com/kontrast)

14 Deleuze and Guattari (1986) *Kafka,* 17.

15 O'Hara, Craig (1999) *The Philosophy of Punk: More Than Noise.* San Francisco: AK Press; Haeffler, Ross (2006) *Straight Edge: Hardcore Punk, Clean-Living Youth, and Social Change.* New Brunswick, NJ: Rutgers University Press; Hurchalla, George (2005) *Going Underground: American Punk 1979–1992.* Stuart, FL: Zuo Press; Jenkins, Mark and Mark Andersen (2000) *The Dance of Days: Two Decades of Punk in the Nation's Capital.* New York City: Akashic Books.

16 Home, Stewart (1991) *The Assault on Culture: Utopian Currents from Lettrisme to Class War.* Edinburgh: AK Press; Blissett, Luther (2005) *Q.* London: Harvest Books.

17 Deleuze and Guattari (1986) *Kafka,* 18.

18 Holtzman, Ben, Craig Hughes, and Kevin Van Meter (2004) "Do It Yourself… and the movement beyond capitalism," *Radical Society* Volume 31 Number 1: 7–20. Also see McKay, George (1998) *DIY Culture: Party & Protest in Nineties Britain.* New York: Verso; Leblanc, Lauraine (1999) *Pretty in Punk: Girl's Gender Resistance in a Boy's Subculture.* New Brunswick, NJ: Rutgers University Press.

19 Stansill, Peter and David Zane Mairowitz, Eds. (1999) *BAMN (By Any Means Necessary): Outlaw Manifestos & Ephemera, 1965–1970.* Brooklyn, NY: Autonomedia, 88.

20 Thoburn, Nick (2003) *Deleuze, Marx, and Politics.* London: Routledge: 44–45.

21 Thoburn, Nick (2003a) "The Hobo Anomalous: Class, Minorities and Political Invention in the Industrial Workers of the World," *Social Movement Studies*, 2(1): 61–84

22 Maher, Kris (2006) "IWW Branches Out in Bid to Recruit Starbucks Baristas," *Wall Street Journal.* May 17, 2006. Available at http://www. starbucksunion.org/node/899. There have also been actions in Edinburgh, Scotland and in Leicester, England.

23 This, however, is not to imply that these processes of symbolic mediation the social creation of the imaginary of the corporation are something new that has occurred in the post-fordist economy, as they are indeed part of a much larger and on-going social processes. It is rather that in the changing na-

ture of the post-fordist economy they have come to play a more central role in the productive process. Thus, it is a change in the composition of economic forces rather than anything resembling a sharp break in regimes of production, as is sometimes claimed. For more information on the process of creating the representation and imaginary of the corporate persona see Roland Marchand (1998) *Creating the Corporate Soul: The Rise of Public Relations and Corporate Imagery in American Big Business*. Berkeley, CA: University of California Press.

24 Elliot, Charlene (2001) "Consuming Caffeine: The Discourse of Starbucks and Coffee," *Consumption, Markets, and Culture*. Volume 4 Number 4: 369–382.

25 One must be clear, however, about the *way* that Starbucks goes about hawking its wares. It is not the old direct sell, which at times almost takes on a carnivalesque atmosphere of its own, but rather something that is more subtle and insidious—what might described more as a tactic of immersion and spreading: becoming the background, becoming the context in which activities and interactions takes places.

26 Information about the Starbucks Workers Campaign (www.starbucksunion.org) and Billionaires for Bush (www.billionairesforbush.com). For more on other related forms of culture jamming, see Dery, Mark (1993) *Culture Jamming: Hacking, Slashing, and Sniping in the Empire of Signs*. Open Magazine Pamphlet Series; Lasn, Kalle (2000) *Culture Jam: How to Reverse America's Suicidal Consumer Binge*. New York City: Harpers. Reverend Billy (2003) *What Should I Do if Reverend Billy is in My Store?* New York: New Press.

27 Denz, Diva (2005) "Billionaires Rush to the Aid of Starbucks," *NYC Indymedia*, August 10, 2005. Available at http://nyc.indymedia.org/en/2005/08/55275.html.

28 Harvie, David, Keir Milburn, Ben Trott, and David Watts, Eds. (2005) *Shut Them Down! The G8, Gleaneagles 2005 and the Movement of Movements*. West Yorkshire and New York: Dissent! and Autonomedia. See also Gavin Grindon (2006) "The Breath of the Possible," *Constituent Imagination: Militant Investigations // Collective Theorization*. Ed. Stevphen Shukaitis and David Graeber. Oakland, CA: AK Press: 91–104.

29 Holmes, Brian (2004) "Artistic Autonomy and Communication Society," *Third Text* Volume 18 Issue 6, 552.

30 Information on the Chainworkers (www.ecn.org/chainworkers), EuroMayDay (www.euromayday.org), and San Precario (www.sanprecario.info). Also see the precarity-themed issue of *Greenpepper Magazine* (Number 31, Fall 2004) and *Mute Magazine* (Issue 29 Spring 2005) as well *fibreculture* Issue 5 (2005), "Multitudes, Creative Organisation and the Precarious Condition of New Media Labour." Available at http://journal.fibreculture.org/issue5/.

31 Drew, Jesse (2004) "Technopranks. Carving Out a Message in Electronic

Space," *Processed World 2005*: 39–43; Cleaver, Harry (1998) "The Zapatistas and the Electronic Factory of Struggle," *Zapatista! Reinventing Revolution in Mexico*. Ed. John Holloway and Eloina Peláez. London: Pluto Press: 81–103. Fore information on these various examples please see Yo Mango (www.yomango.net), Super Size My Pay (www.supersizemypay.com), and Molle Industria (www.molleindustria.org)

32 Castoriadis, Cornelius (1997) *World in Fragments: Writings on Politics, Society, Psychoanalysis, and the Imagination*. Ed/Trans David Ames Curtis. Stanford, CA: Stanford University Press.

33 Taylor, Charles (2004) *Modern Social Imaginaries*. Durham: Duke University Press, 23.

34 For instance, activists who have moved a march on to the streets frequently are heard to chant "this is what democracy looks like," sometimes drawing queries of whether a street demonstration is really an embodiment of democracy — and perhaps more often the ambivalently curious / slightly disdainful stares of those nearby who try to figure out just what the protest is about (for often this is not readily apparent). But this overlooks that the chant about democracy also refers to the process of formulating and organizing that led to the action in question, through a series of consultas, gatherings, and planning. It is this process of creating new forms of horizontal organizing and participation distinct from the often alienating realm of electoral politics which is often the most difficult to communicate, but that which is referred to by chants, leaflets, and the information circulated. Paradoxically this constantly refers to experiences which are integral to the overall organizing but nonetheless never seen within its most visible manifestations.

35 Brewer, Norman (2005) "Victorious Students Unleashed Rally — Next Stop: May Day Rally and Contingent," *Melbourne Indymedia*. May 1, 2005. Available at www.melbourne.indymedia.org.

8
Anti-Capitalist Movements

The Leeds May Day Group[1]

> Communism is not for us a state of affairs which is to
> be established, an ideal to which reality [will] have to
> adjust itself. We call communism the real movement,
> which abolishes the present state of things —Marx
> and Engels 1970, pp. 56–7.

WHAT'S MY NAME?

From Seattle to Gothenburg and Genoa, from Evian and Gleneagles, and from Argentina 2001 to France 2006, a new movement has come into existence: and one of the labels to which it has been attached is "anti-capitalist." We should not underestimate the significance of this terminology. Following years of defeat and disarray among oppositional movements, we've enjoyed new-found energy and experienced moments which have punctured the world of money and power. Once again we can just make out the spectre of communism haunting the world.

But what does it mean to talk of an "anti-capitalist movement?" What do we mean by the word "movement?" Its most straightforward meaning is a collection of individuals connected by means of some shared ideology or practice. This new anti-capitalist movement is, then, quite simply composed of those individuals who consciously, collectively and actively opposed to capitalism. By this definition, it clearly includes those who danced in the streets at the J18 Carnival against Capitalism in London in 1999, and those who took to the streets of Genoa and Gothenburg in 2001. But beyond this things get more problematic. The movement may also include those on the streets of Seattle in 1999, but would it *also* incorporate those who attempted to defend Nike stores from the violence of some of the Seattle demonstrators? More recently, where can we place those who took part in the Make Poverty History mobilisations of 2005? Or those who went to the Live8 concerts? Or Bob Geldof and Bono?

Even such a simple understanding of "the movement" soon starts to unravel. For one thing, it quickly falls into the trap of playing the numbers game: this many demonstrators, that much damage. As one contributor to *Reflections on J18* sarcastically notes: "we congratulate ourselves through commodifying our resistance, 2 million quid of damage — good demo!" (G. 1999). It's an approach that tends to exclude those who can't or won't attend the big spectacular demonstrations and actions, or who aren't even aware of their happening. In fact it dovetails neatly into the recruitment practices of much of the organised Left, as well as the "activist" mentality of many in the current movement. Both perspectives suggest that just one more paper-sale, one more demonstration, one more action can tip the balance decisively in our favour, as if a real qualitative transformation of our lives will be simply a matter of quantitative change. Despite their protestations to the contrary, both are driven by the same underlying attitudes:

> The activist is a specialist or an expert in social change. To thing of yourself as being an activist means to think of yourself as being somehow privileged or more advanced than others in your appreciation of the need for social change, in the knowledge of how to achieve it and as leading or being in the forefront of the practical struggle to create this change....
>
> Defining ourselves as activists means defining our actions as the ones which will bring about social change, thus disregarding the activity of thousands upon thousands of other non-activists. Activism is based upon this misconception that it is only activists who do social change (Andrew X. 1999).

A further problem with this numbers approach is that it tends to be Eurocentric, and almost always privileges those groups that have been identified in advance as "political formations," regardless of whether such groups style themselves as an "organisation" or "party" (for example, the Socialist Workers Party), a "network" (for example, People's Global Action), a "disorganisation" (for example, Reclaim the Streets) or something even looser. In fact the vast bulk of the movement is made up of people who do not consider themselves "activists" or "political" but who nevertheless have to struggle against oppression and exploitation in their everyday lives — people who, just like us, are struggling for new ways of living.

However, simply expanding the definition of movement—to include millions of workers and peasants and any other number of social groupings across the world — is still limited by the fact that it conceives of movement as "a thing."

As something that can be defined, whose boundaries can be clearly mapped, and which stands *outside* and *against* something else called "capital." We may argue over the exact terms of the definition (for example, do we include Make Poverty History?) and we may agree that these definitions will shift but this movement is still seen as a "thing." It is increasingly difficult, though, to reconcile such a static, "thing-like" view of the anti-capitalist movement with the realities of everyday life — not least our own — where the vast majority of the world's population exists both *within* and *against* capital.

In trying to rethink this, we have drawn heavily on our own political experiences (mainly but not exclusively within the libertarian revolutionary milieu) and on the analysis developed by "autonomist Marxists." We have found two aspects of the autonomists' analyses particularly helpful: first, the idea of workers' autonomy — the potential autonomy of labour from capital — and, second, the understanding that "capital is nothing other than the *product* of the working class" (Holloway 1995: 163) and hence, as we mentioned above, we exist *within-and-against* capital.

While many orthodox Marxists emphasise the power of capital, taking at face value the "inevitable" unfolding of its laws, this first insight — that of workers' autonomy —reverses the perspective entirely. It instead asserts the primacy of *working-class struggle* and recasts capital in a reactive role. As one of its earliest theorists puts it:

> We too have worked with a concept that puts capitalist development first, and workers second. This is a mistake. And now we have to turn the problem on its head, reverse the polarity, and start again from the beginning: and the beginning is the class struggle of the working class. At the level of socially developed capital, capitalist development becomes subordinated to working class struggles; it follows behind them, and they set the pace to which the political mechanisms of capital's own reproduction must be tuned (Tronti 1979: 1).

If the first insight reverses the polarity between capital and labour, the second attempts to dissolve this polarity entirely. Instead of seeing capital as a "thing" external to the working class, the relationship between capital and labour is viewed as *internal*. Fundamental is the view, developed from Marx, of capital as a social relation, one that contains labour within it. As Marx characterises workers:

> Their co-operation only begins with the labour process, but by then they have ceased to belong to themselves. On entering the labour process they are incorporated into capital. As co-operators, as members of a working organism, they merely form a particular mode of existence of capital. *Hence the productive power developed by the worker socially is the productive power of capital.* (Marx 1976: 451; our emphasis.)

"Capital" is not something "out there," something that we can fight against as if it were external to us and part of someone or something else — even if we sometimes talk about it as if it is. "Capital" is not a person or group of people, nor an organisation or group of organisations. It's not the sum total of "capitalists" or "capitalist enterprises." Capital is a social relation mediated through commodities. Capital is the way we live, the way we reproduce ourselves and our world — the entire organisation of the "present state of things" as they are today.

But capital is reliant on the expenditure of our labour power to valorise itself. What lies under capitalist development is the social production of co-operative labour. While labour can never be autonomous from capital, through its constant insubordination it tries to affirm itself as the social subject beyond capital. Conversely capital constantly tries to contain the working class within the limits of its form as a mere living container of labour power, reducing the whole of life to work — for the sake of work. This forms the fundamental cycle of what is termed "class composition": our struggles provoke capital to restructure the production process and the division of labour in order to reassert its command. This in turn leads to the development of new antagonistic subjectivities, a "recomposition" of the working class, not as a wage-labouring class demanding a better, new deal, but as the multitude-in-resistance that demands the end of class. The only possibilities of escape from this cycle of decomposition and recomposition, of imposition of work and resistance to this imposition, lie in the asymmetry at the heart of the relationship between capital and labour: while capital needs labour, labour does not need capital. Instead of the familiar view of capitalism as confident and monolithic, we are left with a picture of a social order constantly forced to recompose itself in attempt to co-opt, channel and cap the "creative unrest" of human labour.

In short, it is human practice — what we do — which is central. Although we do not choose our conditions, nevertheless we do, collectively, make our own history: "Men make their own history… not under circumstances they have chosen but under the given and inherited circumstances with which they are directly confronted" (Marx 1973, p. 146). Or, as the graffiti in Genoa expressed it: "You make plans. We make history!" Orthodox Marxist thinking has tended to read off human action as a function of class, or as a function of some other social category. But if human practice—doing—is central, then we should begin with the doing. Class and "movement" then become truly dynamic categories which develop with the doing. As an English historian put it, "[class] is a *historical* phenomenon. I do not see [it] as a 'structure,' nor even as a 'category,' but as something which in fact happens (and can be shown to have happened) in human relationships" (Thompson 1968: 8). Or, in the words of autonomia: "We don't start with the class: we come to it. Or better, we reach a new level of class composition. We begin with struggle….We go from the struggle to the class" (Tronti 1976, pp. 126–27).

It is far more fruitful then to conceive of movements as the moving of these social relations of struggle — in crude terms, movements not of people, but of people *doing things*: that is, the multitude-in-practice. This dynamic approach allows us to sidestep many of the traps that lie in wait for more orthodox theorists. For instance, from this perspective what people do is far more important than what they say. We no longer have to rely on people's own self-definition ("I'm a communist, therefore everything I do is anti-capitalist"). Communism is, after all, not a label but critical, purposeful social practice.

Moreover, if movements are the *moving* of social relations of struggle, it no longer makes sense to talk of static boundaries or limits ("these people are in the capitalist movement, those people aren't..."). But it makes no more sense to adopt a simple anti-identity position (one which would itself offer an "identity"). Living a life will always involve some sort of definition, however temporary and tentative, if only to ward off entropy. More crucially, social movements (the moving of social relations) travel through moments of expansion and contraction. In this, the act of drawing boundaries, of defining ourselves in some way, can prove immensely productive, by generating further moments of expansion as we fight to overcome the limits we have set ourselves. In the UK, the trajectory of the anti-roads movement is a good example. What started out as an "environmentalist" struggle in the early 1990s became an explicitly "anti-capitalist" one within a few years, not through a conscious adoption of a communist ideology but simply because people's practices kept coming up against, *and overcoming*, the limits set by capital.

Finally, the dynamic approach to "movement" opens our eyes to the everyday activities, both individual and collective, of millions upon millions of "ordinary" people. Closer to our own political histories we can start to see how, in the rush to abandon the "lifestylism" and "single issue politics" that were so pre-dominant in the mid to late 1980s, many of us also jettisoned its actual social practices — practices which were in retrospect far more radical than those of the more formal "revolutionary" groups (in our case Class War) to which we gravitated. (See, for example, Anonymous 1999). Here we can also see a way out of the traditional "means and ends" dichotomy. Historically anti-capitalist movements have too often thrown up organisational forms which ran counter to their long-term objectives. We only need to glance at the history of the "communist" movement in the twentieth century, for example, to see party being put before class with devastating consequences. This is a theme to which we will return later.

LOST IN THE SUPERMARKET

Anti-capitalist movements, then, are movements of social relations. As such they occur across a number of dimensions, both spatial and temporal. One of the key characteristics about the current movement is its immediately global nature. In this respect "globalisation," far from being a one-sided extension of capital's power, entangling the whole world in the logic of the market, is actually a response to the flexing of *our* muscles in the 1960s and 1970s — which temporarily forced capital on to the defensive. From capital's perspective globalisation is an inevitable corollary of its ceaseless self-expansion. From our perspective it is as much a *flight from* our insubordination as a *flight to* new untapped markets (see Holloway 2003). And here it is useful to think of circuits of struggle, of the ways in which struggles in one country reverberate and are amplified around the world. This process can occur simultaneously at a number of levels—for instance the Zapatista uprising, besides inspiring many thousands, even millions, around the globe, gave birth to the *encuentros*, which in turn inspired many similar events across the globe. On another level, labour militancy in, say, South Korea may cause some sectors of capital to relocate to South Wales, while other elements move to Seoul to assist in decomposition of the class there. Of course, as some have argued, the current "anti-globalisation" tag is a misnomer: "it should not be called an anti-globalisation movement. It is pro-globalisation, or rather an alternative globalisation movement, one that seeks to expand the possibilities of self-determination" (Hardt and Negri 2001, pp. 102–03). The current phase of globalisation is a real response by capital to our own ongoing dissension and revolt across the world, to the ways in which we have attempted to undermine the capital relation, to refashion social relations in our own interests.

Movements of social relations also occur across time. It may appear a truism, but anti-capitalist movements of the early twentieth century are vastly different from those of the present day. Again, just as at a global level, what we see here is the operation of that spiralling "double helix" identified by Tronti: working class composition and capitalist restructuring chase each other over the span of historical periods in ever more complex ways. More specifically, we can reconsider Negri's historical phases of capitalist development in the light of our new understanding of movement. At the risk of being over-schematic, Negri identifies three broad phases. First we have the era of the "professional worker," which we might characterise as running from the middle of the nineteenth century to the outbreak of World War One. This is the "classic" period of large-scale industry which sees the dominance of productive factory labour ("skilled workers") and the formation of the first workers' political parties. The second phase is the age of the "mass worker," which we could say runs from 1918 to the late 1960s. This phase is characterised by increasingly alienated work processes (Taylorism), mechanisation and mass production (Fordism), and a heavily interventionist State model (Keynesianism). The third, current, phase is that of the "socialised worker." In this phase the factory is dispersed into society, giving rise to the "social factory" and the "real subsumption" of social labour under capital.

In the era of the professional worker, capitalist command and control is based firmly within the factory, and outside of this there are areas which are left relatively untouched (although that is not to say they were havens of peace and freedom as they were subject to other forms of hierarchy and domination). We can see the transition from this era to that of the mass worker as a result of, on the one hand, labour's flight *of* insubordination and, on the other, capital's flight *from* insubordination. Through its struggles over the length of the working day and over "skills," labour sought to escape the discipline of the factory. Capital, in its turn, was forced to respond on two fronts. Within the factory, it sought to flee labour's insubordination by "displacing" workers with machines and by increasing its control over the remaining labour-power with those self-same machines. But capital can only exist through labour, through dominating living labour. As labour fled the factory, capital was forced—to secure its very existence — to pursue it and thus developed the political, economic and social strategies associated with the era of the mass worker.

Turning now to the late 1960s and '70s, the transition from the era of the mass worker to that of the socialised worker, we can see how this too was a product of the flight of and from insubordination, as the movement of the capital relation. Throughout society, insubordinate labour refused capitalist domination. While factory workers practised strikes, go-slows and industrial sabotage, there was an explosion of new social movements, typified by the rise of the Black Power, women's and lesbian and gay rights movements, and importantly also the anti-nuclear movement off the 1970s. Some factory workers, besides demanding more money and less work, experimented with alternative uses for the factory; the new social subjects fiercely proclaimed their autonomy, their difference, their individual and collective identities; beyond the factory floor, all the activities associated with the "counter culture" were nothing other than explorations in new ways of being. Once more, capital was forced to flee, yet also to chase. Taking flight from insubordinate waged workers in the North, it has relocated much physical production to the South and East (cf. Bonnet, 2002). And it has "taken on" the counter-culture, commodifying what previously appeared unruly and domesticating "dissent" by making it a profitable and marketable asset in the burgeoning "culture industry." Labour power as a category and capitalist command is extended throughout society to such an extent that it now makes sense to see the whole of society functioning as a moment of production. Time for ourselves is increasingly time spent either preparing for work or time spent engaging in "leisure" — regimented forms of "free time" that seem closer to break time at school than periods when we can decide what we really might want to do with our lives. In short, capital is now entirely social and its power is almost completely diffuse throughout every level of society. Negri (1996: 157) captured this development well when he argued that "productive labour is no longer 'that which directly produces capital,' but that which reproduces society."

Of course it is important to recognise that the most modern and technological expressions of this "social factory" sit side by side with more brutal forms of capitalist domination. No matter what the hype says, we are not all web designers now, and in some parts of the world capital is still attempting to carry out the enclosures and expropriation of common land that it enforced in the UK over three hundred years ago. Elements of "primitive" and "developed" are frequently intimately entangled: the new technology worker's lunch-time latte is made by close-to-minimum-wage employees, while the metallic ores — cobalt, copper, coltan — which end up in computers, cell phones and other electronic equipment are frequently mined in conditions that would have been unthinkable even in the darkest hours of the pre-Chartist nineteenth century. But even where capital is struggling to impose itself, it's impossible to deny that capital is starting to suffuse all forms of social life: when TV images show those resisting expropriation are wearing last year's Nike cast-offs from the west, how can the principled distinctions of the past be maintained?

In this nightmare vision of invisible, even "totalitarian" control, it might appear hard to see what space is left for anti-capitalist movements. But if capital is primarily a social (class) relation, and if the capital relation is a global relation, then capital is contested everywhere. Or, in a neater summation, "[t]he proletariat is everywhere, just as the boss is" (Negri 1989: 178). A vicious circle develops: because capital is so diffuse, so the sites of resistance and antagonism become generalised and diverse — and are automatically social. In contrast to the earlier periods, the state's primary role is now one of decomposition, of neutralising our resistance to capital, rather than one of mediation. Thatcherism and Reaganomics were just early expressions of this deep structural shift. Low intensity conflicts and "slow riots" are the order of the day — "low intensity" both because they rumble on and on without end and, crucially, because there are no longer any Winter Palaces to storm. In fact the real subsumption of labour under capital means that there is no space left between capitalism and anti-capitalism — there is no "outside" any more, if indeed there ever was. So while capital might appear stronger than ever, its grip is more precarious than ever. Without the safety valves of the past, everything now goes straight to the heart of its mode of domination. As one of our former Class War comrades succinctly put it, "There's now only one question worth asking: what sort of world do we want to live in?" This formulation is echoed elsewhere: "How are we to become what we already are?" (Smith 1996: 154); and: "What is it to live in a society completely constituted on the basis of freedom?" (Surin 1996: 203). It is on this basis that a whole new anti-capitalist politics has started to flourish.

COMPLETE CONTROL

With the development of the social factory, the entire terrain of politics has shifted to what could be described as the abstract and the universal. Capital has "socialised" itself to escape the battles we waged in the factory, and in so doing has unwittingly opened the way for a new form of politics ("postpolitical politics" in Surin's words). For us the key issue here is not just the emergence of a self-defined "anti-capitalist" movement. It is also the real experimentation with social practices and organisational forms that can prove adequate to the task.

Here we think of the tendency to develop horizontal networks, non-hierarchical information and skills exchanges; the imaginative attempts to move beyond sterile, ossified positions (e.g the efforts of *Tute Bianche* (White Overalls) to transcend the violence/non-violence issues in Genoa); the shift to more flexible, informal ways of organising; the rejection of representation (other people doing things on our behalf) in favour of direct action; the reintroduction of notions of pleasure and fun into "politics"; the increasing recognition of our vulnerability as human beings and attempts meet the need that spring from that (as shown by the Activist-Trauma support group at Gleneagles); and, above all, the willingness to be open and honest, to think sideways, and to do things differently. As De Angelis (2001) has pointed out, two interdependent fronts have been opened up: "one is of the limit to capital, and therefore against the limit that capital places upon us — the other is that of relations with the other, a network based on respect, dignity and direct democracy." This simultaneous struggle *against* capital and *for* new, unexplored and diverse ways of being is encapsulated in the Zapatista slogan: "One *No*, Many *Yes*es." That is to say, the "anti-capitalist movements" fight on the one hand *against* capital, and on the other *for* us. And it is the shift to the second front which seems to be the most decisive. Having created a space from where we can start to pose limits to capital, we have also created a space from where we can start to create situations which go beyond capital.

Here we return to Marx's formulation from his *German Ideology* with which we began, or as it has been more recently expressed: The aim is not to force the creation of something which has never existed but to free those forces which already exist, to "develop potentialities slumbering within" existing social being. The task is to discover, hidden inside the chaos of modern life, the elements of a set of relations between human beings, including their relations with the natural world, which are "worthy of their human nature" (Smith 1996: 165).

From this perspective, anti-capitalist movements are concerted attempts to discover what we already are.

However, we need to introduce a note of caution. Neat as this scheme might appear, it would be foolish (and dangerous) to mistake the map for the territory. Anti-capitalist movements at particular points in time throw up new forms of political organisation, but these organisational forms also have a life and a power of their own. They quickly become limits which react back upon the real movements of social relations from where they arose — the Bolshevik model, for example, is an organisational practice which still has an enormously damaging effect on our ability to organise ourselves effectively against capital (cf. The Free Association 2006). In this respect, it's possible to talk of a third front opening up, one against outdated and alienating political forms. After the attempted criminalisation of the entire movement in Genoa, and increased repression and marginalisation by the "war on terror," there has been pressure on the movement to define itself, to offer up its programme for inspection and negotiation. Crucially, part of this pressure has come from "within" the movement, from political organisations which can only think in terms of "demands," "lobbying" and more of the same old mediation (see Schnews 2001, De Angelis 2001, Harvie et al 2005). Outright repression and clumsy attempts to freeze and channel these movements of social relations both belong to the same strategy of enclosure. In refusing to be defined and limited, we both defend and deepen a process that represents the dynamic, self-expanding unfolding of our power—a real attempt to work out in practical terms new ways of being.

NOTES

[1] The Leeds May Day Group/Free Association is an ongoing collective project. This is a revised version of a document originally written by Alex Dennis, David Harvie, Nette Humphreys, Brian Layng and Keir Milburn. Thanks to Werner Bonefeld for help in re-editing. Comments, criticisms and communication are welcomed and can be sent to <the.free.association@gmail.com>. Our virtual home is www.nadir.org.uk.

REFERENCES

Andrew X. (1999), "Give Up Activism," in Reclaim the Streets (eds) *Reflections on J18*. London: RTS. Also at www.infoshop.org/octo/j18_reflections.html. Reprinted with a new postscript in Earth First! (eds) (2000), *Do or Die*, 9: 160–170.

Anonymous (1999), *Beasts of Burden: Capitalism—Animals—Communism*. London: Antagonism. Also at www.geocities.com/CapitolHill/ Lobby/3909/ and at www.geocities.com/CapitolHill/Senate/7672.

Bonnet, A. (2002), "The Command of Money Capital and the Latin American Crisis," in Bonefeld, W. and S. Tischler, *What is to be Done?*, Ashgate, Aldershot.

De Angelis, M. (2001), "From Movement to Society." *The Commoner*, 2, at www.commoner.org.uk. Also in Anonymous (eds), *On Fire: The Battle of Genoa and the Anti-Capitalist Movement*. London: One-Off Press.

G. (1999), "June 18th —If I Can Dance It's Not My Revolution?" In Reclaim the Streets (eds), *Reflections on J18*. London: RTS. Also at: www.infoshop.org/octo/j18_reflections.html.

Hardt, M., and Negri, A. (2001), "What the Protesters in Genoa Want," in Anonymous (eds), *On Fire: The Battle of Genoa and the Anti-Capitalist Movement*. London: One-Off Press.

Harvie, D, Milburn, K., Trott, B. and Watts, D. (eds) (2005), *Shut Them Down! The G8, Gleneagles 2005 and the Movement of Movements*, Autonomedia and Dissent!, New York and Leeds.

Holloway, J. (2003), "Capital Moves," in Bonefeld, W. (2003), *Revolutionary Writing*, Autonomedia, New York.

Holloway, J. (1995), "From Scream of Refusal to Scream of Power: The Centrality of Work," in W. Bonefeld, R. Gunn, etal. (eds.), *Open Marxism III: Emancipating Marx*, London, Pluto.

Marx, K. (1973), "The Eighteenth Brumaire of Louis Bonaparte," in *Surveys from Exile*. Harmondsworth: Penguin. Also at www.marxists.org.

Marx, K. (1976), *Capital: A Critique of Political Economy*, Volume 1. Harmondsworth, Penguin.

Marx, K. and Engels, F. (1970), *The German Ideology*, London, Lawrence and Wishart. Also at www.marxists.org.

Negri, A. (1989), *The Politics of Subversion: A Manifesto for the Twenty-First Century*. Cambridge, Polity.

Negri, A. (1996), "Twenty Theses on Marx: Interpretation of the Class Situation Today," in S. Makdisi, C. Casarino and R.E. Karl (eds), *Marxism Beyond Marxism*. New York, Routledge.

Schnews (2001,) "Monopolise Resistance?: How 'Globalise Resistance' Would Hijack Revolt." Brighton: Schnews. Also at: www.schnews.org.uk.

Smith, C. (1996), *Marx at the Millennium*. London, Pluto.

Surin, K. (1996) "'The Continued Relevance of Marxism' as a Question: Some Propositions," in S. Makdisi, C. Casarin and R.E. Karl (eds), *Marxism Beyond Marxism*. New York, Routledge.

The Free Association (2006), *What Is A Life?*, at www.nadir.org.uk/whatisalife.html.

Thompson, E.P. (1968), *The Making of the English Working Class*. Harmondsworth: Penguin.

Tronti, M. (1976), "Workers and Capital," in Conference of Socialist Economists (eds), *The Labour Process and Class Strategies*. London: Stage One/CSE Books.

Tronti, M. (1979), "Lenin in England," in Red Notes (eds), *Working Class Autonomy and the Crisis: Italian Marxist Texts of the Theory and Practice of a Class Movement, 1964–79*. London: Red Notes/CSE Books.

9

Deep Currents Rising
Some Notes on the Global Challenge to Capitalism

Harry Cleaver

Despite neo-conservative illusions of a hegemonic Pax Americana, the persistent efforts of supranational state institutions such as the IMF and the WTO to impose neo-liberal policies throughout the world and the US government's efforts to use its post-9/11 "war on terrorism" to leverage the power of capital against all opponents, the basic institutional structures of modern capitalist society continue to be challenged on all levels by diverse currents of grassroots struggle. In their increasingly common rejection of business priorities these struggles recall Marxist notions of class warfare. Yet the common opposition to capitalism is not accompanied by the old notion of a unified alternative project of socialism. On the contrary, such a vision is steadily being displaced by a proliferation of distinct projects and a common understanding that there is no need for universal rules. In response to these struggles, the threatened global order is responding in various ways, sometimes by military and paramilitary force, sometimes by co-optation aimed at reintegrating the antagonistic forces. The problem for us is finding ever new ways to defeat these responses and continue to build new worlds. To find those new ways, we need to understand the character of the currents of struggle now in motion. Among such diverse currents conceptual approaches have naturally differed. In the notes that follow I evaluate a few of those concepts and offer some new ones.

1. GLOBAL CHALLENGE AND THEORETICAL INNOVATIONS

There can no longer be any doubt that proliferating interconnections among diverse, geographically dispersed, grassroots social struggles — e.g., those of waged workers (often precariously waged), indigenous peoples, human rights advocates, ethnic and cultural minorities, environmentalists, women, students, immigrants — are resulting in a deepening and broadening threat to the contemporary capitalist social order. On the one hand, it is the very proliferation, intensity and interlinkages of struggles attacking one or another dimension of capitalist domination that is so striking — virtually all types of existing social relationships of control are being challenged. On the other hand, one of the most important and widely recognized dimensions of increased collaboration is its global or transnational character. Those involved in local and national struggles, who have fought local and national battles, are quite consciously seeking and finding ways to connect up with those struggling elsewhere and to make their efforts complementary and visible. This has taken at least three main forms: first, increasingly effective transnational mobilization in support of particular struggles in specific locations, e.g., support for the Zapatista rebellion, second, global convergences of thousands of protestors besieging various supranational state institutions and their meetings, e.g., those of the World Trade Organization, the International Monetary Fund and World Bank and the G8, and third, coordinated, simultaneous actions in diverse locations with a common purpose, e.g., the June 18, 1999 "global ambush of capitalism."

One dimension of this multi-pronged, increasingly global attack on capitalist hegemony has been the effort to grasp theoretically what is new about this situation. This project has occupied both those involved in or sympathetic to the attacks and those threatened by them and desperate for counter-strategies. New metaphors and concepts about social conflict are born with insights flowing from the recognition of new situations that don't seem to fit existing theories. One kind of new situation involves hitherto unknown or unrecognized phenomena; another occurs when some known, but previously secondary phenomena have taken on a new importance and have become progressively more central in the challenging of existing institutional structures and mechanisms of control. The genesis of new theoretical approaches then results from efforts to imaginatively resolve apparent contradictions between existing theory and these new perceptions and insights in order to inform strategy and tactics for dealing with the new situations. In recent years there has been a veritable scramble to grasp the nature of the dizzying array of new disjunctures, connections, contradictions and complementarities that make up the current proliferation of interconnected challenges to global capital.

2. Transnational Networks and Social Netwars

Perhaps the most common new theoretical approach has been to interpret the pattern of interconnections among proliferating struggles in terms of "networks." Among those challenging capitalist domination neither what is now called "networking" nor the concept of networks are entirely new. The entire history of challenges to capital has been replete with the efforts of its opponents to break out of their isolation and form mutually beneficial linkages with others in similar situations. This is true of early resistance to its primitive accumulation and true of the rise and development of trades unions, political parties and other organizational forms against its ongoing efforts to accumulate people as workers and labor power. As a general rule the wider and deeper the linkages, the more successful struggles have been, the greater the isolation, the more likely defeat.

As for thinking about such linkages in terms of "networks," some roots of today's common use of the concept by activists can be found in Italy in the 1960s where the Marxist sociologist Romano Alquati in his studies of workers conflicts with the Italian auto giant FIAT meshed the Marxist analysis of class composition with that of networks, at the factory, national and international levels.[1]

Other sociologists and then political scientists took the concept of networks over from mathematical graph theory to analyze a wide variety of social relationships. These have included individual behavior, small group interactions, organizational behavior and social movements — most recently transnational movements.[2] Of these, the last two would seem to have the most salience here. Organizational theorists and observers have traced the emergence within businesses and to some degree the state sector, of network forms of organization that appear distinct from more traditional hierarchies and market systems.[3] Recent applications of network analysis to transnational social struggles have drawn on past sociological studies of local networks, on organizational studies and on empirical work on particular network-based campaigns to knit together a synthetic view of "those relevant actors working internationally on an issue, who are bound together by shared values, a common discourse and dense exchanges of information and services."[4]

Similar work has been done by national security analysts, who have examined the implications of the emergence of network forms of organization for the United States Department of Defense. One early study was that of Pentagon analyst Charles Swett who focused in on the role of the Internet.[5] The most perceptive and influential work has been done by RAND's David Ronfeldt and his co-authors. Drawing on studies of the changing organization of business and the state, such as that of Walter Powell, they have taken over the juxtaposition of networks to markets and hierarchies and argued that a wide variety of contemporary social conflicts have been evolving networked organizations capable of unleashing "transnational social netwars." On the one hand, they were among the first to identify such structures in terrorist organizations, e.g., Al Qaeda, — a recognition that has since become increasingly commonplace. On the other hand, they also pointed to emerging transnational networks of "information age activism" based on associations among non-governmental organizations (NGOs) concerned with modern and postmodern issues such as the environment, human rights, immigration, indigenous peoples and freedom in cyberspace.[6]

3. The Zapatista Rebellion

In much of this recent work, a primary reference point for the study of transnational networks has been the rebellion waged by Zapatista communities in Chiapas, Mexico since the beginning of 1994 and the activities of its supporters around the world. That rebellion — organized by a culturally and linguistically diverse array of collaborating, indigenous communities — was the latest in a long history of struggles by such people to defend themselves from the recurrent efforts to separate them from their land and their means of production.[7] Those efforts date back to the Spanish Conquest but have never been entirely successful.[8] In some periods, such as the Mexican Revolution that began in 1910, such enclosure has been partially reversed and reforms have restored some previously stolen lands. More recently, neo-liberal government policies have increasingly threatened surviving communities by closing legal options for reversing enclosure while facilitating its extension.[9] These deepening threats helped set the Zapatista rebellion in motion.

The first activist analysis of the communicational dimension of that rebellion noted that the "most striking thing about the sequence of events set in motion on January 1, 1994 has been the speed with which news of the struggle circulated and the rapidity of the mobilization of support which resulted."[10] It went on to note how modern computer communications, through the Internet and the Association for Progressive Communications networks, made it possible for the Zapatistas to get their message out despite governmental spin control and censorship. Mailing lists and conferences also facilitated discussions and debate among concerned observers that led to the organization of protest and support activities in over forty countries around the world. The Zapatista rebellion, the analysis concluded, was not only built on local indigenous networks but through much wider networks was able to catalyze the weaving of a global "electronic fabric of struggle."

Subsequent studies at the U.S. Defense Department and at RAND also focused on the networked character of the rebellion and of its supporters as well as the role of computer communications in the mobilization of that support.[11] The lesson they drew was the need for the U.S. government to develop its own "networks" — both military and civil — to counter those of their opponents. In 1998, as a part of their study of the development of transnational human rights networks, Keck and Sikkink reported on how: "the [Mexican] government could no longer control information as it had in 1968…. The press and domestic and international NGOs monitored the conflict closely, and electronic mail became one of the main mechanisms through which the EZLN communicated with the world."[12]

More recently network analysis has been applied empirically in some detail to understand the international struggles connected to the Zapatistas. From hyperlink analysis designed to identify the structures of Zapatista support networks, to more extensive efforts both to discover the nature of, and relationships within the transnational Zapatista support network and to explore the connections with, and impact on, other networks of counter-globalization, we find a variety of sympathetic efforts being elaborated understand this ever-growing set of experiences.[13]

4. FROM STATIC NETWORKS TO THE DYNAMICS OF STRUGGLE: SWARMING

One problem with the application of the concept of "network" to social struggles has been the tendency to think about "networks" in static terms. Even when the noun "network" is turned into a verb — "networking" — it just means "building networks" or "operating through a network" with no specification of the dynamics involved. Recognizing patterns of connectivity is not enough; the key thing is how they work dynamically. Capitalist strategists need to know how networks function to threaten them so that they can develop countermeasures — to block, crush or absorb the threats. Those building opposition to capitalist domination need to understand how networks are established, strengthened and can be used for mobilization and attack, but they also need to understand how and to what degree networks constitute viable approaches to the organization of post-capitalist social relations.

Following up their earlier advice of devising state networks to counter oppositional networks, David Ronfeldt and his primary co-author John Arquilla have also argued for the adaptation by such state networks of one method they have identified as being used by such opponents: "swarming," defined as "a deliberately structured, coordinated, strategic way to strike from all directions, by means of a sustainable pulsing of force." Some examples that they cite are from historical military experience but others are from anti-capitalist social struggle, e.g., Mikhail Bakunin's proposal of "general strikes" and the rapid mobilization of support networks in response to Mexican government moves against the Zapatistas. The concept is also, obviously, evocative of the periodic convergence of thousands from diverse struggles who have gathered to besiege various capitalist institutions. In their essay devoted to this subject, Ronfeldt and Arquilla juxtapose swarming to other types of military tactics, e.g., melee, manoeuvre and massing, and propose "battleswarming" as a successor to current U.S. military doctrines such as LandAir Battle.[14]

The concept of "swarming" has subsequently been appropriated by some activists for their own purposes. One example, hacktivists — whose coordinated "ping" attacks on targeted websites were one example of swarming for Ronfeldt and Arquilla — quickly adopted their adversaries' conceptualization for their own purposes; "digital Zapatismo" became "InfoSwarm Systems."[15]

The responses to such actions on the part of those involved in various social struggles have often been highly critical. One criticism has been that the hacktivists have chosen bad targets and have done so because they are neither connected to, nor did they consult with, the particular struggle their actions were aimed at supporting. A second criticism has been that the use of such tactics could open movements to the charge of violating their own rules of free speech and set them up for being attacked in the same way.[16] A third objection has revolved around the difficulty in demonstrating that such actions are not the rogue actions of a few individuals but do indeed involve thousands of people and are thus politically significant. Although the ping engines can generate information about the numbers and addresses of those who logged into a site and used it, there remain the questions of circulating that information, making it believable and gaining legitimacy for such actions.[17]

When this tactic was used by U.S. activists to attack Mexican government and financial websites, there was protest from within Mexico by activists who had not been consulted and who felt placed at risk by these actions. When it was used within the U.S. to attack newspapers about coverage of the Mumia case, it was severely attacked by lawyers defending Mumia as counterproductive. As a result of such criticisms, no social movement that I know of has generalized the use of this tactic.[18]

Another adaptation of "swarming" explores the dynamics of real-time mobilization during protests and demonstrations in the streets. An essay written by the activist group "Why War?" recognizes and adapts the work of Ronfeldt and Arquilla to their own purposes:

> Swarming, for the purposes of protesting, can be thought of as the technique of quickly massing a large number of individuals from all directions onto a single position in order to attain a specific goal. There are roughly four different phases in a successful swarm: locate the target, converge, attack, disperse. For these four phases to work correctly they must be synchronized between a diversity of seemingly disconnected individuals. Therefore, there must be a layer of instantaneous communication between these individuals.[19]

The essay also offers detailed analysis about how swarming can be facilitated by protestors using portable communication devices such as cell-phones and text-messaging. This adaptation of flash mobs analyzes possible police counter-measures and discusses some concrete cases.[20]

5. The Dynamics of Struggle: Rhizomes

As an alternative to "networks" and "networking," the theoretical work of Michel Foucault, Gilles Deleuze and Félix Guattari offered a quite different set of metaphorical and conceptual approaches for analyzing the dynamics of struggle. Leaving behind some traditional orthodox Marxist frameworks, such as structuralism, dialectics and a preoccupation with the overall war between capitalists and workers, they elaborated a number of new concepts to explore and illuminate the micro-politics of both individual psychology, class power and interconnected social conflicts. For my purposes here, the most salient of their ideas — because the most widely taken up by others — are the ones associated with the metaphor of the *rhizome*: a subterranean system of horizontal roots and above ground stems.[21] Deleuze and Guattari juxtaposed this to more familiar form of trees. Obviously, both trees and rhizomes grow, they propagate dynamically; the difference lies in the pattern of growth. Trees grow vertically with their branches radiating from the central trunk; rhizomes propagate horizontally elaborating tuberous root systems in all directions — from which new sprouts arise. (These botanical examples provide the core of their metaphor in *Thousand Plateaus*, although they also called rats and their burrows rhizomes.) Through the metaphor of the rhizome they explored the characteristics they argued could be found in horizontally linked human interactions: connectivity, heterogeneity, multiplicity and rupture.

Closely related to the metaphor of rhizome are two other concepts they elaborated: deterritorialization and nomadism. Like "rhizome" both obviously evoke not only space (as does "network") but movement through space. Whereas capital has tended to impose specific "territorializations" — fixing people in particular positions where they can be controlled as workers, the struggles of those people, elaborated rhizomatically, tend to rupture that fixing by finding or creating new spaces for autonomous activity. Thus deterritorialization is an autonomous prison-break and nomadism is another way of thinking about such autonomous movement.[22] Just as traditional nomads, e.g., the Roma of Europe or the herders of the Sahel, have escaped the control of centralized Powers, whether kings, emperors, or national governments, so do modern workers sometimes escape specific institutions and mechanisms of capitalist control, e.g., school drop-outs, precarious workers, trans-sexuals and immigrants.

This dynamic metaphor and these concepts of the kinds of dynamism involved have been taken up by those involved in such struggles and used for thinking about and organizing their own activity, both locally and internationally.[23] Rhizomatic self-organization and "rhizomatic" thought have quite explicitly challenged older conceptions of organization, e.g., the welfare state or Leninist party, and the associated kinds of thinking that accompanied and justified those kinds of social organization. Acolytes of those older kinds of thinking, not surprisingly have condemned these newer approaches.[24]

If we compare and contrast Deleuze and Guattari's concepts of the dynamics of rhizomes with Ronfeldt and Arquilla's concepts of the dynamics of networks we can see how the latter reflect and pertain mainly to moments of attack, while those of the former provide much more insight into the dynamics of political recomposition that not only make attack possible but possibly establish organizational points of departure for alternatives to capitalism. These differences undoubtedly flow from the different locations of the authors amidst contemporary social struggles. Whereas Deleuze and Guattari's concepts were enunciated by men who were trying to think from within opposition to capitalist ways of organizing the world, Ronfeldt and Arquilla's work for the Pentagon has situated them most firmly within the defense of the current order.

6. The Dynamics of Struggle: Currents

Every metaphor, like every analogy, has its limits. Even with the analysis of swarming we can see how the concept of networks used by both the theoreticians of "netwar" and some of their opponents grasps only part of the reality of those loosely connected, yet restless, actors and sets of actors who share a common, creative opposition to contemporary capitalism and sometimes seek to go beyond it. What is missing is the sense of ceaseless, fluid motion among those antagonistic actors who make up that opposition in which "organizing" may not take the form of "organizations" but rather of an ebb and flow of contact at myriad points that only sometimes results in massed or simultaneous attack.

On the other hand, Deleuze and Guattari's fecund metaphor of "rhizome" does evoke ceaseless growth in various directions, albeit a slow and subterranean kind. But despite its horizontal propagation and connectiveness, the plant rhizome is a fixed form (and the restlessness of rats is obviously quite limited.) The iris rhizome in flowerbeds or the cattail rhizome in ponds do propagate themselves in all directions and send up shoots from old and new nodes, year after year. But the shoots with their leaf structures, flowers or heavy heads of pollen, are always the same. So here too restlessness exists only at the margins as a given structure reproduces itself. Indeed, the truth is that many of Deleuze and Guattari most creative insights escape their own metaphor. The deterritorialization of the plant rhizome is obviously very limited, as are the metamorphoses of which the rhizome is capable. The insight into nomadism definitely evokes a degree of mobility far beyond its possibilities. These important concepts are quite separable from the metaphor of the rhizome.

An alternative metaphor for thinking about the ceaseless movement that forms the political life and historical trajectory of those resisting and sometimes escaping the institutions of capitalism, is that of water, of the hydrosphere, especially of ever restless ocean currents. Currents are masses in motion, not just masses of homogeneous water but of whole ecologies of differentiated water molecules and the myriad forms of life that thrive and perish amidst them — floating or swimming with the flow or struggling across or against it. Everything thing is in motion, nothing is stable, deterritorialization is virtually constant, there is no "safe haven," no "secure foundation" other than familiarity with the ever-rushing, ever-changing flows.[25] Yet nomadic whales sing and dolphins play as they traverse thousands of miles of ocean.

In some places these flowing ecologies move faster, in others more slowly, in some places they are warmer, in others colder, in some places they run deep, in others on the surface. The most visible currents — those that run on the surface of the ocean — are warmer, while the deeper currents are colder. Ocean waters also differ in both salinity and in the array of life that populates them. But precisely because they are in constant motion all these things change. Sometimes deeper and colder nutrient-rich water rises in an upwelling that brings it to the surface where its molecular components warm up and grow more agitated. On the other hand, when ocean water enters polar regions it gets colder, becomes saltier, denser and either freezes or sinks. When water does freeze, it crystallizes into rigidity, but mostly it melts again, undoing one molecular form to return to a process of dynamic self-organizing that refuses crystallization yet whose currents, of varying directions and power, can be observed and tracked. When currents connect in the ocean they sometimes interact to form giant eddies: "gyres" or circular movements that pile up water in "mounds" whose surfaces rise above that of the nearby ocean. Or, more dramatically still, crosscurrents may interact to form killer "rogue waves," mini-tsunamis capable of destroying and sinking huge ships.[26]

Finally, the movement of ocean currents are affected not only by the makeup (temperature, salinity, density, nutrient load) of different masses of water but by the topology of the ocean's floor, gravity and also, especially for surface currents, by sun, wind and the coriolis force.[27] In other words, currents move according to the nature of the water that composes them, but that movement is shaped by surrounding forces.

All of these characteristics are evocative of the behavior of those forces in opposition to capitalism. Like ocean currents, social struggles have both their internal dynamics — shaped by the class composition and imaginations of the people involved — and they are shaped by the forces that surround them: capitalist institutions that constrain them or other struggles that may counter or reinforce them. They are fluid, often changing and only momentarily forming those solidified moments we call "organizations" — sometimes small, like patches of ice, sometimes quite large, like icebergs. However, such moments are constantly eroded by the shifting currents surrounding them so that they are repeatedly melted back into the flow itself. There is, of course, a certain kind of power in rigidity — frozen seas block ships and an iceberg sank the Titanic — but recognizing the inevitably transitory character of organizations necessarily must broaden our attention to the flows out of which they have crystallized and to which they must sooner or later return.

Some currents of opposition are quite visible, on the surface as it were, sometimes steady, sometimes turbulent. When they connect reinforcing each other the social equivalent of rogue waves and gyres are the swirling turbulence of public struggle: short term upheavals such as massive protests, e.g., the Battle of Seattle against the World Trade Organization, or the heady, intense days of the Zapatista intercontinental encounters, or more protracted, widespread upheavals such as insurgencies.

But, it is worth remembering that oppositional movements on the surface of society are like the surface currents of the oceans — they only involve a small percentage of the total mass.[28] Most currents of opposition run deep, below surface appearances, but like deep waters that are rich in salt and nutrients they can be rich in social connections, anger and creativity.[29] When such deep currents surface in surprising, massive upwellings of social struggle they can change the world and nourish wider conflict. Such were the world shaking eruptions in the 20th century of the Mexican, Russian, Chinese, Cuban and Hungarian Revolutions; such too were sudden appearances of Solidarity in Poland in 1980, 0the Zapatistas in 1994 or the Oaxaca City Commune of 2006.[30] In every case the biggest mystery and the hardest thing to explain have been what was going on in those invisible, deep, but rich currents of struggle that made possible and led to their sudden, explosive and world changing upwelling. Thus the importance of the various kinds of study that have sought to understand these largely invisible forces, e.g., analyses of everyday life, of the "weapons of the weak," of class composition, of certain aspects of popular culture.[31]

It has always been easier to identify the outside forces shaping social struggles — the social equivalents of seafloor topology, gravity, wind and solar energy — than their internal dynamics. Just as undersea landslides and earthquakes can cause abrupt changes in seafloor topology and trigger tsunamis, so social analysts often look for events that trigger social upheavals, e.g., the Mexican government attack on communal lands and the imposition of NAFTA that convinced the Zapatistas that they had to act quickly or see their lands privatized and their communities dispersed. Marxists, in particular, have often devoted far more time to analyzing the "laws of motion" of capitalist development and its consequences for workers than they have the internal, self-organization of the working class.[32] They have more readily seen and understood how capitalist imposed patterns of development, exploitation and institutional structures have confined and shaped the development of social struggles than they have grasped the internal relationships of those struggles. When those relationships have frozen into overt organizations, e.g., political parties, labor unions, NGOs, guerrilla groups, they have become the focus of intense research. Unfortunately, the molecular dynamics of the flows that have gestated self-organization but have only occasionally resulted in visible organizations have remained, all too often, largely out of sight and unanalyzed.

Many have also tended to think in terms of a one-sided causality between changes in capitalist institutions, policies and actions and working-class reactions rather than seeing how the self-activity of workers may bring about those changes. Within the framework of my oceanographic metaphor, for example, capitalist policy changes, e.g., attacks on peasant land holdings, may be seen as the result of persistent resistance to enclosure and success at reversing it — just as undersea landslides may be triggered by the erosion caused by turbulent ocean currents. Or, just as hurricanes are intensified by warming ocean water, so too is capitalist desperation and murderous flailing about often the result of their loss of control due to suddenly visible, rapidly circulating struggles.

Such invisible, deep currents — the inevitable consequence of alienation and exploitation throughout the history of capitalism — have been a source of endless frustration to those who would harness the power of those flows, whether the institutions of Western capitalism or the Leninist party. Power would harness power, but power lies in the flow itself, in the broad, deep and partly invisible currents that traverse society. Imagine the challenge to these would-be dictators or managers, standing in the middle of a world of swirling, powerful social currents, trying to manage the flows. It is easy to see how the frustration of early capitalists who had very little grasp of the flowing, living ecologies they sought to dominate would often drive them to desperate, violent efforts. It is also easy to see how later capitalist policy makers, although more experienced, have often been at a loss as to any other way to handle those ecologies and resort, once again, to force — thus the cruel brutality of much of capitalist history.

7. Harnessing Flows

But, over time, the more perceptive of capitalist policy-makers have fostered and financed the development of an array of "social sciences" whose primary purpose has been to identify and analyze the social currents that have given rise to overt attacks on business' domination of society. In many Western countries, such as the United States, anthropologists, sociologists, political scientists, psychologists and economists have all been drawn, by ideology or financial reward, into the study of such threats, either potential or actual, with a view towards providing policy-makers with both understanding of the struggles that threaten and strategies for coping.[33]

As a result, in its more genial moments capital, like engineers who have designed devices to harness the power of ocean waves, currents, tides and even salinity gradients, has understood enough to design institutions to harness antagonistic social flows without trying to simply dam or crush them. One example of such harnessing can be found in the Keynesian period when workers' struggles were used to stimulate capitalist investment, productivity growth and accumulation. By shaping worker-formed unions into institutions that would not only negotiate but impose contracts on workers, capital was able, at least to a degree, to convert struggles over wages and working conditions into motor forces of its own development.[34]

Much earlier Marx captured such harnessing in his adaptation of Quesnay's metaphor of circulation to sketch the "circuits of capital."[35] While those circuits — whether of money, commodity or productive capital — represent flows of capital, at the heart of the flows is the living labor of workers. The various moments of the circuits and their interconnections constitute the general framework through which capital organizes or manages life as living labor. The metaphor returned, to a small degree, in mainstream macroeconomics' portrayal of the circular character of economic relationships and its sharp distinction between flows and stocks. In both cases social relationships are conceptualized as flows, but they are harnessed flows, like rivers or ocean tides diverted into hydroelectric plants to drive turbines.

Such harnessing and the constraints it imposes, quite unsurprisingly, are endlessly resisted by the restlessness of a humanity that has so many, many different ideas about interesting forms of self-organization. From shop-floor to street, from rice paddies to mountain forests people have organized and reorganized to escape this harnessing. As a result, some contemporary Marxists have not only recognized the autonomous power involved in this resisting and these efforts to escape but have analyzed how such struggles "circulate" from sector to sector of the working class, rupturing capitalist circulation in the process — thus taking over and using the metaphor of "circulation" for their own purposes.[36]

In line with this metaphor we can think about the conflicts described above not so much in terms of wars between set pieces (chess, go, military confrontations) or wars between classes for Power (Leninist revolution versus the capitalist state), but rather in terms of the vast imagination and capability of self-organization of a multiplicity of struggles straining against capitalist rules that bind, limit and distort.[37] There is a kind of class war here that involves increasingly resistance to the unity of global capitalism. But the resistance flows not from an increasingly unified class seeking a new unified hegemony, but rather from myriad currents seeking the freedom of the open seas where they can re-craft their own movement and their interactions with each other free of a single set of constraining capitalist rules.

Given the diversity of approaches to thinking about the emergence around the world and connections across borders of such a wide variety of social struggles, that have increasingly challenged capitalism, there have also been a variety of approaches to the characterization of the subjectivities involved in those struggles.

8. CIVIL SOCIETY?

Ever since East European dissidents resurrected the concept of "civil society" as a way of talking about social initiatives that escaped the control of Soviet-style states, the use of the term has proliferated across the political spectrum. From Left to Right, from opponents of capitalism to its defenders, the concept has been deployed, as it has in the past, in a variety of ways. "International civil society," "transnational civil society" and "global civil society" have all been evoked to characterize the kind of widespread challenges to contemporary capitalist policy I have been discussing. But when we examine what people mean by these terms we find the same varied meanings as when the concept of "civil society" has been applied to local social structures in the past.[38]

Many have tended to reduce the meaning of "civil society" to formal NGOs.[39] This reduction has been more or less severe, largely depending on the interests of those using the words. For many state agencies, either national or supranational, the term NGO is used so broadly as to include the private business sector. For others the term refers only to non-governmental and non-business organizations. In this case, however, there is often a failure to distinguish between NGOs that are obviously integral parts of capitalism such as the Rockefeller and Ford Foundations from grassroots organizations opposed to it. Conceptualizing "civil society" only in the form of NGOs is a reductionism not surprising in a society where political Power is usually vested in formal institutions. It is not, however, satisfactory. Oppositional NGOs should be seen as only particular organizational crystallizations of a much more general and fluid social struggles. Indeed, partly in reaction to the growth and behavior of some transnational NGOs, various critiques have emerged along with a quite conscious search for alternative ways of organizing. One such critique has been of an observed tendency for NGOs to become bureaucratic and self-preserving institutions, increasingly operating above and independently from their supporters. This critique parallels similar ones that have been directed at traditional labor unions and political parties by the Zapatistas who have been unusually successful in articulating these critiques in ways that have resonated widely among those who have become disenchanted with such organizations.

A second critique has been that such NGOs have cut deals with the state and with business in ways that have betrayed the purposes for which the organizations were formed. One example has been the willingness of some big environmental organizations to collaborate with the World Bank or the World Trade Organization — thus lending legitimacy to those institutions whose policies have generally been ecologically destructive. Here again, parallels can be drawn with the behavior of "business" unions and political parties.

These critiques have effectively recast the notion of "civil society" in a narrower sense. "Civil society" has become, for the Zapatistas and many others, a term applied *only* to those moments and struggles within society that resist subordination to capitalist institutions and, in many cases, fight for alternative ways of organizing society.

Unfortunately, both historically and in the contemporary world the concept of "civil society" has been given so many different meanings as to render its meaning opaque. When you have to go into a long discourse to explain the particular meaning of your use of a term — as opposed to the way many others use the term — it's usually a good time to seek a different vocabulary. Although what interests me here is most closely approximated by the last definition of "civil society" given above, I prefer to eschew the use of the term altogether to avoid misunderstanding.[40]

9. Social Movements?

Conceptualizing widespread but interconnected challenges to existing institutions in terms of "social movements," rather than just unusual "collective behaviors," grew out of the experience of the "civil rights," "black power," "counter-cultural," student, women's and other "movements" of late 1950s and 1960s. Those of us engaged in struggle thought of ourselves as being part of a "movement" and so did those many who analyzed us from within or from without, whether sympathetically or critically. The very term "movement" not only evoked struggle for change, but also the absence of any center, of any hierarchical organizational structures that could command the widespread, frequent protests and related actions. Cohesion in movements has often been thought to derive from common goals and shared collective identities.[41]

The identification of separate organizing by separate movements, e.g., black power groups organizing separately from civil rights groups, women organizing themselves autonomously from men, led many to speak of "new" social movements — as distinct from the traditional labor movement — and sometimes to skeptical characterizations of these movements as being balkanized, essentially reformist efforts that ultimately posed no real threat to "the system" as a whole, however much this or that aspect of it was being contested. Whether enthusiastic or skeptical, the number of academic researchers, especially in sociology, focused on "new social movements" multiplied rapidly and churned out a huge body of work, first articles and then collections of those articles. Books with titles such as *Social Movements and Culture* or *Cultural Politics and Social Movements* began to appear in the mid-1990s.[42] Political scientists and historians joined in and a variety of approaches have been offered to explain patterns of movement development and behavior. Among the most influential have been those of "political process" and "resource mobilization" where the former emphasizes changes in the larger political situation that opens up or closes down opportunities for movement formation and action and the latter focuses on how movement activity is shaped by all the resources available, including political, economic and communicational ones.[43]

As recognition has grown of how struggles for particular changes have been flowing together into collaborations whose impact is already larger than the sum of the individual influences. Many have come, therefore, to speak of a "movement of movements" and optimistically, for the first time in quite a while, to declare that "another world is possible" or "other worlds are possible."[44]

As one might expect both the commonplace use of the term "movement" to characterize these struggles as well as the academic "social movement" literature on them have been critiqued in various ways. One example is the paper by the Leeds May Day Group in this volume that sees this characterization as too restrictive because it highlights the actions of activists while ignoring much more widespread actions on the part of "people who do not consider themselves "activists" or "political" but who nevertheless have to struggle against oppression and exploitation in their everyday lives — people who, just like us, are struggling for new ways of living."

More generally, because these "new" social movements have been identified as falling outside the labor movement, they have also been identified as falling outside the Marxian concept of class struggle. While this has permitted such "post-Marxist" approaches to successfully create an accepted space for their work within an overwhelmingly anti-Marxist academic establishment, it has done so only by defining "class struggle" very narrowly and marginalizing it as one kind of conflict among others. As with the broader space of "post-modern" studies — which has executed a similar strategy — the overly simplified characterization and abandonment of Marxist thought has often led to an identity politics blind to, and thus vulnerable to, the threat of a common enemy.

10. WORKING CLASS?

Although the "post-Marxist" and "post-modernist" characterizations of Marxian thought has rung true among those who have identified Marxism with its orthodox varieties — e.g., Leninist, Maoist, Trotskyist — it has rung quite false among those familiar with less orthodox and more adaptive varieties of Marxist thought. Whereas orthodox Marxists have tended to react to the struggles of those outside the waged industrial proletariat — and there have been such throughout the history of capitalism — by demanding that they get a waged job, join the working class and *its* struggles, other Marxists, long ago, saw the political and theoretical flaws in such a response. On the one hand, critical theorists of the Frankfurt School and those who followed them, recognized and analyzed how capitalist mechanisms of domination had been extended to the sphere of culture and everyday life — even if they were not always able to either recognize or analyze the struggles against those mechanisms. On the other hand, first Marxist feminists and then others began to recognize how "the" working class has always included the unwaged as well as the waged and how varied struggles have been among both. As a result, for many Marxists the concepts of working class and working class struggle have been so widened beyond its orthodox association with waged factory labor as to encompass all of those struggles that have threatened the rules and institutions of capitalist domination throughout society and frequently sought to go beyond them. Beyond Marx's "collective worker" at the point of production, they saw a collective worker acting in both spheres of the "social factory": production and reproduction.[45] One name for this collective worker was bestowed by the Italian Marxist Antonio Negri: the "social" or "socialized" worker.[46]

Such a broadened concept of working class has made possible Marxist analyses of the wide variety of social struggles around the world that have challenged capitalism in ever more interconnected ways. Such analyses have employed Marxist analytical and political categories, e.g., value, exploitation, alienation, class struggle, but have elaborated and adapted them in ways that take account of the breath and variety of the struggles among both waged and unwaged. Among the first examples of such analyses were those of class conflicts of the Fordist or Keynesian period in which the factory model had been extended to, and hence contested, throughout society. In other words both deskilled industrial workers and others outside industry — but whose lives were shaped in ways designed to feed into (schools), or support (nuclear families), or manage the reserve army of (the welfare state, foreign aid, neocolonialism) industry — were organized as effectively as Keynesian planners could manage as one great social factory. The result, of course, was the inevitable, equally thorough appearance of class struggle against such shaping and all of its miserably constrained conditions of life.

The point of departure for analyzing the complexities of such a multi-dimensional working class and its struggles was, naturally, Marx's own analysis of the way capital imposed a division of labor in production and the way it pitted some groups of workers against others, e.g., Irish against English or the unemployed and unwaged (the reserve army) against those with jobs and wages. But whereas Marx's focus was on the methods of capitalist control and exploitation, the need of those in struggle against such control demanded an inversion of perspective, from top-down to bottom-up. Just as Marx had studied everything he could find on division of labor, including theoretical essays by economists and engineers and factory inspector reports, so a new generation of Marxists in the post-WWII era undertook to study, sometimes in similar sources, sometimes at actual points of production (and later at the points of reproduction) the contemporary shape of class relationships.[47]

The result was the elaboration of a "workerist" analysis of "class composition" that looked at the division of labor explicitly in terms of the power relations between capital and workers and among the latter with a view to providing theoretical concepts for grasping changes in those relations brought on through workers' struggle. Thus workers' efforts to tip the scales of power in their favor were conceptualized as processes of "political recomposition" while capitalist attempts to thwart or reverse such efforts were seen to involve the imposition of new divisions in processes of class "decomposition." Similarly, attempts to theorize the ability of workers to take the initiative in the class war and to craft alternative non-capitalist relations among themselves led from the concept of workers' autonomy to that of self-valorization — an appropriation and inversion of a term Marx used to describe capitalist expanded reproduction.[48] Methodologically, these ideas implied taking workers struggles, in all their variety and interrelationships, as points of departure for understanding both particular organizational crystallizations, e.g., unions, political parties, NGOs, and capitalist strategies and tactics.

Applied to the international level such an analysis tended first, to recognize how supranational institutions such as the International Monetary Fund, the World Bank and the General Agreement on Trade and Tariffs were not merely vehicles of post-WWII U.S. imperial hegemony but were intended to manage a global Keynesian hierarchy of development and underdevelopment and therefore, second, to bypass traditional orthodox theories of imperialism to focus on the commonalties and interconnections among particular struggles. Thus, for example, while some viewed the anti-Vietnam war or anti-apartheid mobilizations in the United States as examples of anti-imperialist solidarity, others came to see them as interconnected moments of class struggle challenging a global capitalist order. Similarly, this approach led to an analysis of the crises of Keynesianism in the late 1960s and 1970s as political crises of that global order brought on by an international cycle of those interconnected class struggles.[49] In turn, "economic" crises since the 1980s must be understood in part as the product of capitalist counterattacks and in part as the result of continuing working class resistance. In other words, from this Marxist perspective the global drama of the last thirty years or so has not only been — in the words of Subcomandante Marcos — a "Fourth World War," but a class war between capitalists trying to wield neoliberal policies to regain control around the world and a diverse working class resisting those policies and fighting to build new worlds.[50]

11. MULTITUDE?

The kind of analysis of class struggle sketched above was taken by some Marxists, mostly working in France and Italy, and crossed with concepts from some "post-modernist" thinkers such as Michel Foucault, Gilles Deleuze and Felix Guattari. The primary products of this melding that deal with conflict at the global level and are known in the English speaking world are the later works of Antonio Negri and especially his two books with Michael Hardt, *Empire* (2000) and *Multitude* (2004).[51] These works are the outcome of over twenty years of efforts to understand precisely the nature of the processes of "political recomposition" that brought on the crisis of Keynesianism and shaped capitalist efforts at "decomposition" in the years since. From a wide-ranging series of studies of diverse struggles, mostly in Europe, whose results have been published in several European journals including *Futur Anterieur* and *Multitudes* in France and *Derive Approdi* in Italy, these writers elaborated a theory of the nature of contemporary class relationships that reformulated the concept of working class into that of "multitude" and that of capital into "empire."

The concept of empire designates a new organization of command, beyond imperialist competition between national blocs of capital backed by nation states, in which, through both national governments and supranational state institutions capital has begun to act as a more unified whole at a global level. A ferocious debate has followed this thesis — one that is strongly reminiscent of that which followed Karl Kautksy's proposed theory of ultra-imperialism just before World War I — as it was attacked those who argued 1) national rivalries are still very much alive, 2) the United States government still dominates all "supranational" state institutions and 3) American imperialism is obviously rampant in the invasions of Afghanistan and Iraq and in neoconservative plans for a new Pax Americana.[52]

The concept of multitude for Negri and Hardt designates the new collective subject that overthrew Keynesianism and imposed a new organization on capitalism. Their concept of that new subject is clearly a variation on that of the collective worker in the social factory theorized more than a decade earlier. Historically, multitude designates a metamorphosis of what Negri earlier had called the "socialized worker." The difference between the world of the social factory and the "socialized worker" and that of empire and multitude, would seem to lie in their perception that worker successes in rupturing and fleeing the social factory and capital's successes in adapting to those ruptures and checking that flight have resulted in a more thorough domination of every aspect of life. Their theorization of this supposedly new, thorough domination is based on two related concepts: biopower — a concept taken over from the work of Michel Foucault — and immaterial labor — a concept adapted from Lyotard.

In a manner similar to the work of Deleuze and Guattari, Michel Foucault's research on capitalist domination shifted focus from macro-class forces to the micro-politics of control. His study of Bentham's proposal for the management of prisons via panopticon arrangements led to his investigations into how such control was spread throughout society, the bodies and brains of those living within it.[53] In the process he revealed hitherto invisible arrangements of power through which individual lives were subtly managed through induced forms of internalized control. In Hardt and Negri such bio-political arrangements are presented as thorough and complete; all of life, within formal work places, but also in the home and in the community have become places of work for capital. "Power is thus expressed as a control that extends throughout the depths of the consciousnesses and bodies of the population — and at the same time across the entirety of social relations."[54] As a result, they argue, Marx's labor theory of value is no longer relevant because if it is no longer possible to differentiate between work and non-work, between work time and non-work time, then there is no way to measure "labor," and hence Marx's value.[55]

But what is the nature of this work to which all of life is reduced? While they recognize that older forms of work still abound — such as manual labor in fields or factories — they argue that the most important capitalist adaptation to the emergence of the multitude's subjectivity has been capital's ability to capture, organize and subordinate the increasingly important mental labor of generating information and managing communication flows and the affective labor through which personal and social relations are constructed and managed. Hardt, Negri and Maurizio Lazzarato call these kinds of work "immaterial labor."[56]

While this sounds like a more thorough variation on the vision of critical theorists who saw total capitalist domination as having spread not only through the sphere of production but through that of culture, Hardt and Negri insist that the "multitude" thus subsumed by capital is nevertheless a subject capable of revolt. The source of the power of the multitude to revolt, they argue, lies in its "constitutive power" — a formulation taken over from their, and Deleuze's, reading of Spinoza where they identify the power to create or constitute (*potentia, puissance, potenza, potencia*) being distinguished from the Power (*potestas, pouvoir, potere, poder*) to command.[57] The actual generation of information, communication and affect is, like more traditional forms of labor, the activity of the multitude. Thus, the bio-political Power of Empire is exercised against the bio-political constituent power of the multitude, but that bio-power — which can only be harnessed but not eliminated — not only breaks free from time to time, here or there, but has the potential to free itself from Power completely. Moreover, "freeing itself" means power destroying all of the mechanisms through which Power has constrained and harnessed it and achieving complete self-determination. And if Empire is world wide, so, necessarily is the multitude on which it is based.

How much of this analysis of multitude is really new? How much does it really differ from the earlier Marxist analyses of class struggle from which it drew? Let's examine some of the key concepts. First, what of (constituent) power vs. Power? While the two linked terms of this dichotomy may have originated in Spinoza, is it really that different from Marx's own dichotomy of living-labor and dead-labor? In Hardt and Negri's analysis it is power that is constitutive and Power that merely controls and manages. In Marx's analysis the living labor of the working class is the real life force within capitalist society and capital's ability to survive and expand depends entirely on its ability to control, subordinate and exploit that force. That subordination, in turn, had to be exercised, from the beginning, throughout society, starting with the expulsion of people from previous social relations (primitive accumulation) and then finding ways to continue to control the dislodged in factories, fields and communities. Although the array of skills and creative forces of living labor have evolved over time, including the communicative abilities essential to cooperation and collective work, these things have always been present. Applying Spinoza's term constituent power to living labor merely emphasizes its creative and productive character that was already highlighted by Marx. Hardt and Negri's location of the revolutionary potential of the multitude in its constituent power thus appears as a mere reformulation of Marx and many autonomist Marxists' grounding of the revolutionary potential of the working class in its own self-activity (only temporarily harnessed by capital as labor power).

Second, what of "immaterial labor," of kinds of work that can be characterized as productive of information, communication and affect? To begin with, the adjective "immaterial" here is clearly designed to differentiate this kind of mental work from manual labor that produces durable physical commodities; indeed the adjective is simply taken over from the idea of "immaterial goods" such as services and communication. However, there is really nothing immaterial about the various kinds of work that produces services, information and communication, so the adjective is confusing. Although the perspective is reversed (Hardt and Negri see immaterial labor as absolutely central to contemporary work) this distinction between material and immaterial labor reminds one of the Soviet distinction between real work that produced real physical commodities and other kinds of activity, not worth counting as value production, that produced services. The "immaterial" work of information production, processing and communication clearly involve considerable mental labor which is every bit as material as manual labor.

The same is true of "affective labor" — a term that highlights the emotional dimension of mental labor (as opposed to its rational component). Whether affective labor is understood as producing services (e.g., health care, entertainment) or social networks and community through direct, or indirect, human contact, it is every bit as material as any other kind of work. Nor is this kind of work new. To begin with Marx recognized, though analyzed far less than he might, the necessary work of producing and reproducing human life as labor power.[58] Hardt and Negri even admit that "affective labor" has been around for a long time, acknowledging how "Feminist analyses in particular have long recognized the social value of caring labor, kin work, nurturing, and maternal activities."[59] A recent, excellent example of such recognition and analysis by a Marxist feminist is the book *Caliban and the Witch* by Silvia Federici, who has shown how, from the very first, capital sought to control not only production but the labor of reproduction.[60] What they do claim is new is "the extent to which this affective immaterial labor is now directly productive of capital and the extent to which it has become generalized through wide sectors of the economy."[61] If "directly productive of capital" refers to the direct production of profitable commodities, then this corresponds to the growth of the service sector and certainly it has grown as a proportion of capitalist industry. If it means directly productive of capital understood as class relation then it has been true from the beginning. As to becoming generalized, clearly the work of reproduction has always been necessary in every sector even if its modalities have changed over time.

Third, what of the contention that capital has succeeded in so extending its bio-political control throughout all of life to the point where it is no longer possible to distinguish work from non-work or to measure either? Clearly the imposition of capitalism has always involved the imposition of the work of producing the commodity labor power as well as the work of producing other, profitable, commodities. The question is what was the basis for distinguishing these different kinds of work in the past and has that basis disappeared? Hardt and Negri argue that because communicative or affective activities in the sphere of reproduction have come to play a larger and larger role in the sphere of waged work, the distinction has been breaking down. However, in Marx's analysis any and all activities that produce labor power, i.e., the willingness and ability to work, have fed into what goes on in the sphere of production! What actually distinguished work in these two spheres was that one had to be paid for and one did not. Thus the acute capitalist preoccupation with measuring the time of work. Those who performed unwaged work had to be supported, of course, or the reproduction of labor power would falter and collapse, thus the family wage, charity and eventually welfare and unemployment insurance. Quite clearly this distinction between work that is directly paid for and work which is not still exists.

The classic "working day" discussed by Marx in Chapter 10 of Volume I of *Capital* is the waged working day, but it was by no means the entire working day. The rate of surplus value, or the rate of exploitation measured only the ratio of the work time that capital had to pay for over and beyond that required to reproduce labor power (in the aggregate, that required to produce goods and services consumed by workers) and ignored the work time in the sphere of reproduction. At the same time, neither was the entire time of waged workers actually spent working for capital, nor was the time spent by others, e.g., spouses or children, entirely filled with the work of reproducing labor power. Within the factory, Marx discussed the "pores" of non-work in the working day and the endless efforts of capitalists to eliminate them to avoid paying for non-work.[62] Although he never analyzed them, the same kind of "pores" of non-work have always existed in the home, school, community and so on.[63] The "pores" in his discussion were temporal ones — time momentarily freed from capitalist imposed work — but they must also be spatial ones as well; time spent not working has to take place somewhere, whether directly on the shop floor, at the water fountain, in a restroom or in specially appropriated spaces away from the workplace.

As the ability of workers to hammer down the time of waged work grew, the capitalist preoccupation with time outside that sphere grew apace, thus countless efforts to shape "leisure time" and "culture," i.e., to turn society into a social factory, to make sure that as much unwaged time as possible has been used to produce and reproduce labor power rather than being used for non- or anti-capitalist activities. Thus, too, multiplying efforts to measure how time is actually spent in various spheres of reproduction, e.g., homes, schools and communities.[64] Those efforts demonstrate a capitalist awareness of the importance of a continuing difference between work and non-work that disappears in the writings of Hardt and Negri.[65] This disappearance, although consistent with their emphasis on the thoroughness of capitalist bio-political control, is odd considering their contention that the multitude has the power to rupture that control through the exercise of its own bio-power. Does rupture actually occur? If so, then capitalist bio-political control is not omnipresent but full of "pores" blown open by struggle and what we need are detailed analyses of the methods of rupture and of the actual exercise of the multitude's bio-power to constitute new kinds of social relationships autonomously of capital. Many of the studies of actual struggles whose results have appeared in the journals mentioned above do provide useful information on such issues but, unfortunately, little of it makes its way into Hardt and Negri's books.

12. CONCLUSION

The array of concepts discussed above has included sketches of several different approaches: 1) to thinking about the interconnectedness of struggles in terms of networks, of the dynamics of struggles in terms of swarming, rhizomes or currents, and 2) to characterizing the subjectivities in motion in terms of civil society, social movements, the working class or multitude. What do I make of these? Let me answer briefly in terms of two criteria: first, their usefulness in understanding the spreading, interconnected struggles that are challenging capitalism around the world, and second, their usefulness in terms of helping us figure out how to do better.

The concepts of de-centered networks and rhizomes do provide attractive metaphors for the patterns of interconnectedness that can be identified in a wide variety of grassroots struggles. But while the people and organizations in networks or rhizomes may sometime converge or swarm to focus protest or disruption against some moment of capitalist domination, understanding how such networks or rhizomes have developed to the point where such behavior is possible leaves something to be desired. Similarly, it's one thing to point, as I have done here, to the fluidity of self-organization through the metaphor of currents of struggle, and quite another to identify exactly how such currents form, how they gather or lose strength, how they interact and how and why organizations sometimes crystallize into being or melt back again into the flow. The concept of civil society, in all of its permutations, is of no help here. The work of social movement theorists is helpful in identifying permissive or restrictive parameters of such growth but less so in revealing its internal dynamics. Those analyses of everyday life, of the weapons of the weak, and of certain aspects of popular culture mentioned above help us understand something of the social dynamics that gestate networks or rhizomes but generally have been unable to specify the actual processes of quickening that brings these to life. Again, some Marxist analyses of the general patterns of the capitalist organization of social life, like some of the restrictions on self organization identified by students of social movements, are helpful in understanding constraints on self-activity but not on understanding the dynamics of self-activity itself.

On the other hand, both the Marxist theory of political recomposition and the theory of multitude — which I see as a mutation or hybrid of class composition theory — provide concepts that focus our attention precisely on the character of self-activity involved in the genesis of networks, rhizomes or currents of struggle. Both theories, of the autonomous power of the working class (in production and reproduction) or the bio-power of the multitude throughout society, are formulated in ways intended to provide an understanding of how struggles shape and reshape themselves.

What is all too scarce, however, in the elaborations of all these theories are concrete analyses of *how* networks, rhizomes, currents or organizations have been formed, of their growth and of their effectiveness, strengths and weaknesses. In other words, far too much of the work done so far has focused on understanding the general character of these struggles and far too little on examining exactly how they have emerged, grown — and sometimes withered — in such ways as to permit drawing useful lessons from them about how to improve our abilities to bring about the changes we seek. The work that has been already done analyzing these struggles can, I think, be mined for material that can help us draw such lessons. But there is also a need to reorient our efforts away from crafting general theories and toward figuring out, on the one hand, what has worked, to what degree, why and how, and on the other hand, what has failed, to what degree, why and how.

For example, at the beginning of this essay I mentioned three main forms through which global connections among diverse struggles have been organized and surged upward into public view. One of those has been the physical convergences of thousands of protestors. Now, the massive convergence against the G8 that took place in Genoa in July 2001 arguably involved the greatest number of participants since such mobilizations first began. How exactly was that degree of mobilization achieved? Some of the approaches discussed above provide general suggestions about where to look to answer that question, but we need concrete answers. This is especially true because, as has been widely remarked, since Genoa there has been an apparent lessening in the participation and intensity of such mobilizations against capital's global policy makers. Protests have continued right up through the September 2006 meetings of the IMF and the World Bank in Singapore, but on a much smaller scale. What has happened? Some have attributed this to the events of September 11, 2001 and the subsequent actions of the Bush administration: the invasion and brutal occupation of two other countries and repression at home, e.g., blatant violations of civil rights, refusal to protect workers rights, attacks on environmental activists, and the not-so-secret CIA kidnappings and torture, all justified by the rhetoric of a "war on terrorism." But such an appeal to a change in the political climate does not explain how any of this has changed the behavior of the forms of self-organization and mobilization that gave rise to such protests prior to this new capitalist offensive.

It seems more likely that the judgments of participants and sympathetic observers, based directly on the experiences of the mobilizations, that what has been gained through these actions has been limited enough to warrant redirecting one's efforts into finding or elaborating alternative forms of struggle. Certainly the sharing of experience, multiplication of contacts and increased collaboration that has occurred at each of these events has been almost universally judged positive, even exhilarating. Eventually, a few of the positive demands made by protestors at these convergences have born fruit, e.g., debt reduction, but clearly most have not been achieved despite the enormous resources, personal and collective, expended in these efforts. But has there been such a consensus over the results (if not the factors taken into account) of such cost-benefit calculations as to explain the reduced participation in such efforts? One approach to testing this hypothesis involves examining the ex-post discussions and evaluations of the experience at Genoa (and other such convergences). The few evaluations that I have read suggest that this is indeed the case, but real verification would require more extensive investigation than I have undertaken.

Two examples, on a smaller scale, of how and why shifts in the direction of struggle have taken place can be found in the reorientations of Zapatista struggle that occurred in the wake of their extremely well organized and extremely public, 3000-mile-long March for Indigenous Dignity in 2001. The March took the form of a sizable caravan to Mexico City to demand from the Mexican congress the enactment into law of the San Andrés Accords on indigenous autonomy agreed to in 1996 but never implemented. This was understood by those in the Zapatista communities as a reformist demand but desired as a step that would facilitate further struggle. The caravan was a huge undertaking involving not only the movement of Zapatistas and the many supporters who accompanied them but also the organization of dozens of stops and encounters with thousands of people involved in local struggles along the way, and in Mexico City when they arrived — organizing undertaken not by the Zapatistas alone but by dozens of local groups. Despite these day-after-day displays of widespread public support the Mexican congress refused to pass a law or constitutional amendment that would implement the Accords. The Zapatistas returned to their communities in Chiapas.

The first shift in Zapatista struggle that occurred in the wake of these events was a turning inward and abandonment of any dialogue or negotiation with any wing of the Mexican government. From their point of view the March had been both a stunning success and an abject failure. The success lay in the mobilization of thousands of other people that demonstrated not only their continuing power of convocation and support for their demands but also extremely widespread opposition to Mexican government policies. The failure lay in the effort to leverage that support and opposition into sufficient pressure on Mexican politicians to achieve the long-sought legalization of indigenous autonomy. The professional politicians in all three major parties, including the so-called leftist PRD, ignored the voices rising from the streets of Mexico and refused to recognize indigenous autonomy. In the discussions that ensued within the communities agreement was reached to abandon the struggle for the legalization of their autonomy and to proceed 1) with concrete projects that would strengthen their actual autonomy, i.e., their ability to organize themselves autonomously from Mexican capital's plans for their assimilation and cultural genocide and 2) to protect themselves from future attacks.[66] Among the more striking of those projects was the organization of regional governments they call *caracoles* or "Good Government Councils" to coordinate activities among their various autonomous communities.[67]

The second shift in Zapatista struggle came after four years of the above kind of internal work. In the summer of 2005, they issued a "Red Alert," closed their communities to the outside world and engaged in intensive internal debate over strategies of struggle. The result was the issuance in June of the "Sixth Declaration of the Lacandona" that recounted what the Zapatistas had been doing, analyzed and condemned capitalism in general and neoliberal Mexican capitalism in particular and announced plans for a new outward-oriented offensive.[68] The reasons given for this new offensive are clear: the war with capital is global, what can be accomplished in isolation is too limited (even for struggles as well organized internally as that of the Zapatistas), so people must organize themselves across space and differences to win the war. As a step toward such organization, they proposed: a series of dialogues with others in struggle throughout Mexico. They also called for a series of meetings in August and September to discuss what others in struggle thought about this proposal for dialogue and if they approved, contributions as to how it could be achieved. Their idea for organizing such dialogues directly involved what they dubbed (during a year of presidential elections) an "Other Campaign" in which a handful of Zapatistas, led by their spokesperson Subcomandante Marcos would travel to community after community, wherever the people involved in local struggles would invite them to come, to listen, to learn from and to share experience. The meetings were held, organization began and the Other Campaign was launched in January 2006.

While an analysis of Zapatista communiqués clarify the reasons for these two shifts in strategies of struggle, it is also true that because the Zapatista communities have been besieged by police, military and paramilitary harassment and violence ever since 1994 the internal discussions that led to these shifts were closed to outsiders. As a result, those of us on the outside know more about the decisions made than we do about the processes through which they came to be made. The above brief account, moreover, provides few details on exactly how these strategies were, and are being, implemented. (A more detailed account can be found in Patrick Cuninghame's contribution to this volume.[69]) Nevertheless, it seems to me that the kinds of evaluations of experience, discussion of lessons to be learned and possible new strategies based on those lessons that can be found in the Zapatista communiqués provide an approximation of the kind of concrete analysis that we need to complement the more theoretical conceptualizations sketched in most of this essay. At the same time, those theoretical approaches lead us to ask questions about these struggles whose answers are not found in those communiqués and therefore prompt us to further investigation.

In short, and to truly conclude, whatever inspiration and insights we may draw from general theories of the growing interconnectedness and global character of our challenges to world-wide capitalist domination, what we really need in order to advance our struggles is more concrete investigation of how we have achieved what we have, what limits we have encountered, what others have achieved and how, what limits they have encountered and what we can learn from each other through a multiplicity of dialogues about where we are and what to do next.

REFERENCES

1 See the collection of Alquati's studies: *Sulla FIAT*, Milano: Feltrineli, 1975. Although this work has never been translated, a synopsis of its ideas on networks has circulated widely and influenced many. See: http://libcom.org/library/network-of-struggles-italy-romano-alquati.

2 A useful overview of the development of network theory, from mathematics to sociology, can be found in the introduction to J. Clyde Mitchell, *Social Networks in Urban Situations: Analyses of Personal Relationships in Central African Towns*, Manchester: Manchester University Press, 1969, pp. 1–50. An adaptation of this approach to the understanding of social struggles was made in Italy by the Marxist sociologist Romano Alquati in his studies of workers conflicts with the Italian auto giant FIAT. Alquati meshed the Marxist analysis of class composition with the sociological one of networks, at factory, national and international levels. See: Romano Alquati, *Sulla FIAT*, Milano: Feltrineli, 1975.

3 An influential moment of this literature is Walter W. Powell, "Neither Market nor Hierarchy: Network Forms of Organization," *Research in Organizational Behavior*, 12 (1990), pp. 295–336.

4 Of particular relevance here are: Manuel Castells, *The Power of Identity*, Vol. II of his *The Informational Society: Economy, Society and Culture*, London: Blackwell, 1997, Margaret E. Keck and Kathryn Sikkink, *Activists Beyond Borders: Advocacy Networks in International Politics*, Ithaca: Cornell University Press, 1998, Martha McCaughey and Michael D. Ayers, *Cyberactivism: Online Activism in Theory and Practice*, New York: Routledge, 2003, Wim van de Donk, Brian D. Loader, Paul G. Nihon and Dierter Rucht, *Cyberprotest: New Media, citizens and social movements*, New York: Routledge, 2004, Sidney Tarrow, *The New Transnational Activism*, New York: Cambridge University Press, 2005 and Clifford Bob, *The Marketing of Rebellion: Insurgents, Media and International Activism*, New York: Cambridge University Press, 2005. See also the earlier work by Cathryn Thorup, "The Politics of Free Trade and the Dynamics of Cross-border Coalitions in U.S.–Mexican Relations," *Columbia Journal Of World Business*, Vol. XXVI, No. 11, Summer 1991, pp. 12–26

and (with David Ronfeldt) *North American in the Era of Citizen Networks: State, Society, and Security*, RAND, 1993. Not surprisingly Thorup went on to work for both the United States Agency for International Development and the National Security Council on building relationships with NGOs.

5 Charles Swett, "Strategic Assessment: The Internet," July 17, 1995.

6 The RAND researchers are by no means alone among policy makers in being concerned about the growing power of such networks. Reviewing the Keck and Sikkink book on transnational advocacy networks for the elite journal *Foreign Affairs*, Francis Fukuyama warned: "Like Stalin, one might ask 'how many divisions do transnational networks have?' The answer is that they have information, greatly abetted by modem communications technology, and thus the ability to set agendas for nation-states and transnational organizations like the World Bank, Shell Oil Corporation, or Nestle." Francis Fukuyama, review of *Activists Beyond Borders: Advocacy Networks in International Politics*, in *Foreign Affairs*, Vol. 77, no. 4, July–August 1998, p. 123.

7 Such separation was analyzed by Marx as an essential moment in the creation of a "working" class dependent on the labor market for survival under the rubric of "primitive accumulation" — a variation of Adam Smith's term for the same process: "original accumulation."

8 The recurrent capitalist efforts to impose and maintain such separation, sometimes blocked and sometimes reversed by resistance, has resulted in a debate over the transitory or permanent character of primitive accumulation. For more on this see the papers in this volume by de Angelis, Zarembka and Bonefeld.

9 The prime example of recent years was the gutting of Article 27 of the Mexican Constitution that protected indigenous and peasant *ejidal* (communal) lands, and hence communities, from privatization. This was intended to set the stage for the final enclosure of the Mexican countryside and was executed by the Salinas government as a gift to multinational corporations to help get the North American Free Trade Agreement enacted.

10 Harry Cleaver, "The Chiapas Uprising and the Future of Class Struggle in the New World Order," *Riff-Raff: attraverso la produzione sociale* (Padova, Italy), marzo 1994, pp. 133–45. English versions have been published in *Common Sense* (Edinburgh) No. 15, April 1994, pp. 5–17, *Canadian Dimension* (Winnipeg), Vol. 28, No. 3, May–June 1994, pp. 36–39 and *Studies in Political Economy* (Toronto), No. 44, Summer 1994, pp. 141–57. This early essay has been followed by a series of others most of which are available at: www.eco.utexas.edu/faculty/Cleaver/ hmchtmlpapers.html.

11 John Arquilla and David Ronfeldt, *The Advent of Netwar*, Santa Monica: RAND, 1996, p. 73. David Ronfeldt and Armando Martínez, "A Comment on the Zapatista 'Netwar'" in John Arquilla and David Ronfeldt, *In Athena's Camp: Preparing for Conflict in the Information Age*, Santa Monica: RAND, 1997, p. 371. David Ronfeldt, John Arquilla, Graham Fuller and Melissa

Fuller, *The Zapatista "Social Netwar" in Mexico*, RAND Publication MR–994–A, 1998, (henceforth referred to as Ronfeldt et al.).

[12] Keck and Sikkink, op. cit., p. 115.

[13] See, for example, Maria Garrido and Alexander Halavais, "Mapping Networks of Support for the Zapatista Movement: Applying Social-Networks Analysis to Study Contemporary Social Movements," in Martha McCaughey and Michael D. Ayers, *Cyberactivism: Online Activism in Theory and Practice*, New York: Routledge, 2003 or the broader and more detailed study by Thomas Olesen, *International Zapatismo: The Construction of Solidarity in the Age of Globalization*, New York: Zed, 2005.

[14] See John Arquilla and David Ronfeldt, *Swarming & the Future of Conflict*, Rand: National Defense Research Institute, 2000, p. vii.

[15] See: Ricardo Dominguez, Stefan Wray, Brett Beestal and Osea, "SWARM: An ECD Project for ARS Electronica Festival '98" at: www.thing.net/~rdom/ecd/swarm.html.

[16] The September 1998 counterattack by the Pentagon's Defense Information Systems Agency has demonstrated precisely the kind of dangers feared. See report by computer security writer Winn Schwartau, "Cyber-civil disobedience," *Network World*, January 11, 1999. For more on the debate see the archives of the Chiapas95 listserv beginning in May 1998 at: www.eco.utexas.edu/faculty/Cleaver/chiapas95.html.

[17] See my intervention into the debate on the net in the Chiapas95 archives: "H. Cleaver, A Contribution to the Discussion of ECD," May 1 (1998).

[18] Such methods have been used from time to time, especially in Italy where "netstrikes" have been called in support of local struggles and international ones, e.g. against Turkish government and business sites in support of Kurdish rebels in Turkey whose leader had recently been seized.

[19] See: "Swarming and the Future of Protesting," at: www.why-war.com/features/read.php?id=4#part4.

[20] For a brief history of flash mob protests of various kinds see: http://en.wikipedia.org/wiki/Flash_mob.

[21] "Rhizome" in Gilles Deleuze and Félix Guattari, *A Thousand Plateaus: Capitalism & Schizophrenia*, Minneapolis: University of Minnesota Press, 1987, pp. 3–25.

[22] As Deleuze and Guattari's analysis makes clear, capital can also intentionally deterritorialize, i.e., uproot people from one location to fix them in another as a method of achieving and managing exploitation or displace its fixed capital with the aim of exploiting people in other locations. The slave trade, the recurrent use of immigrant labor, runaway shops and outsourcing are obvious examples on an international scale.

[23] See, for example, Rolando Perez, *On An (archy) and Schizoanalysis*, Brooklyn: Autonomedia, 1990 or the webpage of the Rhizome Collective of East Austin, Texas at: www.rhizomecollective.org/. One example of the direct

application of this kind of thinking to a particular series of struggles is: Andre Gattolin and Thierry Lefebvre, "Stopub: analyse proviso ire d'un rhizome activiste," *Multitudes 16*, Printemps 2004.

24 A good example of such clashes are two articles in the journal *Multitudes* by Richard Barbrook who attacks the work of Deleuze and Guattari and Bifo who defends it: Richard Barbrook, "Le cyber-commnisme, ou le dépassement du capitalisme dans le cyberspace" and Bifo (Franco Berardi), "Techonomadisme et pensée rhizomatique," *Multitudes 5*, Mai 2001.

25 We can also add, with Werner Bonefeld, that everything is uncertain. See: Werner Bonefeld, "Notes on Movement and Uncertainty," in D. Harvie, K. Milburn, B. Trott and D. Watts (eds) *Shut Them Down! The G8, Gleneagles 2005 and the Movement of Movements*, New York: Autonomedia, 2005, pp. 265–72.

26 See the analysis by the Department of Mathematics at the University of Bergen, Norway: www.math.uio.no/~karstent/waves/index_en.html or, for a dramatic account, the program on the subject produced by the History Channel.

27 The physical configuration of seafloor topology obviously affects currents, sometimes channeling them, sometimes deflecting them. Earth's gravity affects all water but pulls denser water toward the bottom of the ocean. Lunar gravity causes tides. The sun's rays warm surface waters — more in some areas than others — and indirectly, and to an ever lesser degree the deeper waters beneath them. Wind pushes surface water through friction. Wind blown surface water in turn affects water below it, also through friction; its differential impact according to depth produces the Eckman Transport Spiral that helps form gyres and mounds of water in the ocean. It also contributes to upwellings of deep water where the wind blows offshore and downwellings where it blows onshore. The coriolus effect is a deflection of wind patterns caused by the earth's rotation.

28 In the case of the oceans the surface currents are only 10% of the total ocean water mass. As a result wind only affects, directly and indirectly, some 20% of the mass.

29 This is akin to Karl Marx's "old mole" — a proletariat whose subterranean struggles periodically erupt onto the surface of society, bringing revolution — or Sergio Bologna's "tribe of moles" in Italy of the 1970s, or his more recent metaphor of invisible "termites" eating away wooden beams from within, in ways that are free of mediation and can bring about the ultimate collapse of a whole structure. See Sergio Bologna, "The Tribe of Moles: Class Composition and the Party System in Italy," in *Working Class Autonomy and the Crisis*. London: Red Notes and CSE, 1979, pp. 67–91 and in *Semiotext(e)* Vol. III, No. 3, 1980, pp. 36–61. Originally in *Primo Maggio*, No. 8, Spring 1977, pp. 3–18 and "An Interview with Toni Negri" by Giuseppe Cocco and Maurizio Lazzarato, translated from the French jour-

nal *Multitudes*, No. 7, December 2001) by Thomas Seay and Hydrarchist, at: www.nettime.org/Lists-Archives/ nettime-bold-0202/msg00006.html. Hardt and Negri, (more or less following Deleuze, who more or less follows Foucault, on the crisis of the "society of discipline" leading to the "society of control") have argued that the "old mole" is being replaced by a "snake" because all of today's struggles take place on the surface of "superficial, imperial landscapes." While it is true enough that all the "environments of enclosure," and hence of discipline, have been thrown into crisis by struggle, it is not at all obvious that all struggles are clearly visible "on the surface." Unfortunately, we rarely see or understand the underlying turbulence that gives rise to those clearly visible struggles that we can not help but recognize. See: Michael Hardt and Antonio Negri, "Marx's Mole is Dead!" Eurozine, February 13, 2002 and Gilles Deleuze, "Postscript on the Society of Control" (1990) both available at: www.eurozine.com/articles /2002 –02–13–hardtnegri-en. html and www.nadir.org/nadir/archiv/netzkritik/societyofcontrol.html.

30 At this writing the popular occupation of Oaxaca City has now shut down the governments of both city and state and substituted its own self-organization for longer than the Paris Commune of 1871.

31 Well-known among such studies are those of Michel Foucault, Pierre Bourdieu, Michel de Certeau, James Scott, Romano Alquati, and John Fiske. Included here must also be the work of those historians who have unearthed the hitherto buried histories of everyday struggle out of which impossible-to-ignore insurrectionary uprisings have emerged, e.g., Christopher Hill, Edward Thompson, Peter Linebaugh, Marcus Rediker, Silvia Federici and contributors to "subaltern studies."

32 This way of thinking has involved a clear-cut dichotomy between capital and the working class such that the dynamics of the former, including its crises, could be theorized independently of the activity of the latter. Fortunately, in recent years this approach has been progressively superseded by an understanding of capital as class relationship that allows us to see how the struggles of workers have shaped, and sometimes ruptured "capitalist" development bringing crisis, threatening its very existence and elaborating possible alternatives.

33 The failure of Soviet-style regimes to use social scientists in this way — as opposed to using them for mere ideological justification of policies — was one reason for the ignorant and ultimately self-defeating brutality of the state's response to all forms of struggle. The brutality drove the currents of resistance deep below the surface where, out of sight and out of the state's mind, they circulated, interacted and gradually gained the strength to surface and overthrow the regime.

34 The classic texts that most clearly articulated this analysis were: Mario Tronti, *Operai e capitale*, Torino: Einaudi, 1966 and Antonio Negri, "John

M. Keynes and the Capitalist Theory of the State in 1929," in Toni Negri, *Revolution Retrieved: Selected Writings on Marx, Keynes, Capitalist Crisis and New Social Subjects, 1967–83*, London: Red Notes, 1987. Originally published in *Contropiano*, 1968. A much elaborated analysis along these lines is Massimo de Angelis, *Keynesianism, Social Conflict and Political Economy*, London: Palgrave Macmillan, 2000.

35 Quesnay's "circulation" was essentially a biological metaphor adapted from Harvey's analysis of the flow of blood in the human body.

36 Such analysis of the "circulation of struggles" was a factor in my coming to re-think the Zapatista and counter-globalization "networks" in terms of currents.

37 In one line of contemporary Marxist thought this imagination and capability is conceptualized in terms of "a general intellect" (a concept plucked from "the fragment on machines" in Marx's 1857 *Grundrisse*) and is manifest not only in the increasingly central role of mental labor, but in its tendencies to autonomy. See, for example, Paolo Virno, "Notes on the General Intellect," in S. Makdisi, C. Casarino and R. E. Karl, *Marxism Beyond Marxism*, New York: Routledge, 1996 and Paolo Virno, *A Grammar of the Multitude: For an analysis of contemporary forms of life*, New York: Semiotext(e), 2004.

38 There are any number of books outlining and analyzing the history of the concept of "civil society" and that history is much to long to recapulate in his essay. See, for example, the following: John Ehrenberg, *Civil Society: The Critical History of an Idea*, New York: New York University Press, 1999.

39 See, for example, Howard Frederick, "Computer Networks and the "Emergence of Global Civil Society," in Linda M. Harasim (ed) *Global Networks: Computers and International Communication*, Cambridge: MIT Press, 1993.

40 For a different critique of the common evocation of "civil society" as the prime agent of anti-globalization movements see Werner Bonefeld, "Anti-globalization and the Critique of Socialism," *Critique*, Vol. 34, No. 1, April 2006, pp. 39–59.

41 See Alberto Melluci, "The Process of Collective Identity," in Hank Johnston and Bert Klandermans, (eds), *Social Movements and Culture*, Minneapolis: University of Minnesota Press, 1995. See also: Alberto Melluci, *Challenging Codes: Collective Action in the Information Age*, Cambridge (UK): Cambridge University Press, 1996.

42 Ibid., and Marcy Darnovsky, et. al., (eds) *Cultural Politics and Social Movements* Chicago:Temple University Press, 1995. Similar titles are: Leo d'Anjou, *Social Movements and Cultural Change: The First Abolition Campaign Revisited*, New York: Aldine, 1996, Rick Fantasia, *Cultures of Solidarity: Consciousness, Action and Contemporary Workers*, Berkeley: University of California Press, 1989.

43 For a sketch of the variety of approaches see: Doug McAdam, et. al, (eds) *Comparative Perspectives on Social Movements: Political Opportunities, Mobilizing Structures and Cultural Framings*, Cambridge (UK): Cambridge University Press, 1996.

44 For example: Tom Mertes (ed), *A Movement of Movements: Is Another World Possible?* New York: Verso, 2004, Susan George, *Another World is Possible IF...*, New York: Verso, 2004 and D. Harvie, K. Milburn, B. Trott and D. Watts (eds) *Shut Them Down!*, op. cit.

45 For one very brief sketch of the international development of such non-orthodox Marxisms see the introduction to Harry Cleaver, *Reading Capital Politically*, London: AK Press and AntiTheses, 2000, at: www.eco.utexas.edu/facstaff/Cleaver/357krcp.html. But also see the much more detailed account of the emergence of such recognition among Italian Marxists in Steve Wright, *Storming Heaven: Class Composition and Struggle in Italian Autonomist Marxism*, London: Pluto Press, 2002 as well as such detailed historical explorations of the long history of the role of the unwaged in working-class struggle in studies such as: Peter Linebaugh, *The London Hanged*, London: Verso Press, 2003, Peter Linebaugh and Marcus Rediker, *The Many-headed Hydra: Sailors, Slaves, Commoners, and the Hidden History of the Revolutionary Atlantic*, Boston: Beacon Press, 2000, and Silvia Federici, *Caliban and the Witch: Women, the Body and Primitive Accumulation*, New York: Autonomedia, 2004. See also: Ana C. Dinerstein and M. Neary (eds) *The Labour Debate: An Investigation into the Theory and Reality of Capitalist Work*, Aldershot: Ashgate.

46 See R. Alquati, A. Negri and A. Sormano, *Università di ceto medio e proletariano intellectuale*, Torino: Stompatori, 1976, and A. Negri, *Dall'Operaio Massa All'Operaio Sociale* (1979), and his "Archeologia e proggetto: L'operaio massa e l'operaio sociale," in *Macchina Tempo* (1982). This last is also available in English as "Archeology and Project: The Mass Worker and the Social Worker, " in *Revolution Retrieved: Selected Writings of Toni Negri*, London: Red Notes, 1988.

47 Among those who went into the factories to discover what was the actual state of the class composition of their times were the members of the Johnson-Forest Tendency in the United States, those of *Socialisme ou Barbarie* in France and associates of *Quaderni Rossi* in Italy (especially Romano Alquati). These interlinked efforts are described briefly in the introduction to Harry Cleaver, *Reading Capital Politically*, op. cit. For a more detailed discussion of Alquati and his work, see Chapter 2 of Steve Wright, *Storming Heaven*, op. cit.

48 On self-valorization see: Antonio Negri, *Marx Beyond Marx: Lessons on the Grundrisse*, New York: Autonomedia, 1992 and Harry Cleaver, "The Inversion of Class Perspective in Marxist Theory, from Valorization to Self-Valorization," in W. Bonefeld, R. Gunn and K. Psychopedis (eds) *Open Marxism*, Vol. II, London: Pluto Press, 1992.

49 A now classic example of this kind of analysis is laid out in the two issues of the American journal *Zerowork* (1975 and 1977).

50 Subcomandante Marcos, "The Fourth World War," November 20, 1999. Available at: www.inmotionmagazine.com/auto/fourth.html.

51 Michael Hardt and Antonio Negri, *Empire*, Cambridge: Harvard University

Press, 2000 and Michael Hardt and Antonio Negri, *Multitude: War and Democracy in the Age of Empire*, New York: Penguin Press, 2004.

52 Kautsky's classic essay is online at: www.marxists.org/archive/kautsky/1914/09/ultra-imp.htm. One collection of articles critical of the "empire" thesis is Gopal Balakrishnan, *Debating Empire*, New York: Verso Press, 2003.

53 See Michel Foucault, *Surveiller et punir: Naissance de la prison (1975)* or *Discipline and Punish: the birth of the prison*, New York: Pantheon Books, 1977; *Histoire de la sexualité, 1: la volonté de savoir* (1976) or *The History of Sexuality*, Volume I, New York: Pantheon, 1978. See also Gilles Deleuze, *Foucault*, Paris: Minuit, 1986.

54 *Empire*, op. cit., p. 24.

55 Negri's attack on the "law of value" pre-dates *Empire* and goes back at least to his 1971 article on the "Crisis of the Planner State: Communism and Revolutionary Organization," available in English in: Toni Negri, *Revolution Retrieved: Selected Writings on Marx, Keynes, Capitalist Crisis & New Social Subjects, 1967–1983*, London: Red Notes, 1989.

56 Maurizio Lazzarato "Immaterial Labour," (1996) in Paolo Virno and Michael Hardt, (eds), *Radical Thought in Italy*, Minneapolis: University of Minnesota Press, pp. 132–46. Available at: www.generation-online.org/c/fcimmateriallabour3.htm. See also: Maurizio Lazzarato and Toni Negri, "Travail immatériel et subjectivité," *Futur Antérieur* 6 : Été 1991.

57 See Antonio Negri, *The Savage Anomaly: The Power of Spinoza's Metaphysics and Politics*, Minneapolis: University of Minnesota Press, 1991, Antonio Negri, *Il potere costituente*, Milan: Sugerco, 1992, Antonio Negri, *Insurgencies: Constituent Power and the Modern State*, Minneapolis: University of Minnesota Press, 1994 and Antonio Negri, "Constituent Republic," in W. Bonefeld, *Revolutionary Writing: Common Sense Essays in Post-Political Politics*, New York: Autonomedia, 2003.

58 See, for example, his analysis of simple reproduction in Chapter 23 of Volume 1 of *Capital*.

59 A seminal text in the history of such recognition is Mariarosa Dalla Costa, *Women and the Subversion of the Community*, December 29, 1971, now available online at www.eco.utexas.edu/facstaff/Cleaver/357kDallaCostaSubversion.html, and www.eco.utexas.edu/facstaff/Cleaver/ 357kDallaCostaSubversionTable.pdf.

60 Silvia Federici, *Caliban and the Witch*, op.cit.

61 Michael Hardt, "Affective Labor" (n.d.) at: http://makeworlds.org/node/60.

62 This discussion is in the discussion of the intensification of labor in Chapter 15 of Volume I of *Capital*. As has been often pointed out, it was partly against such pores — as well as in order to intensify work itself — that Frederick Taylor and Henry Ford reorganized work with stop watch and assembly line.

63 Marx also failed to examine the flip side of capitalist "nibbling and cribbling"

to lengthen the working day pointed out in Chapter 10 of Volume I of *Capital*. Pitted against such efforts, workers have also found innumerable ways to shorten their work time, not only at the beginning and at the end (showing up late, leaving early, taking long lunches) of a working day but in the middle, by carving out precisely those "pores" that have so preoccupied their bosses. They have done the same within the working week through fake sick leave and other forms of absenteeism.

64 See the recent paper by Massimo de Angelis and David Harvie, "Cognitive Capitalism and the Rat Race: How Capital measures ideas and affects in UK Higher Education," (2006) available at: www.geocities. com/immaterial-labour/angelisharviepaper2006.html. For another discussion of the "measuring" of various kinds of unwaged schoolwork see: Harry Cleaver, "Schoolwork and the Struggle Against It," (2006) available at: www.eco.utexas.edu/facstaff/Cleaver/OnSchoolwork 200606.pdf.

65 For a different, but useful, critique of Hardt and Negri's thesis of immeasurability see: George Caffentzis, "Immeasurable Value? An Essay on Marx's Legacy," *The Commoner*, No. 10, Spring–Summer 2005, available at: www. commoner.org.uk/10caffentzis.pdf.

66 This protection took the form, primarily, of clearly separating the EZLN from community self-governance. The story of their worries about possible attack and the preparatory steps they took has now been told in Subcomandante Marcos, "The Zapatistas and the Other: The Pedestrians of History," (2006).

67 A fairly detailed description of these caracoles, why they were formed, how they operate, their successes and failures can be found in two series of communiqués issued by the Zapatistas in 2003 and 2004 and available at: www.eco.utexas.edu/facstaff/Cleaver/aguascalientes.html and www.eco. utexas.edu/facstaff/Cleaver/leerunvideo.html.

68 The Sixth Declaration is available at: www.eco.utexas.edu/facstaff/Cleaver/SixthDeclaration.html.

69 Patrick Cuninghame, "Reinventing an/other anti-capitalism in Mexico: The Sixth Declaration of the EZLN and the "Other Campaign." Thanks to both the Zapatistas and to journalists, the progress of the Other Campaign has been closely followed and reported. See the series of reports and articles available at: www.eco.utexas.edu/facstaff/ Cleaver/TheOtherCampaign.html and in the archives of Chiapas 95 at: www.eco.utexas.edu/~archive/chiapas95/.

10
The Crisis of the Classical Canon of the Class Form and Social Movements in Latin America

Sergio Tischler[1]

> *The future is not a blank page,*
> *it is an errata*
>
> Mario Benedetti

I

One of the most important issues regarding social movements in Latin America — especially some of the indigenous movements — is related to the question of class and class struggle in current capitalism. This is a thorny theoretical issue that is usually left aside as a consequence, amongst others, of the dramatic changes associated with the end of the Cold War and the fall of the so-called Really Existing Socialism of the former Soviet Union and its satellite states. There is no need here to offer a detailed analysis of the ideological impact of these events. We experience it in everyday life, from the announcement of the "end of history," to the identification of utopia of human emancipation with Stalinism, and to the much-praised spread of liberal democracy across the world. We are told that we are finally living in the best of all worlds, a world beyond class and "ideological" challenges.

Talk about revolution has fallen on hard times. The concept is deemed to have lost its meaning; and revolutionary struggles are said to have vanished with the disappearance of classes and class struggle. Social conflicts still occur but these are understood not in terms of class. This conception has vanished. The ruling discourse says: we know this world is not full of roses, but it is the best there is and the best there can be. Nobody has as yet made the absurd claim that our pleasant world is a world devoid of social conflicts. However, these are no longer deemed to be irreconcilable class conflicts. Instead, conflicts are said to be reconcilable within the framework of the new liberal global order. That is to say, existing conflicts are no longer deemed to be of an antagonistic sort — they no longer express the *fissures* or *contradictions* of a perverted world. Instead, conflicts are deemed to be "functional" and thus themselves a force for the good, the good of a dynamic, capitalistically organised society (on the notion of functional conflict, see Agnoli, 2003). The functionalist understanding of conflict derives from neo-liberal conceptions of the market as a competitive system. Competition makes strong people stronger, free people freer, and allows the best to succeed. Success is a matter of individual will. Egoism is endorsed as intrinsically good. What is my destiny? What do I want? But, as if that were not enough, liberal democracy celebrates the egoistic market individual by emphasising its tolerance, one might even say "progressive" tolerance, vis-à-vis well-defined group interests, the interests of the so-called social minorities. The atomistic market individual may coexist with movements and different actors, from gays, lesbians, urban tribes, graffiti artists, etc. This only proves the plurality of social definitions that befits the "open" society of a free world. Its political correctness is a mere posture, a mere pretence. It pretends that bad human conditions do not need to be changed. All that needs to be done is to interpret them more favourably. No wonder the new-found discourse of liberal tolerance finds the talk about class and class struggle so distasteful. It does not want to be reminded of the class struggle. Class struggle disturbs its posture of liberal tolerance and respectfulness, and reveals it as a mere mask that hides the true purpose of its stance. In the face of misery, it proclaims the political correctness of conditions.

It is also said that our global liberal society presents not only the victory of freedom against totalitarianism but, also, the overcoming of history. History smacks of struggle and evil. With the end of history, the *locus* of conflict and evil has disappeared, too. Nevertheless, the end of history is precarious and has therefore to be defended against the enemies of freedom. It is said that the language of "evil" and "totalitarianism" is seductive, and that the danger of "evil" and totalitarianism is therefore always latent. There is thus need not only for action but also for pre-emptive action, just in case! We know about the struggles of the dispossessed and their demands for the necessities of life, to say nothing about their demand for the equality of human needs. Here the discourse of political correctness really shows its true colours. We hear of individual empowerment, and individual self-responsibility, and individual achievement. Each person is encouraged to compete against the other. Everyone still inclined to disagree with conditions is gently reminded to wrap his or her everyday scream in cellophane and place it at once where it belongs — in the rubbish bin of history. We are told that the very idea that our scream is part of a collective scream capable of transforming reality, is simply wrong. There is no collective scream. That there ever was such a collective scream is sheer ideology, a perverse invention like class struggle.

There is some truth in all this. A new capitalist hegemony has arisen, and this new hegemony has forced into crisis the traditional forms of social and political organisation of the working class, forms that resulted from great and long struggles. The so-called globalisation of capital cannot just be understood as a mere phenomenon of market expansion or of the creation of global systems of communications (which are also a part of the market). Globalisation is a form of class struggle, of the breaking of the social limits that the working class had imposed on capital, be it in the form of the Welfare State in the central capitalist countries, or in the form of *development-ism* and populism in Latin America. Hence a first idea: the so-called end of history does not amount to the end of class and class struggle, but to a *constitutive movement of a new form of class struggle and a different hegemonic project.*

In other words, the discourse on the end of history has a social and political reference point: the destruction of the classical working class forms of organization on the part of capital and its ongoing attempt at decomposing labour on a global level. To put it in other words, this discourse is part of a process of re-configuring social reality, at the centre of which is the attack on the classical organisational forms of collective resistance, such as the trade unions, trade union confederations and so on.

One of the achievements — though contradictory, as is well known — of this hegemonic project *(considered to be an advance or rooting of liberal democracy)* has been the generation of a "new civil society," in which citizenship appears to be liberated from the burden of class and history. In the case of the Welfare State, this liberation of civil society entailed the destruction of collective forms of social protection that had been fundamental for the stabilisation of capital in the face of working class struggles. Destruction entailed a process of re-commodification and market expansion on a global scale. It is obvious that the fall of the Soviet Union was a fundamental factor in this process. It liberated, as it were, the capitalist world from the need to incorporate labour by means of material concessions. "Liberation" also entailed a fundamental shift from the recognition of class antagonism towards a politics of political correctness in the discourse of modernity. In short, it proclaims that class struggle leads to totalitarianism, and that the struggle for human emancipation produces perverse effects.

II

Nevertheless, for us the central question is this: can we still think in terms of classes and class struggle, can the social movements still be interpreted in these terms? The answer is complicated. One can say: Yes, it is possible, but...and the "but" is enormous. Obviously, in this short text we can only formulate some starting points. One of them can be expressed in the following terms: the crisis of the concepts of class struggle and revolution is itself not just linked to but is in fact a moment of the class struggle. That is to say, it indicates a crisis of the forms of struggle and of their ruling theoretical principles. In this context we would have to approach the "crisis-ridden" concepts of class and class struggles, its changing forms and movements of decomposition and recomposition, at both a historical level — the forms of class struggle pertaining in a specific historical period — and a conceptual level — the dominant theoretical principles that formulate and articulate the pertaining forms of class struggle.

It is not easy to balance these two dimensions, and conceptualise class composition. Simply put, the conceptualisation of class composition is not a matter of deploying a series of abstract formulations that facilitate the establishment of the relation between a social group, for example, defined by its relationship to the means of production, and the type of political action it generates (a kind of Marxist sociology or sociological Marxism). Such an approach succumbs to a sociological study of society and its positivist definitions of "social groups." The critical dimension of Marx's critique of class society is lost, and instead, the theory of class would rest on definitions of class. These are applied to class as if the definition is itself beyond theorisation. The analytical framework is treated as if it really is autonomous from the very society to which it is "applied" (see Gunn, 1992). The implied assumption is thus that theoretical tools of understanding society can be applied as if they have the force of nature. However, analytical tools are neither universally valid nor do they have a trans-historical validity. Concepts are bound up with the society that requires them. It is therefore important that we submit the concepts class and class struggle to criticism, and that we once more reflect on what is to be understand by class struggle.

One way to begin is by arguing that the concept of class struggle has always been a polemical one. We can observe a difference, for example, between its gnoseological and its critical usages. It is not a novelty to declare that there exists a great difference between the concept of class struggle of a Karl Kautsky and a Rosa Luxemburg. The same occurs with Lenin and Anton Pannekoek, Lukács and Benjamin, to name a few, starting from Marx himself. Nevertheless, the revolutionary movement produced a kind of conceptual consolidation of the concept. That is to say, it produced an identitarian conception of history and a canon-like understanding of class struggle. That is to say, the institutionalisation of Marxism entailed the definition of a canon of revolution. The canon came about as part of the defining processes of tradition and political identity that accompanied the transformation of the proletarian movements into stable and lasting structures, crystallised in the form of political parties. The Russian Revolution was a crucial event in this regard. The Bolshevik seizure of power led to the consolidation of Marxism-Leninism as the doctrine of revolution, class, and class struggle. The historical experience of the Russian revolution was thus generalised and as the canon of class and revolution.

An important element of this "canonisation" of the Russian revolutionary experience is the form of the revolutionary party as the form of revolutionary organisation. It was the party form that gave expression to the true interests of class, to class consciousness *versus* the psychological or empirical (false) consciousness, as Lukács puts it (1971). Here the issue of *form* is fundamental, for it involves a process of abstraction (real abstraction) where "form" finally dominates and stabilises the political on the basis of alienation. Predominance of the form entails reification. Class-consciousness appears as a universal attribute of the party or the state; it is not the working class-in-struggle that forms the content of experience but the party as organisation or the (workers) state as the collective "consciousness" of the working class. In this sense, the theory of class struggle has undergone a period of stasis, a stasis of a specific historical experience, which was canonised and thus achieved hegemonic position. The institutionalisation of class struggle is precisely this. Institutionalisation in the state *form* or in the *party form* replaces the self-organisation and self-determination of the working class. In short, canonisation entailed the constitution of a vertical subject.

The divorce between class-consciousness and empirical consciousness, or between the party and the spontaneity of the working class in-resistance, opened the space for a hierarchical conception of organisation, based on the leadership principle of the revolutionary party, as the embodiment of class-consciousness. It separates the elite from the masses and grants intellectuals a special and privileged role in the new "organic" hierarchy. Class struggle is made hierarchical and the canon of class struggle is defined: the theory of the party as the most elaborate expression of class struggle is precisely this. The theory of the party as revolutionary vanguard was consolidated in the ideology of Leninism. Thus, to think revolution was to do so from the standpoint of this ideology, the classical canon (see Tischler, 2002).

The canonisation of the ideology of Marxism-Leninism perverted in its consequence the category of totality. Totality became identified with those forms of domination that were consolidated in the soviet system. The notion of totality was thus deprived of its critical dimension and instead of demystifying the relations of power, it became affirmative in its conception of power.

III

One of the ideological consequences of the fall of Really Existing Socialism was the crisis of the classical canon of class struggle and, with it, of the concepts of revolution and class struggle.

Against the background of this ideological climate, it is understandable that the resistance movements of the subaltern classes in Latin America should gradually abandon the classicist discourse that characterised them for many decades, largely motivated by the Cuban Revolution. This change, however, was not a kind of post-modern "discursive turn." The crisis of the *class form* of social movements was preceded by the most violent cycle of counter-revolution in Latin America. One of the main tasks of the military regimes was to end the cycle of the class struggles of the 1960s and 1970s. The various forms of worker organisation were destroyed through the use of state terrorism.

The so-called transition from dictatorship to democracy took place in a context where the *class form* of "civil society" had been dismantled from the organizational point of view. On the ideological level, there was a rejection of the discourse of class due to the identification of the fall of Really Existing Socialism with the end of class struggle, and the subsequent substitution of class with the liberal subject as the embodiment of universal freedom. This, then is the context in which the new social movements came to the fore. In other words, revolution (in the sense of radical social change linked to the struggle of subaltern classes) disappeared from the conventional framework of politics as "the art of the possible." Instead, the movements promoted their particular interests within the "universal" order of liberal democracy.

Nevertheless, struggle, the history of the oppressed and the exploited, has always exposed the fundamental fallacy of liberal politics. Recent struggles in Latin America, especially those of the Zapatistas, of the peasants and of indigenous populations, the urban experiences of the *Piqueteros* (unemployed worker's movement) and the *Asambleas de Barrio* (neighbourhood councils) in Argentina, have again done this. In fact, these movements are a response to a politics that considers them disposable. By demanding their right to exist, they have again revealed the irreconcilable contradiction between liberal democracy and collective subjects.

One of the most important issues that these movements have brought to the fore is this: By reactivating a long tradition of resistance and struggle, they have created a space for the redefinition of collectivity based on a notion of struggle that eludes the equivocal post-modern discourse; i.e. that points towards a critique of existing social relations, and that thereby recuperates the *principle of hope*, the *not-yet* (Bloch, 1986). The not-yet is entailed in the ¡YA BASTA! of their battle-cry. The ¡YA BASTA! is, one could say, the contemporary "countermovement" to existing conditions of misery. It is a movement forged in confrontation with the state, against neo-liberal policies that have aggravated the forms of rule and exploitation of capital.

To a greater or lesser extent, these movements have created an *atmosphere* that brings the issues of class and class struggle to the fore.

In this brief essay we can discuss only a few aspects of this complex issue.

First, there is the real possibility of a consciousness focused on the concept of struggle. The emphasis on struggle as the nerve-centre of collectivity entails a way of thinking the force of resistance that consists in the meeting of the exploited and the dominated as a liberation from capitalist oppression. But this liberation also amounts to the self-consciousness of the potentialities of collectivity. If collectivity is not a mere sum of individuals, of groups, of movements, but a kind of "illumination" (Benjamin) that gives rise to a new subjectivity and a new subject, then what is the element that gives meaning to it? In other words:

what makes possible this self-consciousness and collectivity, an emergent self-conscious collectivity in-and-against the existing order?

Is it struggle? Is it resistance? Immediately the question arises about the content of these concepts and, along with that, the question of the *who*. It is very likely that we discover that there are many "who's," many struggles, and that collectivity is not an abstraction, but a real form of existence that is produced as an "instance" of the negation/overcoming of the "logic of separation" upon which the rule of capital rests (separation of subject/object, labour/capital, state/society, etc.). In this sense, collectivity is an action that goes beyond and explodes the form of appearance of social objectivity, an appearance that suggests that society is divorced from the human being and that human social practice is therefore a mere derivative of structural laws. And this "instance" of negation/overcoming amounts to the class-practice of insubordination, that is to say, of human *doing* as opposed to *being* (cf. Holloway, 2002).

In other words, the notion of class does not express its critical content in distinction from struggle: class as a critical form of existence in capitalist society is struggle. This is one of the issues Marx underlines in the famous chapters on manufacture and modern industry in Volume One of *Capital*. The traditional separation between class as objective existence and class as a subject is part of the separation effected by the domination of capital, embedded in the marrow of revolutionary thinking. In the same sense, the tendency to slip towards a positivist objectivism can become as gratifying as the projection of scientific certainties that cover faraway mythical fears (see Horkheimer and Adorno, 1972). But the key to the question is that class, according to Marx, is not an object but a subject that struggles against its reduction to an object. It can only be conceived in a radical and critical way as part of this struggle, of this dialectic.

Indeed, a dialectic of alienation exists, that is, the dialectic of power or of the forms of appearance. Modern fetishism, reification, conceived as "metaphysics" of the object or movement of the object in the form of the subject, is the essence of this dialectics. In it, class appears as an object, as labour force defined by the laws of capital. Dialectics as the rupture of the reified forms of appearance is the critical nerve of class struggle as a practice and as a theory. It is a dialectics of freedom, of the destruction of the object in and through the realisation of the subject. The subject constitutes itself and realises itself in and through struggle. It springs from struggle and necessity but it is not reduced to the latter, it overcomes it in the form of the self-determining subject. In this sense, one can claim that the horizon of class struggle does not consist in the switch from the domination of one class to that of another, but in the end of domination and of class as a form of the existence of power.

Class struggle, the history of the struggle of the oppressed and the exploited, is filled with these "instances" we referred to previously.

Following Walter Benjamin (1973), we could argue that these "instances" are times that cut the duration of domination and suspend the *everyday-ness* of a fragmented reified objectivity. They are times in which a new subjectivity is produced that — although it has affirmations in its immediate practice (expressed in a disruptive language, in new concepts, in organisational experiments) — is predominantly negative. Their meaning is the struggle *against* the various forms of domination. It is a going against the current, a counter-current.

When does this process end? When will the "illuminations" permanently light up the night sky? We do not know.

In the classical canon of revolution, history is realised with the taking of power and the consecration of class. In this sense, class struggle is defined as a struggle for taking power and for the stabilisation of the figure of class. Or, better, the separation class/party, state/society is the ratification of power based on class as the relationship of domination/subordination. The state freezes this rupture in the form of a paralysing myth. This conception of revolution was a product of political pragmatism accompanied by a positivist conception of class struggle, a conception that identifies struggle with power.

In terms a "counter-current," class can be conceived as the creation of a new subjectivity whose radicalism implies the illumination of power as the consciousness of what has to be negated. Thus, class struggle points towards freedom and not towards domination. What unifies the collectivity of the exploited and the dominated is the struggle against the conditions that negate their freedom. Hence, class struggle is not dominated by the category of necessity (raw objectivism and power), but by the category of freedom: collectivity involves class as a movement of negation against capital, which is simultaneously a movement of negation of class. Radical collectivity points towards the elimination of class, not its assertion.

In a political sense this notion of class entails a radical critique of the *state form* as the central *locus* of revolutionary politics. It entails thinking of the *soviet form* (council, *Räte*) as a radical criticism of the forms of domination (see Debord, 1995). For the soviet is the intent of ending the rupture, the rule of the form over the content: the soviet is a form that posits the liberation of the content from perverse forms of existence, like that of the *state form*. Breaking with the rule of the object implies, using Holloway's terminology, struggle by doing as opposed to the classical dogma of submission to objective rules, that is, submission-of-doing. The state is a form of submission-of-doing to the flow of capital. In this instance, form acquires an abstract, objective, independent and mystical dimension, for it is part of the divorce between doing and power. The *soviet form*, the form of the *Räte*, is an effort to end the separation that renders form a relation of ruling.

IV

What we have commented until now could be conceived in the sense that all past struggles for socialism have been a total failure, a rebuff of destiny that reveals to us the smallness and the perverse nature of our human condition.

But no. This is what liberalism wants us to infer. However, to argue that our conception (the classical canon) of revolution remains immaculate, and that it conserves all its conceptual force until the time when the "objective conditions" are ready once again, does not help much in the breaking of the myth of destiny. This has partly been so because the classical canon was construed as another myth of the historical destiny of human kind. "Revolution has to occur by historical necessity." Recipes look good on destiny, but for revolution they spell death.

When we criticise the concept of revolution codified as Leninism, it is not a question of saying that the struggles conceived and oriented on this basis have not been true and morally legitimate. In many aspects, these struggles are truthful expressions of the insubordination of the subject. In this sense they are, as Badiou (1988) says, "truth events." However, these struggles have also been contradictory and their results have not always been the most desired, not only as defeats but also as crystallisation of a new power.

We can see this clearly in the case of the Russian Revolution and Lenin's theoretical trajectory. In *What Is To Be Done?*, Lenin defines revolution as the work of the proletariat led by a vanguard, the revolutionary party. The party is responsible for taking "class consciousness" to the workers, for "spontaneously" they can only achieve trade union consciousness. The taking of power by the party on behalf of the working class is the focal point of its theory of class struggle. Thus, revolution is conceived in terms of a general theory of revolutionary organisation.

Nevertheless, the experience of the Russian Revolution of 1905 forced a change in Lenin of this — let us say abstract — perception, based on the predominance of the form, the form of the party. Through this experience, Lenin was able to see in the *soviet* a revolutionary form that rises directly from working class struggle without the mediation of the party. In other words, the "spontaneity" of class struggle produces, according to Lenin, forms of consciousness and a kind of subjectivity that could not be attained by the party, based on a theory of organisation. This idea stayed with him throughout the first phase of the 1917 revolution. The watchword of the April Theses ("All power to the soviets") was the recognition that revolution amounted to the self-determination of the working class in the form of councils. Nevertheless, the process that goes from the taking of power by the Bolsheviks to the massacre of Kronstadt marks a radical change: from a conception of the soviet as the nucleus of revolution to the conception of the party and the state as its centre.[3]

The result was the destruction of the soviets as the political form of worker self-determination. And, along with it, the installation of the dictatorship of the party (of a small elite) in the form of the proletarian state. The crisis of the Russian Revolution was resolved by means of a new form of domination over the workers; that is, in a reactionary way. We can now look at the issue with relative clarity, but in the immediate years of the taking of power by the Bolsheviks it posed a true political and theoretical dilemma that even the most lucid revolu-tionary theorists could not escape. Think, for example, of how the crisis of the his-torical form of the soviet (its negation in the form of the party-state) permeates the ideas of the young Lukács, who for more reasons than one can be considered the principal philosophical exponent of the October revolution. We refer, of course to his work *History and Class Consciousness*. One could argue that the ten-sions in the making of the concepts of "psychological consciousness" and "class consciousness" are affected by the problem that the party-centred definition of class struggle entails. But, simultaneously, they recognise the soviet as the form of organisation of the proletariat that amounts to the "political and economic de-feat of reification" (Lukács, 1971, p. 80). Nevertheless, political Leninism pre-vents Lukács from radicalising this aspect of class struggle, for it introduces the question of class-consciousness as an issue of theoretical and organisational me-diation that is radically different from the "empirical" movement of class. The foundation of Lukács is not real class struggle, but a theoretical (hypothetical) subject, the "knower" of class-consciousness. Thus, as in Lenin, the initiative in struggle must be this theoretical-political subject, the party.[4] From a similar per-spective, Zizek (2001) defines the pertinence of Leninism today as the instance that (consciously) assumes the historical responsibility for the taking of power with all its possible ethical and moral consequences.

John Holloway's *Change the World Without Taking Power* provides the most up-to-date discussion of revolution. There is no need here to discuss the book or the polemic that it has provoked. There is no doubt that the book develops a new formulation of revolution that goes against the Leninist canon and that, in this sense, develops a theory of class struggle from the radicalism of the *soviet form*. Thus, the accusations by some of the critics of the book that it lacks his-torical perspective are quite groundless (see, for example, Borón, 2003). These critics conceive the bourgeois canon of history as a historical perspective, a lin-earity that suppresses the multiplicity of times contained in a historical "con-stellation." On this basis, history is what-came-to-be in terms of pragmatism and power, suppressing what-could-have-been in the sense of the struggle of the sub-ject against power (cf. Tischler, 2005). In this sense, the recovery of the dy-namics of the struggle that the soviet form entails retrieves for revolution a "suspended" form of "doing" that was "suspended" ever since its forceful de-struction in the name of the workers' state.

In sum, in order to think revolution in our time, we have to be conscious that the *party form* and the *state form* contradict and so pervert the ends of revolution. We know what the imposition of the state form upon the soviet form meant and to what it led. In order to think revolution in our time, we have however also to learn from the revolution that really was. That is, we have to learn from the *ex-perience of truth* that the *soviet form* entailed. Under current circumstances the issue of revolution is not something that can be formulated solely in empirical or prag-matic terms; on the contrary, it is an updating and reconstitution of theoretical reflection as a moment of practice. Instead of separating the theory of revolution from its practice — a separation that tells us what revolution *must be* according to some canonised doctrine — critical reflection is part of the struggle as a *true criticism in motion.*

V

In the aforementioned sense, one can argue that revolution is reinvented by the radical social movements of our time.

To reinvent revolution under the current circumstances is to change the meaning of words, to create a new language for naming radical change.

The EZLN (*Ejército Zapatista de Liberación Nacional*, Zapatista Army of National Liberation) has been particularly groundbreaking in this effort. Imagining revolution against the background of the crisis of the classical, Leninist canon, entails an effort of creation. This is one of the meanings we find in the Zapatista critique of *the struggle for power and of the categories of avant-gardism and the classical revolutionary* forms of organisation.

Does this new language exclude the concept of class struggle? There is obviously a rejection of its dogmatic, classificatory and formal use, for Zapatismo does not intend to be a kind of contemporary figure of "class-consciousness." It rather tries to break the canon. Nevertheless, as we already argued, the radical quality of the concept of class struggle is not the replacement of one power by another, but the realisation of the social subject in and through the destruction of all forms of power, all forms of domination. In this sense, when Zapatismo talks of struggle against power, it is applying an *open* concept of class struggle, as opposed to the closed concept of the classical canon. Revolution is no longer considered from the standpoint of the category of power, but from the constant struggle of the social subject against power, against its different forms — amongst them that of politics as the culture of reification.

The *rebel* subject creates a language that tells us that the desired change will no longer be trapped in the form of a vertically constructed power, but that it will be one of the self-organisation and self-determination of the exploited and the dominated. Self-determination and self-organisation is something that cannot be constructed in subordination to a repressive totality. Such subordination subsumes the multiplicity of "doing" to a homogenous and hegemonic universal — the part that always knows best.[5] The text of Marcos, "Durito and one on statues and *birds*" is eloquent regarding this issue:

> *"In order to tell the story of Power"* says Durito, *"it is enough to describe the statues that exist in the world in the geography of time and space."*
>
> *"For"* says Durito *"where there is a lack of reasons there is an abundance of statues. When Power is not yet Power but is still in the struggle to become such, its dogmas are rendered declarations of principles, programs, plans of action; they are,*

in sum, statues in projection. When Power takes the seat of Power, its dogmas turn into laws, constitutions, regulations; they are, in sum, paper statues that then turn into stone statues."

"But as it turns out, history turns round in circles, full of bumps, but it turns," says Durito, *"and today's winner of the statue is not even remembered in the tomorrow that we are, no matter how much the signs uselessly say 'this is the statue of the Marquis of Eternal Truth, etc.' The 'intelligent' world of Power is seemingly complex but indeed quite simple, it is made up of dogmas and statues. And the genealogy of power is based only on the intellectual discussion of what came first, the dogma or the statue."*

"There are those who make of our words a statue (or a dogma, but it is the same). Some turn our thinking into stone, in order to later demolish it in front of many spotlights, round tables, journals, journalistic columns, café reunions. Others transform our idea into a dogma, they put some incense on it and then change it for some other dogma, one that is more fashionable, more appropriate, more ad hoc."

Durito says that in both instances the fact that Zapatismo is neither a dogma nor a statue is ignored. Zapatismo, as rebelliousness, is but one amongst thousands of birds that fly.

"As any bird, Zapatismo is born, it grows up, sings, reproduces itself with and in another, dies and, as is the law amongst birds, shits on statues," says Durito while he flies and uselessly tries to adopt an *"air between tender and tough, like a sparrow"* (Marcos, 2003a, pp. 1–2).

A similar insight can be found in the *piquetero* movement of the MTD of Solano. The struggle is conceived as the process of destroying power relations and of constructing a horizontal collective subject. This subject is constituted in practice by means of direct democracy amongst its members and in relation to other organizations (see MTD Solano/Colectivo Situaciones, 2002).

In Zapatismo, as well as in the movement of the MTD of Solano, struggle is conceived as *collective democracy in action*. As such, it implies the transformation of sociability, producing *spatial-temporal forms* of a subjectivity in struggle against power and capital (see MTD Solano/Colectivo Situaciones, 2002). The critical line of this democracy in action radicalizes the collectivity of the subject and thereby reveals the limits and myths of liberal, representative democracy.

In this struggle, the concepts and categories of our world undergo a radical transformation. One could say, they are "resignified." For example, the concept "civil society" transforms into a notion that captures the self-determination of the indigenous communities of the EZLN. Similarly, the notion of dignity transforms. For the Zapatistas dignity does not amount to the achievement of "respectability," which maintains them unaltered, and which for that very reason is so highly valued in liberalism (see Bonefeld, 2002). Instead, dignity amounts to the struggle against contemptible conditions (see Holloway, 1998).

What these movements are doing is not completely new. They feed on experience and recover old notions and ideas that the left "had given up on," such as freedom, democracy, justice or dignity (see Rodríguez Lascano, 2003).

But the transformation of words is not a simple, rhetoric game. What it in fact amounts to is an exploding of the utopian nucleus of meanings, of that which they secretly keep as a *principle of hope* (Bloch). This "exploding" is a part of the struggle against power, that is, of the self-activity of the social subject.

The contemporary class struggles force us to think revolution in a new way. We are living in a time of liberation of revolutionary imagination. The demolition of the fetishes of power is part of the complex process of elaborating a new revolutionary subject. This elaboration is taking place here and now, and it does so in the form of the new social movements.

NOTES

1 I thank John Holloway and Cecilia Zeledón for their comments on this paper. I also wish to thank Werner Bonefeld.

2 On this see the contributions to Dinerstein and Neary (2002).

3 On this see the contributions to Bonefeld and Tischler (2002).

4 For Lukács, the consciousness of the proletariat is not the "psychological," but the "possible" consciousness. In the struggle against the opportunism of social-democracy and of its political consequences in the midst of the European proletariat, especially the German one, the issue of possible consciousness involved the issue of struggle for power, already abandoned by social-democracy. But then, the question of possible consciousness slides towards a revolutionary theory of organization. Who creates this consciousness? If according to Leninism it is not spontaneously produced by the proletariat, then the relationship between struggle and consciousness entails a theoretical mediation (as the space of truth) linked to the figure of the intellectual of the party. In this process, there exists the risk of introducing the idea of separation (class/knowledge) as the inevitable condition of revolutionary practice, which implies the legitimizing of the construction of a vertical, hierarchical subject.

5 In the *communiqué* of the 12 of April, 2003 of the EZLN, Marcos severely criticizes the concept of hegemony as part of a left-wing culture the EZLN wishes to overcome. He says: "To the political and social organizations that participate today in this march, and in other parts of Mexico, we say to them that the EZLN does not wish to hegemonize and homogenize rebelliousness in Mexico.... We well understand that rebelliousness has many colors and follows many paths.... To all organizations we offer a mirror. If they respect us, they shall in turn receive respect.... For a long time we have been told that the fragmentation of the social movement is lethal for the struggle to transform society.... Whoever says this does so because he or she wishes

to be the one to lead and hegemonize the movement, most of the time in order to then hand it in for a few coins; or, alleging unfavorable junctures and conditions, replace mobilization with deceitful cheating and agreements between leaders.... We do not know if the plurality and diversity of political and social organizations can achieve a transformation that is possible and that we need and deserve.... But we do know that hegemony, however disguised as 'unity of program' has not achieved it and, rather, it has spread skepticism and disappointment. The multiply mentioned union of the left, according to the Zapatistas, cannot be constructed based on one criterion only, with a structure that merely obscures the mutual piracy of activists and militants, cannibalism between political proposals, the open competition to see who is the most radical in words and the hidden competition to see who shall sell out at the best price.... The efforts of unity, constructed with the goal of hegemony, have only ended in ruptures, divisions and sterile rivalries.... Unity is possible if plurality and diversity are respected.... Our idea is not of one sole organization, but of a movement with many organizations, with a basic agreement, resistance, and a common flag, rebelliousness." (Marcos, 2003b).

REFERENCES

Agnoli, J. (2003), "Destruction as the Determination of the Scholar in Miserable Times," in W. Bonefeld (ed) *Revolutionary Writing*, Autonomedia, New York.
Badiou, A. (1988), *L'Etre et l'Evénement. L'ordre philosophique*, Seuil, Paris.
Benjamin, W. (1973), "Theses on the Philosophy of History," in *Illuminations*, Schocken Books, New York.
Bloch, E. (1986), *The Principle of Hope*, Basil Blackwell, Oxford.
Bonefeld, W. (2002), "¿Dignidad versus respetabilidad? Marx y la ciencia," in *Bajo el Volcán* No.5, Posgrado de Sociología, Benemérita Universidad Autónoma de Puebla, México.
Bonefeld, W. And S. Tischler (eds) (2002), *What is to be Done? Anti-Leninist Marxism and the Question of Revolution Today*, Ashgate, Aldershot.
Borón, A. (2003), "Poder, 'contrapoder' y 'antipoder.' Notas sobre un extravío teórico-político en el pensamiento crítico contemporáneo," in *Chiapas* No.15, Instituto de Investigaciones Económicas of the UNAM, Ediciones Era, Mexico.
Debord, G. (1995), *The Society of the Spectacle*, Zone Books, New York.
Dinerstein, A.C. and M. Neary (eds), *The Labour Debate*, Ashgate, Aldersthot.
Gunn, R. (1992), "Against Historical Materialism: Marxism as First-Order Discourse" in W. Bonefeld etal. (eds) *Open Marxism*, Vol. II, Pluto Press, London.
Holloway, J. (1998), "Dignity's Revolt," in Holloway, J. and E. Peláez, (eds) *Zapatista! Reinventing Revolution in Mexico*, Pluto Press, London.

Holloway, J. (2002), *Change the World Without Taking Power. The meaning of revolution today*, Pluto Press, London.

Horkheimer, M. and T. W. Adorno, (1972) *Dialectic of Enlightenment*, Herder and Herder, New York.

Lenin, V.I., (1988) *What is to be Done?*, Penguin, London.

Lukács, G. (1971), *History and Class Consciousness*, MIT Press, Cambridge MA.

MTD Solano/Colectivo Situaciones (2002), *La hipótesis 891. Más allá de los piquetes*, Ediciones De Mano en Mano, Argentina.

Rodríguez Lascano, S. (2003), "¿Puede ser verde la teoría? Si, siempre y cuando la vida no sea gris," *Rebeldía* No. 8, June, México.

Subcomandante Marcos (2003a) "Durito y una de estatuas y *pájaros*," *Rebeldía* No. 7, May, México.

Subcomandante Marcos (2003b), "Comunicado del Comité Clandestino Revolucionario Indígena-Comandancia General del Ejército Zapatista de Liberación Nacional. México, 12 de abril de 2003," *La Jornada*, 13 April 2003.

Tischler, S. (2002), "The Crisis of the Leninist Subject and the Zapatista Circumstance," in Bonefeld, W. and S. Tischler (eds) *What is to Be Done? Leninism, Anti-Leninist Marxism and the Question of Revolution Today*, Ashgate, Aldershot.

Tischler, S. (2005), "Time of Reification and Time of Insurbordination," in Bonefeld, W. and K. Psychopedis (eds) *Human Dignity. Social Autonomy and the Critique of Capitalism*, Ashgate, Aldershot.

Zizek, S. (2001), "Can Lenin Tell Us About Freedom Today?," in *Rethinking Marxism* Vol. 13, No. 2, Indiana.

PART III

THE QUESTION OF THE MULTITUDE
ARGENTINA, MEXICO & THE UNITED STATES

11

The War on Terrorism & The U.S. Working Class
From Septemeber 11, 2001 to
the "Si Se Puede" Insurrection of 2006

George Caffentzis

INTRODUCTION

The Bush Administration's "war on terrorism" has been often criticized as an attack on both "enemy combatants'" and US citizens' civil and human rights. There is now a large literature concerning the many ways in which it violates previously widely shared norms of privacy and advocacy in the US (Cole 2003). Indeed, the Bush Administration's post-September 11 "coup" is frequently seen philosophically as the opening of a growing arena of "emergency powers" that is increasingly being arrogated by the Neoliberal state in a time of crisis. Parallels between the collapse of the World Trade Center towers and the 1933 Reichstag fire abound. The Reichstag fire cleared the way for the Nazis' imposition of Emergency Laws that obliterated the notions of legality worked out in the German class struggle after the end of the anti-socialist laws in the 1870s. In the same way, "9/11" gave license to the Bush Administration's exercise of emergency powers. Without a doubt, then, the main critical discussion of the "war on terrorism's" impact in the US has been through legal and civil liberties categories, with all the virtues and limitations of such an approach.

In this chapter, instead, I analyze the war on terrorism as a class strategy used by Capital in the US in a way reminiscent of the "anti-communist" campaign of the 1950s that also had legal and political-economic faces, as well as domestic and foreign applications. The questions motivating this essay then are: *how have the events of September 11, 2001 been used to transform class relations in US and why did this transformation reach its own crisis in the Spring of 2006?*

A Wage/Profit Crisis at the End of the 20th Century

Answers to the above questions clearly depend on an understanding of the composition and relations of force between the classes in the years before September 11, 2001. A quick, though dry, way of understanding the class relation inherited by the George W. Bush Administration is through studying the wage/profit profile of those years.

The most salient feature of the U.S. class struggle in the quarter century from 1973 to 1997 was the decline of real wages that laid the foundations for the surprising revival of profitability of US capital in the early 1990s. The average weekly real wage (in constant 1982 dollars) in 1973 was $315 and in 1997 it was $268. This decline of 15 percent took place at a dismally regular pace and, conversely, total corporate profits (both real and nominal) rose dramatically. To get a rough estimate of how differently average wages and total profits fared compare the different rates of increase of their nominal (not real) values in two different periods, the Keynesian (1959–1973) and the Neoliberal (1973–1997):

Dates	Wage Increase	Profit Increase
1959–1973	85%	115%
1973–1997	192%	577%
1997–2000	12%	-6%
2000–2005	13%	60%

Table 1

All quantities are nominal. They are calculated as the percentage change between the initial and final year of the period. Calculated from Tables B–47 and B–90 of *The Economic Report of the President (2006)*.

Table 1 simply illustrates a well-known fact: in the Keynesian era nominal wages and profits increased at roughly the same rate, but in the Neoliberal period nominal profits increased three times more than nominal wages (which actually fell in real terms).

However, TABLE 1 reveals a surprising development beginning in 1997: for the first time since the 1960s there were three consecutive years of positive, above one percent, increases in real wages (1997, 1998, 1999). Not surprisingly, in these years profits began to fall from $868 billion in 1997 to $801 billion in 1998, to $851 billion in 1999 after more than a decade of uninterrupted nominal (and "real") profit increases. This initiated a crisis period where nominal wages increased while profits decreased which reversed a key feature of the Neoliberal period.

To put some "flesh" on these numbers we should remember that it was during the last Clinton Administration that some important strikes were won, after a long period in which strike activity had dramatically decreased and strikes had become increasingly longer and more risky. There was, for example, the successful UPS (United Parcel Service) strike in 1997 organized by the Teamsters under their "reform" leadership (Prashad 2003). Moreover, the year 2000 saw the highest number of "days idle" due to strikes since the highly conflictual 1970s (*Statistical Abstract of the US 2003*, Table 655).

Here, in numbers, is one source of the relentless hostility President Clinton evoked in the hearts of Right-wing politicians in the "boom years" of the late 1990s. Despite Clinton's statements in support of Neoliberalism, the US economy experienced on his watch a three-year period when real wages went up and total profits declined. It should not be a surprise then if Republican senators demanded his head! In their eyes Clinton was either, at best, so incompetent as to let unemployment fall too low, or, at worst insincere in his pronounced faith in the theological properties of "the market." Many suspected him of being an evil-doing Keynesian in Neoliberal clothing.

This inversion of the ideal Neoliberal wage/profit ratio and the intensification of strike activity could not last, however, in an environment dominated by Neoliberal policies, whether Gore or Bush won the 2000 election. Consequently, beginning in 2000, amid the collapsing stock markets, the dot.com crash, an economic slowdown and a statistically defined recession, the nominal wage/ profit ratio changed as indicated by the last "Bush Administration" line (2000–2005) of TABLE 1. Real wage increases also began to drop; they have averaged about 0.1 % for the last six years: 0 .4% in 2000, –0.1% in 2001, 1.3% in 2002, and 0.0% in 2003, –0.4% in 2004 and –0.6 in 2005 (*Economic Report of the President 2006*, Table B–47). Finally, the number of "idle days" due to strikes from 2001 to 2004 dropped to historic lows (*Statistical Abstract of the US 2006*, Table 646), to the point that almost no young worker has had the experience of being on strike!

These statistics show that the Bush Administration, after September 11, 2001 succeeded in reversing the crisis of Neoliberal economics in the US, at least in the short-run. I claim that this reversal has been in part due to the launching of the war on terrorism.

THE USA PATRIOT ACT AND WAGE SLAVERY

We build machines that act like men and we want to produce men who act like machines. Our danger today is not that of becoming slaves, but of becoming automatons.
— Erich Fromm, "Freedom in the Work Situation," in Harrington and Jacobs (1960:3).

An important first step in the war on terrorism was the almost unanimous, but hasty passage into law of the Uniting and Strengthening America by Providing Appropriate Tools Required to Intercept and Obstruct Terrorism (USA PATRIOT) Act. President Bush signed it six weeks after September 11, 2001. It was sold to Congress and the public as a means to repress Al Qaeda and its allies. But the Act is not specifically directed at Al Qaeda members. Far from having a clear objective—as was the case, e.g., with the legislation of the Cold War that criminalized communism—the USA PATRIOT Act's identification of the "enemy" is extremely vague. Its definitions of "terrorist activity" and "terrorist organization" are so broad that it criminalizes practically anyone who is politically involved and travels, communicates, or sends money across national borders for almost any political purposes not sanctioned by the US government. Thus its scope is wide enough to undermine working class struggle in the US.

"Terrorist activity" is defined as committing any crime involving the use of a "weapon or dangerous device (other than for personal monetary gain)," it includes soliciting funds, soliciting membership, and providing material support for a "terrorist organization," even when the organization has some legitimate political and humanitarian aims. What constitutes a "terrorist organization" is even more problematic. In the past, US State Department decided which organizations were to be considered terrorist and it periodically issued new lists of such organizations. But with the passing of the USA PATRIOT Act, "terrorist organization" is defined as any group of "two or more individuals, whether organized or not," engaging in terrorist activities, as defined above.

As for the crimes that can be prosecuted under the USA PATRIOT Act, the list is potentially endless. It covers:

> ...acts dangerous to human life that are a violation of the criminal laws [if they] appear to be intended... to influence the policy of a government by intimidation or coercion [and if they] occur primarily within the territorial jurisdiction of the US.

This definition can easily include picket-line activities occurring in the context of a public demonstration outside a politician's home, a government office, or an

182

army base. Moreover, a non-citizen can be deported even if s/he provided material assistance to, solicited funds for, or solicited membership for an undesignated "terrorist organization" prior to the enactment of the Act.

Considering how "fluid" and contingent is the US government's classification of its opponents, this clause is a very provocative step. It clearly intends to put the anti-globalization and union movements on the defensive. Activists now must face new risks when engaging in any transnational networking and support work. More than that, as Nancy Chang, from the Center for Constitutional Rights, has noted, the language of the USA PATRIOT Act can be read by federal law enforcement agencies: "...as licensing the investigation of political activists and organization based on their opposition to government policies. It also may be read by prosecutors as licensing the criminalization of legitimate political dissent" (Chang 2002).

However, while many US-born activists and workers can be criminalized under the USA PATRIOT Act, immigrant workers are most under the fire of the new legislation, as their organizing and the requirements of their daily lives demand that they operate on a transnational level, e.g., through engaging in support work for political organizations in their "home" countries. Indeed, when we look at the use that has already been made of it, we see that, behind the "terrorism" rhetoric, the USA PATRIOT Act appears as nothing less than a new tool to keep class struggle in check in the US, and it is especially designed to control a working class that is becoming increasingly multinational.

The USA PATRIOT Act has already been used to raid immigrant neighborhoods, deport or detain an undeclared number of immigrants, especially (but not exclusively) from Muslim countries, and screen tens of thousands more. Most important, its immediate effect—in the period after September 11—was to freeze the organization drives immigrant workers were leading.

This is not accidental. To fully understand why this type of legislation was adopted, two considerations are in order. First, "September 11" occurred at a time of renewed class struggle and union mobilization which, by the year 2000, was beginning to reverse the tremendous decline in union membership that had occurred in the 1980s (by 1999 union membership had fallen to 13.9 percent of waged workers from 25 per cent average of the 1970s). Thus, while in the 1980s workers had seemed defenseless against the anti-union attacks launched by corporate power with the support of both the Republican and Democratic parties, by 2000 unionization and a working class offensive was regaining ground. The stability and, in some cases, growth of unionization in the public sector (including teachers, police officers and welfare workers) — from 36.7 percent in 1983 to 37.5 percent by 2000—has been in part responsible for the resurgence of workers' activism. But the main protagonists of the new class offensive and labor's organizational drive in the 1990s have been immigrant workers, especially from Mexico and the rest of the Americas, whose massive entrance in the US work-force — almost 15 million be-

tween 1981 and 1998 — has radically changed its social and political composition. As a Justice for Janitors rank-and-file leader in Los Angeles put it,
"We Latino workers are a bomb waiting to explode" (Clawson 2003: 101).

For a start, immigrant workers have affected the rate of unionization, as
they are generally more favorable to unions than native-born workers (De Fre-
itas 1993). An example of this preference is the fact that 75 percent of the heavily immigrant Latino population of California voted against the anti-union
Proposition 226 in California (which would have required unions to obtain individual permission from their members to spend any of their dues on political
campaigns), while only 53.5 percent of voters overall voted against it.

Unions are certainly not revolutionary organizations. However, it is indis-
putable that in the US unionized workers earn higher wages (though the exact
amount depends upon the method of calculation). For example, Collins and Yeskel
claim that unionized workers earn an average of 34 percent more than other workers. According to them, "Joining a union raises earnings by 40 percent for [waged]
working women, 44 percent for African American workers, and 53 percent for
Latino workers" (Collins and Yeskel 2000: 83). Mishel, Bernstein and Allegretto
of the Economic Policy Institute calculate that the "union wage premium (the difference between union and nonunion wages after controlling for a variety of
worker characteristics such as amount of schooling) was 15.5 percent (for black
workers it was 20.9 percent and for Hispanics 23.2 percent)" (Yates 2005). Indeed,
a sudden reversal of unionization rate trends and a return to their level in the
1950s would dramatically reduce most US corporations' profits (given their impact on wages). Thus, the increasing presence of immigrants in the US work force
is seen as a mixed blessing by US capital. On the one side, immigrants are the
source of much of the profitability of US industries; on the other hand, immigrant
workers (both documented and undocumented) bring with them an intense experience of struggle that can be applied to wage struggles in the US.

It is rare for politically active immigrants from Latin America or any part
of Asia or Africa not to have been involved in anti-globalization struggles in
their home countries prior to migrating. Very few adults have not participated
in a strike, riot, insurrection, or even rebellion against governments adopting
World Bank privatization and liberalization programs, or IMF-inspired devaluations. Many workers have been hounded out of their countries precisely because of both their anti-globalization militancy and the general impoverishment
which structural adjustment has caused. For example, many Salvadorian workers have come to the US as refugees from the war against a military junta and a
right-wing Neoliberal government, and they maintain deep ties to the politics of
the liberation movement in El Salvador. In other words, the immigrant workers
who come to the US are not defeated, apathetic people. On the contrary, many
are circulating into the "center" of capitalism an enormous experience of struggle from its "periphery" that has been the basis for the revival of trade union
militancy and class struggle in the US of the 1990s.

So powerful has been the impulse immigrant workers have given to the struggle in the US that, by 2000, the AFL-CIO had reversed its century-long hostility to immigrants and taken the unprecedented step of supporting a demand for "Amnesty for the undocumented," recognizing that they were providing the leadership of its organizing drives (Prashad 2003: 44).

It should come as no surprise, then, if the Bush Administration's USA PATRIOT Act targets immigrant workers, and stigmatizes them as (actual or potential) "terrorists." The goal is precisely to interrupt that flow of information, organizational strategies and networking that in recent years—in many cases through the anti-globalization and union organizing movements—has allowed activists to challenge the hegemonic power of multinational corporations, in many cases forcing them to become accountable to their workers through internationally coordinated campaigns such as that against sweatshops, which in the US gained momentum also through a new alliance between students, labor activists, and immigrant organizations. All over the US, in fact, in campus after campus, students organized a movement to protest the use of "sweated" labor to produce the goods (like T-shirts and hats) their universities sold to them.

In this context, the USA PATRIOT Act has been an important step in supporting a new phase of wage slavery in the US, as was indicated by the 2002 US Supreme Court decision in Hoffman Plastic Compounds v. National Labor Review Board (NLRB) which denied illegally-fired undocumented workers the right to back-pay remedy. This decision has behind it an increasing political identification of the immigrants as a "terrorists"—the ultimate right-less demonic beings in contemporary US jurisprudence.

I use the archaic-sounding phrase "wage slavery" for the same reason that other terms like "sweatshop," "enclosures," and "multitude," evoking capitalism's past, have been recently used to refer to some of the major changes in contemporary society (Hardt and Negri 2000; Midnight Notes 1992). This semantic "going back to the future" signals a rupture between capitalist change and social progress, which conceptually recycles both the past horrors of capitalism and the past missed opportunities to break from it.

"Wage slavery" is often misunderstood as a rhetorical phrase referring to a time long-ago when workers' wages were pitifully low, the working day was endless and the discipline of work draconian. But these are only symptoms of wage slavery, they are not its essence, which is a situation in which workers are not legally entitled to collectively bargain the cost and conditions of their labor. In other words, unlike in chattel slavery, the wage slave is not the possession of the employer. S/he gets a wage, but s/he cannot collectively negotiate his/her wage by, for example, joining with other workers to deny his/her labor power to a boss in a strike. In such situations, the wage is effectively determined either by the state or by the employers, and it tends to gravitate to a situation represented by the image of a Victorian Scrooge penny-pinching his helpless workers to death. Wage slavery was quite common in the 19th century in Europe and the US, as the political literature of the period attests. It was only defeated in the late 19th and early 20th centuries, when the workers became enfranchised and gained the right to form unions and collectively bargain wages, hours, and conditions of work. But as the history of the US and Europe shows, every system of capitalist exploitation ultimately tends to wage slavery, given the appropriate circumstances, and the struggle against this tendency is still to be definitively won.

Thus, today as well, we need to examine the space between the wage and slavery to understand work conditions and the class relation in Neoliberal capitalism. Significantly, the conceptual territory between chattel slavery and the protection of workers' bargaining rights has become a focus of attention for activists and social thinkers since the end of Keynesianism in the 1970s. The "chattel slavery" side of the territory has attracted most attention (see Bales (2000) on "disposable people"), while prosecutions for violations (direct and indirect) of anti-slavery conventions have become commonplace in recent years across the planet. But the "wage" side of wage-slavery has also been the object of attention under the rubric of the deprivation of "workers' rights" and the revival of "sweatshops." But even in the face of massive protests, the ideal realization of a free wage-labor regime (as envisioned by the ILO conventions and the more radical part of the New Deal legislation) is receding in the US, as it is throughout the planet.

The fear that Erich Fromm voiced in 1960, in the epigraph cited above about workers turning into automatons, has recently morphed into a fear of the return of wage slavery in the US and internationally. The condition of undocumented immigrant workers, who have no collective bargaining rights, is rapidly becoming identical to that of many other "citizens" who are similarly deprived, like prisoners, parolees and others on probation, as well as those on "workfare," where work imposed as condition for receiving welfare benefits (Caffentzis 2001). As a result of this situation, the fear of obtaining "guarantees" at the price of an alienated and mechanized life, that was so pronounced in the 1950s and 1960s, is giving way, at the beginning of the 21st century, to an older anxiety: the fear of not having *any* rights to negotiate the basic conditions of one's existence in the midst of a jungle of machines. And "the machine" for many has lost any of the attraction it may once have had as something planned, orderly, and beneficial. It now appears instead as a cruel, unpredictable god demanding more and more human sacrifices.

Thus, the critique of capitalism has increasingly turned from an emphasis on alienation to one on exploitation and a reconsideration of the framework of wages, profits, class, and work.

THE HOMELAND SECURITY ACT:
A SUBTLE MIXTURE OF NEOLIBERALISM AND KEYNESIANISM

While the USA PATRIOT Act's violation of workers' rights and attack on unionization is all pervaisive but indirect, the Homeland Security Act's (HSA) hostility to workers' rights and unionization is quite explicit. Passed on November 25, 2002 for purpose of "prevent(ing) terrorist attacks within the United States" and "reduc(ing) the vulnerability of the United States to terrorism," even before its adoption, the Act was at the center of an acrimonious controversy because of its anti-union provisions. The HSA is a direct attack on government employee unions, as it threatens the rights of the 170,000 employees of the newly created Department of Homeland Security (DHS) — resulting from the consolidation of 22 federal agencies — to unionize. (We should here remember that Federal Government workers have no freedom to strike and hence are legally restricted in their power to collectively negotiate their wages.)

One of HSA's many anti-union provisions — buried in Title VIII, Subtitle E, section 842 — specifies that:

> If the President determines that the application of subsections [of the law that involved collective bargaining rights] would have a substantial adverse impact on the ability of the Department to protect homeland security, the President may waive the application of such subsections 10 days after the President has submitted to Congress a written explanation of the reasons for such determination.

In other words, the collective bargaining rights of 43,000 unionized DHS employees must be contingent on a unilateral decision by President Bush! In the debates before the HSA was passed, the Democrats in the Senate demanded that the President be forced either to get approval for such a waiver from the Federal Labor Relations Authority or declare a state of national emergency before issuing it. But President Bush threatened to veto the law if his right to unilaterally waive the DHS workers' collective bargaining rights was in any way diminished, and that threat was sufficient to carry the day.

In this case too, the passing of the Act should be connected with the rising militancy of public sector workers, mentioned above. But what is clearly at work is a broader project aiming to turn back the clock to the pre-Wagner Act, pre-"New Deal" era—that is, to the times of wage slavery and unlimited employers' power, when labor conflicts were "Big Trouble," solved with Pinkerton rifles and occasionally the noose (Lukas 1997).

It is in any case certain that the creation of the DHS has triggered the largest reorganization of the Federal bureaucracy since World War II (the DHS being the third largest Federal Department in terms of employment), and its formation has opened the flood gates for a unprecedented set of administrative decisions both de-legitimating unions in the Federal government and privatizing government services, so that non-unionized corporations, in the future, can become recipients of Federal revenues in a wide variety of areas, something which civil service rules had so far prevented.

One of the first legal challenges to this reorganization was posed on January 27, 2005 when four unions asked for an injunction against the rules the Bush Administration plans to impose on the DHS. Gregory J. O'Duden, general counsel of the National Treasury Employees Union, claimed that the rules "radically reduce the rights of federal employees and deprive them of a voice over important issues like the time and place of work, overtime and the hiring of private contractors to do their jobs." He was joined by many other government union lawyers in criticizing the new rules, that the Bush Administration sees as defining a paradigm for the post-9/11 Government bureaucracy with the watchwords —"flexible," "order," and "discipline"— in an permanent emergency environment of the war on terrorism.

A foreshadowing of this rule transformation was the removal by the Bush administration, in January 2002, of about a thousand Justice Department lawyers from union jurisdiction. This move was justified with the argument that since a small number of these lawyers were involved in "terrorist" litigation, they all could be involved at one time or another in "terrorism" trials that would require them to be privy to "national security" information. Thus they were all subject to "national security" exemptions that barred unionization. This argument could be made because, after September 11, 2001, "terrorism" became defined as a matter of "war" and "national security," instead of a matter of "justice" and "crime control." This means that federal attorneys involved in terrorist cases are now treated as war combatants rather than as court officers responsible prosecuting crime. Indeed, after the HSA, "national security" considerations have been extended to the most innocuous activities, from librarians lending books to janitors repairing boilers in government buildings.

An even clearer example of the use of the logic of the HSA to undermine government employees' unions has been the fate of the airport baggage screeners. By the year 2000 baggage screeners working for private contractors had organized themselves, creating local branches of the Service Employees International Union (SEIU). But one month after September 11, 2001 Congress decided that screeners had to be federal employees and citizens, a move which expelled from the airports many immigrants workers and eliminated SEIU airport locals, as the new federal employees could not bring along their previous union affiliations. The screeners who were then included in the Transportation Security Administration (TSA) created in 2002. They tried to organize a federal employees' union, but they were blocked by the director of the TSA who was given the power to bar them from unionizing, again in the name of the war on terrorism.

An allied example of how "terrorism" has been used to undermine workers' rights is the plan Secretary of Defense Rumsfeld began promoting at the time of September 11, which denies collective bargaining rights to the Department of Defense's (DoD) 640,000 workers (44 percent of whom are already unionized). The Congress gave him, as the head of the DoD, the authority to design a new personnel policy in November 2003 to "support [the DoD's] critical national security mission." After a year of planning "the National Security Personnel System" (NSPS) was introduced with its watchword: "Nothing delays management's ability to act" (DoD 2005: 4). The civil service unions then began a campaign of administrative, judicial and legislative guerilla warfare to stop the NSPS from being implemented. This struggle eventually led to a Federal court blocking the implementation of NSPS in February 2006 and the House of Representatives passed in June 2006 an amendment to the DoD appropriation bill that would refund those portions of the NSPS that are unfair to DoD workers. The Bush Administration is fighting to reverse these defeats in both the courts and the Congress as of the summer of 2006.

Whatever the NSPS's fate, it is an important step in the Bush Administration's campaign to privatize government services and replace unionized government workers with non-unionized workers in the "private sector," an effort that began with the November 2002 decision to open 15 percent of federal jobs, considered "commercial in nature," to competition between federal agencies and private corporations.

Much depends on the success of this operation. Privatization of government services would guarantee that the hundreds of billions of dollars increase in the Federal budget that has taken place since Sept. 11, 2001 due to the war on terrorism would not result in an increase of the predominantly unionized government employment, but would instead consign hiring procedures to private contractors (from cleaning companies to "rent a soldier" operations) heavily relying on non-union labor.

This anti-union privatization would be the solution to the Sphinx's riddle posed by the Bush Administration's revival of military Keynesianism that was voiced by Michael Kalecki in the 1940s: how is it possible for the state to invest in social reproduction without strengthening the working class? Of course, the general preference is to invest in "disciplinary" branches like the police and military rather than in housing, medical care or education, but even military spending creates a guaranteed sphere of employment for millions of mechanics, secretaries and janitors. The massive use of non-union private contractors, that would, at the same time, offer "national security" guaranteed jobs for US citizen workers, would satisfy the conditions of the problem Bush faces. In effect, the Bush Administration is proposing a subtle mixture of Neoliberalism (privatization) and Keynesian deficit spending to get and keep US capital out of a crisis for the near future. This strategy promises non-union jobs, in a hugely expanded and privatized "national security" sector, to citizen workers, further illegality to immigrant workers and wage slavery to both.

The Working Class Response to the War on Terrorism

Together, the USA PATRIOT Act, the HSA, and the other legislated aspects of the war on terrorism had their intended effect by the end of 2005. Real wages were stagnant, profits were up, unionization rates in private industry continued to fall and strike activity had almost vanished in the US since Sept. 11, 2001. Moreover, the signs of a working class recomposition that could be discerned in Seattle in November 1999, seemed to be receding. In the organizing drive that led to the Seattle demonstration a new alliance between unionized workers, students, feminists, and various types of human rights and environmental NGOs was created. This was a historic change with respect to the traditional trade union politics that, for the most part, had always been allied with the CIA and the US government's imperial drive. One especially important ground of recomposition was the "anti-sweatshop movement" which had registered a high participation of both union members and students, who in many campuses had denounced the use of sweatshop labor to make products sold by their institutions and often traveled to the countries in which these articles were produced to support the workers. Indeed, interns at UNITE (the garment workers union) designed the first organizing manual for the anti-sweatshop movement (Clawson 2003: 175–179).

The post-September 11 war on terrorism (from the domestic legislation to the actual wars in Iraq and Afghanistan) caused a rift in the "Seattle movement." The kind of alliance that had been established in the late 1990s, captured by the slogan "Teamsters and Turtles together" (signifying the unity of unionized workers and the ecological movement) collapsed. By the fall of 2001, the "Seattle movement" was retreating and anti-sweatshop efforts were losing ground. For example, the planned demonstration aimed at shutting down the World Bank/IMF meetings in Washington, in late September 2001, was called off and, since then, similar events have registered a low attendance.

We can thus see two conflicting tendencies in the US with respect to the Bush Administration's war on terrorism: on the one side, the growth of a social movement that has refused to cooperate with the USA PATRIOT Act and the police state apparatus of the war on terrorism; on the other, a part of working class giving enthusiastic support to the aims of the war on terrorism. The existence of a rift within the US working class has been variously described and widely discussed. It is often expressed *geographically* as a division between coastal "blue state" versus rural "red state" America, or *psychologically* as "outward-looking worldly America" versus "inward-looking Godly America," or *journalistically* as "Christian Right conservative blue-collar Republicans of Kansas allied with their class enemies, the corporate executives" and filled with irrational, indeed suicidal, wrath against the "pro-union, pro-civil rights, pro-feminist, pro-gay, pro-immigrant elitist Democrats," or *ideologically* as the workers concerned with "family values" versus those concerned with "economic interests."

We should remember that US proletarian politics has historically been often saturated by double-talk, both from the mouths of proletarians themselves and the pens of its commentators. Consequently, a sure path to confusion is to take proffered self-descriptions literally. Right-wing, rural, pro-Bush proletarians exist in the millions, but they are neither irrational nor especially suicidal. They simply assess the class forces in an extremely cold, calculating and, from an anti-capitalist perspective, pessimistic way. Thus the idea that they should unite with black, immigrant, urban workers to take on the most powerful ruling class on the planet is to them irrational and suicidal. Certainly, one can see their point, even though I for one disagree with it. Let us briefly consider each aspect of the Janus-faced US working class.

Although the official AFL-CIO has been nominally critical of the war on terrorism legislation, it has made no consistent campaign against it. Even the bitter struggle concerning unionization in the DHS and DoD has been largely conducted "behind the scenes." Up until the spring of 2006, overt workers' struggles against the new policing apparatus of the state have become local civil society struggles. Since September 11, 2001 residents in more than three hundred municipalities and the Oregon State Senate have passed resolutions defending their residents' civil rights from the threat posed by the USA PATRIOT Act, the HSA, and other pieces of the "war on terror" legislation. In many cases, this legislation is purely symbolic, since Federal law usually overrides state and local law. But these laws have nevertheless some "teeth" since they express workers' and even small capitalists' material interest in defending their local economies and social cohesion in the face of the "slave catching" ethos prized by the war on terror.

The political context of these anti-USA PATRIOT Act laws is worth examining. A good example is the passage of such a law in Portland, Maine, in March 2004 where I live. It was prompted by the surprise descent of the Border Patrol into the city of Portland (which is located about a hundred miles from the Canadian border) in the winter of 2004. The Border Patrol officers went to the markets where African and South American immigrants shopped, demanding to see immigration papers from passers by. Within hours the immigrant community was paralyzed: no one went out to work or shop, children did not go to school, the sick did not go to the hospitals. This paralysis went on for days, to the point that the local police, social service agencies, church groups and civil liberties organizations demanded that the Border Patrol agents leave the city.

A coalition of immigrant rights groups and their supporters drafted the anti-USA PATRIOT Act municipal bill immediately after this incident. The bill, which sanctioned the local officials' resistance to Federal government agencies' "fishing expeditions" in the immigrant community of Portland, even received the support of the local police leadership. A large majority in the City Council passed the bill into law because it became clear that the literal application of the provisions of the USA PATRIOT Act would make life intolerable to the immigrant workers of Portland and in turn jeopardize the economy of the city, which is increasing relying on immigrants to staff low waged jobs (especially in the tourist industry). Aside from the workers' solidarity that the law expressed, its passage was undoubtedly due to the lack of resistance from the many hotel and restaurant owners in Portland, whose greatest terror is not Osama bin Laden, but is the arrival of the Border Patrol in town at the peak of the tourist season!

The resistance to the USA PATRIOT Act was also directly challenged by immigrant workers who refused to become totally invisible in the face of enormous intimidation. For example, in the Fall of 2003, hundreds of immigrant workers undertook a "Freedom Ride" that brought them across the country, from Los Angeles to Washington, D.C., with stops in dozens of towns and cities, to make their case against the provisions of the USA PATRIOT Act and similar anti-immigrant legislation.

THE CLIMAX AND CRISIS OF THE WAR ON TERRORISM: HR4437 AND THE "SI SE PUEDE" INSURRECTION

Between the Fall of 2003 and the Spring of 2006 the immigrant workers' rights movement carried on an intense period of non-spectacular organization, largely ignored by the media, in an environment of maximum intimidation and surveillance (with millions of deportations taking place) stimulated by the anti-immigrant war on terrorism environment. Immigrant workers in this period were testing their powers and allies in a thousand small ways. But when the time came in the Spring of 2006 to massively challenge the attack on their rights sanctioned by the war on terrorism, the result of these organizational efforts was spectacular.

There were more demonstrations in more places with greater participation between March 24 and May Day 2006 than any other six-week period in US history. For a number of days marches of more than half a million people overwhelmed the centers of major cities like Los Angeles, Chicago, New York, and Dallas halting business while there were literally hundreds of smaller gatherings in cities like Charlotte, North Carolina, Milwaukee, Wisconsin, Salem, Oregon, Philadelphia, Pennsylvania. Along with the public outpouring of bodies, there were dozens of student walk outs in high schools around the country as well as a nation-wide immigrants' "general strike" called for May Day that was heeded by hundreds of thousands, perhaps millions of workers, including truck drivers who shut down the Port of Los Angeles (one of the main supply links in the commodity trade with China, South Korea, and Japan). The demonstrators' demands were: amnesty for all undocumented immigrants and the defeat of pending draconian anti-immigrant legislation. In the process, they intermittently stopped or stalled the cycle of production, circulation and reproduction in the US for this six-week period. The slogan of these remarkable demos, whose size consistently surprised both their organizers and the authorities, became "Si Se Puede" ("Yes It Is Possible" in Spanish), implying their awareness of a new political power in the Americas.

Even though the demonstrations, walkouts and strikes were remarkably orderly and non-violent, their harshest opponents, the anti-immigrant vigilante group called the Minuteman Project, described them as an "insurrection." And indeed it was an insurrection, at least in a legal sense of being an "organized opposition or resistance to a government or established authorities," because the demonstrations were largely composed of undocumented workers, their families, friends and immediate supporters who, loosely speaking, were "illegal" and "criminals" but yet were demanding that *they* ought to be "decriminalized"! By their millions they spoke the words, "We are workers not criminals!," implying that the government intent on further criminalizing them is the true criminal. Indeed, in these demonstrations the very symbol of the US, the "stars and stripes" flag, and the one that the right-wing in the US has used insufferably—especially since 9/11—as a weapon of attack on immigrants in the war on terrorism, was overturned and subtracted from the state. If anything burned the Minutemen on May Day 2006, it must have been seeing tens of thousands of USA flags in the hands of an ocean of people they called "criminal thugs" and "an invading army" containing terrorists who now made it a symbol of *their* struggle.

The obvious stimulus for the "Si Se Puede" demonstrators could be read on their banners, again and again, "HR 4437," the designation of a piece of legislation entitled "The Border Protection, Anti-Terrorism and Illegal Immigration Control Act of 2005." It is also often referred to as the "Sensenbrenner" Act after its sponsor, a Republican Congressional Representative from Michigan. The House of Representatives passed this legislation by a vote of 239–182 on Friday, Dec. 16, 2005. The title of the law says it all: this bill is the logical culmination of the USA PATRIOT Act, the HSA, and other war on terrorism legislation, for it melded the attack on immigrant workers with the war on terrorism in a truly devilish manner.

HR 4437 is what is called an "enforcement-only" bill because its conception of undocumented immigration is that of "crime control," i.e., a crime is determined and penalties are devised to punish and "control" it. First, HR 4437 defines a new legal criminal category (similar to older criminal forms of trespassing on private property, as in the game acts, but now designed for the national territory), "unlawful or illegal presence," which is any violation of any immigration law or regulation, even if it is a technical one. This crime would be considered "an aggravated felony" and, as with other aggravating crimes like "terrorist crimes," would lead to extra penalties like, in this case, indefinite detention or expedited removal as well as the denial of ordinary undocumented immigrants of many forms of administrative or judicial review. "In essence, the bill makes every immigration violation, however minor, into a federal crime" (Justice for Immigrants 2006).

Second, "anyone or any organization who 'assists' an individual without documentation 'to reside in or remain' in the US knowingly or with 'reckless disregard' as to the individual's legal status would be liable for criminal penalties and up to five years in prison." Church personnel who provide shelter or other basic needs assistance to an undocumented individual could be prosecuted under this law and "property used in this act would be subject to seizure and forfeiture" (Justice for Immigrants 2006). Union organizers in production sites where undocumented immigrants predominate could also be prosecuted. Included in this bill are also employer sanctions, i.e., it would be a crime for an undocumented person to hold a job in the US and his/her employer would be complicit in this crime. Thus HR 4437 applies the USA PATRIOT Act model in dealing with terrorist crimes to the immigrant workers as if young undocumented Nigerian workers in a North Carolina chicken-processing factory are the equivalent of Mohamed Atta and Co.!

Other aspects of this bill include:

— the DHS is required to erect up to 700 miles of fencing along the Southwest border (and further militarize the 1900-mile-long border);

— "State and local law enforcement officers are authorized to enforce federal immigration laws. State and local governments which refuse to participate would be subject to the loss of federal funding";

— "Document fraud would be considered an aggravated felony and would subject an asylum-seeker to deportation and bars to re-entry" (Justice for Immigrants 2006).

In other words, HR 4437 is the kind of law the anti-immigration movement has been calling for: one that categorizes undocumented workers as criminals and potential terrorists to be tried, convicted, jailed and then deported... pure and simple. If enacted, the bill would transform almost every person in the US (not only police officers) into either its violators, those criminally complicit with its violators, or its enforcers.

After Sensenbrenner's bill passed the House of Representatives in late December 2005, Congress went into recess and not much was immediately done legislatively to deal with it, for the second step in the legislative procedure was to be taken by the Senate. However, alarm about the law spread throughout the Catholic Church, the unions and immigrant rights organizations quickly over the Christmas holidays. I know from my comrades in the immigrant workers' rights movement that, after a decade of legislative defeats, they saw HR 4437 as their endgame. If the Sensenbrenner bill became law, they intoned, they too would be headed for prison, if they continued to do their work!

Two-and-a-half months later an amazing transformation in the immigrant

194

communities of the US took place that could only be seen by those with religious sensibilities as miraculous. The dire message concerning the impact of HR 4437 clearly reached these communities: *unless something drastic was done, the Senate would pass a similar bill and President Bush, after some griping, would sign it into law.* Undocumented immigrants especially had to make an important decision in the winter of 2006, would they take the risk of making themselves socially visible in order to protest HR 4437 after surviving in the US on the basis of their invisibility? They decided by the millions to take the risk both individually and collectively to publicly declare that they are "workers and not criminals."

These decisions marked a crisis for the war on terrorism. For the immigrant worker movement in the Spring of 2006 was no longer going to be deterred by its terrorizing ideology and atmosphere any more than the black civil rights movement in the 1950s and 1960s was held back by nuclear war-laden threats of Cold War ideology. As the black movement demanded "Justice Now!" and an immediate end to US apartheid in the midst of hydrogen-bomb testing and McCarthyite inquisitional tribunals traveling up and down the nation hunting for Communists, so too the immigrants in the "Si Se Puede" demonstrations were standing up for their rights *now* in the face of a similar ideology and atmosphere. This time, however, the atmosphere is generated by the icons of the collapsing World Trade Center towers and Osama Bin Laden instead of the Berlin Wall and Joseph Stalin.

These demonstrations had a powerful effect on the general war on terrorism and on HR4437 in particular. When a vapid ideology like that of the war on terrorism's loses its paralyzing powers, it begins to lose its *raison d'etre*. Surely the immigrant insurrection in the streets of the US slowed the political momentum behind HR 4437 the Spring of 2006. The senators bitterly debated a number of immigration bills, but they decisively rejected the option of passing a copy of the Rep. Sensenbrenner's bill. Many senators undoubtedly recognized that HR 4437 was so sweeping and draconian that it actually helped to unite the immigrants, especially the undocumented ones. They looked at the huge demonstrations and the May Day national strike with apprehension and determined that they must find a way to undermine the most powerful self-defined working class movement since the mid-1970s. On May 25th the Senate passed its own bill, S2611, innocuously entitled "The Comprehensive Immigration Reform Act," by a vote of 62–36. This bill, though it has a wide number of punitive measures similar to HR 4437, still offers possibilities for *some* of the undocumented to gain legal status.

The Senate deployed a classic strategy in this bill to defeat the immigrant workers' new power: *divide and conquer*. S2611 literally divides up the present set of undocumented immigrants into three mutually exclusive subsets: (a) those who have been in the US for less than two years, (b) those who have been in the US between two and five years and (c) those who have been in the US for more than five years. Group (a) members must leave immediately on passage of the bill or face deportation. Group (b) members "must leave the country, and apply to re-enter through some currently unknown process." Group (c) members would be allowed to stay and apply for citizenship, provided they pay back taxes, learn English and have no serious criminal records." This division, the senators clearly thought, would tempt many undocumented immigrants to turn against each other, especially those who were in Group (c).

Though this bill has other less publicized provisions that make it almost as draconian as HR 4437, it does not identify undocumented immigrant workers with either criminals or terrorists. It marks a turning of the political tide. It is not easy to predict what will happen with immigration legislation in 2006, but one thing is certain: a significant section of the US working class—the "Si Se Puede" immigrant demonstrators and their supporters—were no longer going to be controlled by a logic based upon the war on terrorism.

CONCLUSION: THE BEGINNING OF THE END OF THE WAR ON TERRORISM?

> According to some, however, [Janus] is simply the god of doorways (janueae) and in this connexion is the patron of entrances and beginnings....
> *Encyclopedia Britannica*, Eleventh Edition (1910–1911).

The war on terrorism is now facing for the first time a serious proletarian resistance in the strikes and mass demonstrations of immigrant workers, but it has also inspired substantial support from many US workers. These workers include those who are finding new jobs in the branches of industry directly stimulated by this war, from "conventional weapons" manufacturing to "anti-terrorism" accountancy. It is worthwhile to recognize that the most obvious constituency for it are the tens of thousands of US contract workers who are presently in Iraq and Afghanistan working as accountants, cooks, in construction, but especially in security-type jobs. Squads of Americans with Special Forces experience have been hired for tasks ranging from airport security to protecting senior US officials in Iraq. Their salaries can be as high as $1,000 a day, as the news agency Agence France-Presse (AFP) recently reported. For example, Erwin, a 28-year-old former US army sergeant working in Iraq, told AFP: "This place is a gold-mine. All you need is five years in the military and you come here and make a good bundle." But even a truck driver or a fireman can earn more than three times what s/he can in the US. For these workers the war on terrorism has provided (at the cost of great personal risk) the possibility of escaping the debt cycle they and their families have been trapped in.

The war on terrorism is also generating many less risky local jobs for US citizen workers (paying much less, however, than Iraq-duty). Its most obvious employment effect has been (and will be) a tremendous increase in the number of prison guards (from 146,000 in 1983 to 328,000 in 2002), police officers, and security guards. However, much of what is classified under the rubric of "computer and data processing services"—the most rapidly growing employment category in the US (cf. the Statistical Abstract of the US 2003: Table No. 620) — will also be expanded due to the data processing aspects of the surveillance state.

The expansion of surveillance work, demanded by the USA PATRIOT Act and the related Bank Security Act, has already generated a crisis in the banking system. These laws require banks, insurance companies, hedge funds and mutual funds to file "suspicious activity reports" (SARs) with the government, if they detect money laundering or terrorist financing (Kelleher 2004). Thus, one of the oldest banks in the US, the Riggs Bank was fined in a civil court proceeding in May of 2004 a penalty of $25 million for not reporting suspicious activity in the accounts controlled by Teodoro Obiang, the President of Equiritoral Guinea, and Prince Bandar bin Sultan, Saudi Arabia's ambassador to the US. On top of that fine, Riggs Bank pleaded guilty on January 27, 2005 and paid an additional $16 million to a criminal court in order to avoid prosecution on charges related to money laundering under the Bank Security Act. As an expert in the detection of money laundering said of the Riggs Bank, it provides "a textbook case study of most of the money-laundering issues that have surfaced since the Patriot Act." It was certainly not alone in facing sanctions, in October of 2004 AmSouth Bank of Alabama paid a similar $10 million penalty along with $40 million in a deferred prosecution agreement for poor money-laundering controls.

There is a conceptual problem here, for what counts as suspicious, or as John Byrne, a senior lawyer with the American Bankers Association, asked, "What is due diligence?" In other words, the economic sector that has been the driving force behind the exponential growth in globalized financial transactions is now made responsible for monitoring this gigantic planetary flow of money, in order to block a minuscule amount of "terrorist funding" (we have been told that the whole September 11 operation required a mere $500,000). Such monitoring will require another army of analysts, computer programmers, accountants, and lawyers—the more so since the task at hand is so inherently ambiguous. Surely, in this case too, the employment possibilities are endless and will undoubtedly create a self-reproducing constituency supporting the war on terrorism (as well as to continue to generate more internal contradictions within the ruling class!)

Finally, the war on terrorism has brought about a tremendous increase in the US defense budget that in 2004–05 was about $500 billion whereas in 2000–01 it was about $300 million. This too is undoubtedly having a large employment effect and is creating still another constituency for the war on terrorism.

But along with the immediate sources of support from workers on the war on terrorism's payroll there is another, more indirect, but larger source: the segment of US-born workers who are increasingly feeling that they face competition for low waged "unskilled" jobs from immigrants (both legal and illegal). This sentiment is given support by economists like George Borjas who mistakenly claim that there is data to prove that the wages of US-born high-school dropouts are 8 percent lower than what they would have been if there were few unskilled immigrants (Borjas 2004). And surely, many of these US-born workers imagine that if the 4.9% percent of the present working class which is now made up of undocumented immigrant workers were suddenly deported, there would be plenty of jobs at the "lower" end of the labor market for them (Passel 2006). Thus, in December 2005, there were 4.1 million job openings and 7.4 million unemployed workers, a tough situation for an "unskilled" person. However, if suddenly there were millions of new job openings (and fewer unemployed workers) this disadvantage would be reversed and native-born workers could bid up wages. After all, dreams of apocalyptic "solutions" to the problems caused by capitalism are not the monopoly of neo-con intellectuals discoursing in plush seminar rooms.

In fact, these facts have created the humus for the Minuteman Project that claims to represent the interest of all legally authorized US workers. Though rooted in the patriotic white man's mythology — after all "the Minutemen" was the name of the members of the militia that fought the British in the first phase of the Revolutionary War—their self-definition cleverly eschews the traditional right-wing racist paraphernalia and even boasts an Office of Economic Opportunity (OEO)-style disclaimer on its website: "The Minuteman Project has no affiliation with, nor will we accept any assistance by or interference from, separatists, racists, or supremacy groups or individuals, no matter what their race, color, or creed." The Minutemen looked at the millions of immigrant workers demonstrating and striking in the period between March 25 and May Day and saw only "insurrection and mockery of the rule of law."

They claim that in this period "The phone at the Minuteman Project is literally ringing off the hook" and I, for one, believe them. For they clearly speak for many workers who have been facing more than three decades of declining real wages. These workers (and their capitalist allies) have decided to attack other workers *qua* immigrants (especially the undocumented) as the source of their anxiety and powerlessness instead of directing their anger at an increasingly wealthy top 1 percent of the population (which has "grabbed an astonishing 38.4 percent of the total income produced over a [twenty-one, 1979–2000] year period") or attacking the use of union-busting, regressive tax legislation, the declining purchasing power of the minimum wage, and, most important, the impact of "trade-related" reforms which "have given employers a gigantic club with which to threaten workers and obtain wage concessions from them" (Yates 2005).

They apparently believe that if unauthorized workers are stopped at the border and deported from the interior of the country, wages and job security for US-born workers would increase. That conclusion is warranted neither by the facts nor by reasoned argument. Given the present balance of forces between capitalists and workers in the US, any tightness in the labor market will probably not lead to substantially higher wages in the long run, unless rigid controls on the movement of capital are imposed. Without these restrictions on capital movement, capitalists can simply move productive activities out of the country as well as use a savagely divided working class (the result of the anger, bitterness and despair among the "legal" immigrant proletarians caused by the deportation of millions of family members, friends and comrades) and the police powers of a much more draconian "war on terrorism" state to abort the kind of unified struggle required to achieve higher wages and more secure working conditions across the board and for the long-term.

But in class politics a logical failure in strategy can only be explained by the motivations of support for the strategy. In the case of the Minuteman Project it perhaps lies in the character of the white working class in the "Bush recovery" from the 2001 recession. This period has been marked by a number of labor market anomalies. The most important ones for us are the duration of long-term unemployment (more than 20 percent of the unemployed) and the decline in labor force participation rates (66 percent). In both cases, one would have expected a substantial decline for the first and a substantial increase for the second index during a business cycle recovery. As Michael Yates notes, however, "[b]etween 2000 and 2003, the highest growth in long-term unemployment occurred among those with a bachelor's degree or higher, those forty-five and older, those in management and professional occupations, and those in industries such as information and professional and business services, men, and whites" (Yates 2005).

In other words, the anxiety of finding oneself "off the map" in "one's own country" is becoming a reality for more and more white men in the most profound way: through their jobs (or lack of them). The "white man's" deal is being threatened with the crisis of Neoliberalism and in response some of them have not only gone to the border to terrorize and detain border crossers, but to also try to locate and disrupt the typical places where undocumented workers go to be hired within the US.

The legal atmosphere introduced with the war on terrorism has intensified this strategy of the fear of "the alien other" (in a society specializing in the incorporation of others' labor powers). Thus the "leaky" border has become in much right-wing rhetoric after Sept. 11, 2001 an "invitation to terrorists to enter into the US and cause harm." So the Minuteman Project provides an employment strategy for native-born workers who see their future in being the policemen, guards and foremen of the world working class, since the realization of their efforts (the arrest, incarceration and deportation of all undocumented immigrants) will lead to a major building boom of new prisons holding millions of additional prisoners, even though US prisons presently hold 2,135,901 prisoners (the largest number in the world), with an incarceration rate of 724 prisoners per 100,000 inhabitants (the highest in the world) (*International Herald*

Tribune, May 12, 2006: 20). Indeed, earlier this year Halliburton's subsidiary Kellogg, Root and Brown was awarded a $385 million government contract to build "temporary immigration detention facilities" with capacity to hold 5,000 people each with many more contracts to come (migramatters.com). This would be just the beginning, if HR 4437 is passed into law.

The Janus-faced US working class (one composed of immigrants and native-born workers seeing their future in an upsurge of wage struggle based on the achievement of full immigrant rights, and the other seeing their future as the guardians of the US government's role as hegemonic controller and "decider" of the world market and frontline repressor of anti-capitalist aspirations in the US and across the planet) is now in struggle with itself over the fate of the war on terrorism. It is not clear which one of the two faces actually sees the future, but it is clear that this spring's "Si Se Puede" Insurrection has openly challenged the war on terrorism and has taken the initiative from the Bush Administration. Bush's supporters are now involved in their own internal struggle over the proper response to the Insurrection as illustrated by the intensifying division between the supporters of HR 4437 and S 2611. In this fog of struggle, however, the mesmerizing power of the war on terrorism is noticeably waning.

REFERENCES

Bales, Kevin 2000. *Disposable People: New Slavery in the Global Economy.* Berkeley: University of California Press.

Borjas, George 2004. Increasing the Supply of Labor Through Immigration: Measuring the Impact on Native-born Workers. *Center for Immigration Studies* (May). http://www.cis.org.articles/2004/back504.html

Caffentzis, George 2001. From Capitalist Crisis to Proletarian Slavery: An Introduction to the US Class Struggle. In Midnight Notes 2001.

Clawson, Dan 2003. *The Next Upsurge: Labor and the New Social Movements.* Ithaca, NY: Cornell University Press.

Chang, Nancy 2002. *Silencing Political Dissent: How Post-September 11 Anti-Terrorism Measures Threaten Our Civil Liberties.* New York: Seven Stories Press.

Cole, David 2003. *Enemy Aliens: Double Standards and Constitutional Freedoms in the War on Terrorism.* New York: The New Press.

Collins, Chuck and Felice Yeskel 2000. *Economic Apartheid in America: A Primer on Economic Inequality and Insecurity.* New York: New Press.

Dash, Eric 2005. Riggs Pleads Guilty in Money-Laundering Case. *New York Times,* January 28.

Department of Defense 2005. National Security Personnel System—Proposed Regulations. Department of Defense (February 10).

DeFreitas, Gregory. 1993. "Unionization among Racial and Ethnic Minorities." *Industrial and Labor Relations Review,* 46.

Federici, Silvia 2004. *Caliban and the Witch: Women, the Body and Primitive Accumulation*. New York: Autonomedia.

Hardt, Michael and Antonio Negri 2000. *Empire*. Cambridge, MA: Harvard University Press.

Harrington, Michael and Paul Jacobs (eds) 1960. *Labor in a Free Society*. Berkeley: University of California Press.

International Herald Tribune (IHT) 2006. Behind Bars. *IHT* (may 12).

Justice for Immigrants 2006. Major Provisions of HR4437. www.justiceforimmigrants.org/HR4437.

Kelleher, Ellen 2004. The law that outlaws banks. *Financial Times* (July 9).

Linebaugh, Peter 2002. *The London Hanged: Crime and Civil Society in Eighteenth-Century London*. 2nd Edition. London: Verso.

Lukas, J. Anthony 1997. *Big Trouble: A Murder in a Small Western Town Sets Off a Struggle for the Soul of America*. New York: Simon and Shuster.

Midnight Notes (eds) 1992. *Midnight Oil: Work, Energy, War 1973–1992*. New York: Autonomedia.

Midnight Notes (eds) 2001. *Auroras of the Zapatistas: Local and Global Struggles in the Fourth World War*. New York: Autonomedia.

Passel, Jeffrey 2006. Size and Characteristics of the Unauthorized Migrant Population in the US. Pew Hispanic Center. http://pewhispanic.org/reports/print.php?ReportID=61.

Prashad, Vijay 2003. *Keeping Up with the Dow Joneses: Debt, Prison, Workfare*. Boston: South End Press.

The Public Health and Labor Institutes 1997. *Corporate Power and the American Dream: Toward an Economic Agenda for Working People*. New York: The Apex Press.

US Dept. of Commerce 2003. *Statistical Abstract of the US 2003*. Washington, DC: US Government Printing Office.

US Dept. of Commerce 2006. *Statistical Abstract of the US 2006*. Washington, DC: US Government Printing Office.

Wolman, William and Anne Colamosca 1997. *The Judas Economy: The Triumph of Capital and the Betrayal of Work*. Reading, MA: Addison-Wesley Publishing Co.

Yates, Michael D. 1994. *Longer Hours, Fewer Jobs: Employment and Unemployment in the United States*. New York: Monthly Review Press.

Yates, Michael 2005. The Statistical Portrait of the US Working Class. *Monthly Review* (April).

12

Reinventing An/Other Anti-Capitalism in Mexico
The Sixth Declaration of the EZLN & the "Other Campaign"

Patrick Cuninghame[1]

*Well, then, in Mexico what we want to create is an agreement with
people and organizations that are decidedly of the left, because we
believe that it is on the political left where the idea of resisting
against neoliberal globalisation really lives, and the struggle to
make justice, democracy, and freedom in any country wherever it
would be, where there is only freedom for big business and there is
only democracy to put up election campaign signs. And because we
believe that only the left can come up with a plan for struggle so
that our country, Mexico, does not die. And, then, what we believe
is that, with these people and organizations of the left, we will chart
a course to go to every corner of Mexico where there are humble
and simple people like ourselves.*
(The Sixth Declaration of the Lacandona Jungle, 2005)

*The struggles of dignity tear open the fabric of capitalist domina-
tion. (John Holloway, 2003)*

PREFACE

This chapter seeks to draw some lessons at a global level from the ongoing "Other Campaign" (so-called in mock reference to the 2006 presidential electoral campaigns), catalysed by the Zapatistas with their call
for a renewed anti-capitalist resistance movement "from below and to the left"
against neoliberal capitalism in Mexico and internationally, in the Sixth Declaration of the Lacandona Jungle (the Sixth) in July 2005. The chapter also
focuses on how the organization and mobilization of the Other Campaign is
evolving in the trans-border region of Chihuahua–Texas–New Mexico in

Northern Mexico–Southern USA (where the author is based) around the attempted horizontal coordination of autonomists, anarchists, Zapatistas, socialists, indigenous and peasant movements, and the efforts to include independent trade unions and the more radical NGO campaigns against the femicide of some 450 working-class women and girls in Ciudad Juarez since 1993, as well as other issues based around migration, the US–Mexico border, the hegemonic maquiladora (corporate assembly plant for export) hyper-exploitation model and the social violence and urban degradation produced by "savage capitalism."

This "other" organizational paradigm, which includes the "Other on the other side" (of the border), will be also be connected with the May Day Latino boycott movement in the US against the criminalisation of undocumented migrants. The broader socio-political context is framed by the events surrounding the July 2006 presidential elections, which proved to be particularly "dirty" and fraudulent, despite the consensus among the three candidates of the main parties on the need to consolidate through "institutional reforms" the neo-liberal model (constructed on the 1994 NAFTA agreement), which seeks to extend a deepened US economic hegemony over Latin America through the 2001 Puebla–Panama Plan, the 2005 Central Americas Free Trade Agreement (CAFTA) and the recently shelved Free Trade Area of the Americas (FTAA) proposal. The desperate, cynical capitulation of the "vertical" left,[2] both parliamentary and extra-parliamentary (including some ex-Zapatista supporters and much of the post-1968 New Left) to the populist, demagogic presidential campaign of the centre-left Partido Revolucionario Democratico (PRD) candidate Andres Manuel Lopez Obrador (AMLO), some on the basis of keeping the corrupt mafia-linked Partido Revolucionario Institutional (PRI) and Christian right-ultra neoliberal Partido Acción Nacional (PAN) out of power, others in the hope of benefiting personally from future presidential largesse, mirrors a deeper crisis as a divided global anti-capitalism seeks to intensify resistance against an increasingly fragmented and degenerate "global war capitalism." This helps to explain why the EZLN and its global network, under the title of the "Zezta Internazional," are also organizing a third "Intergalactic Encuentro" in late 2006–early 2007, faced with the perceived neo-reformist inefficacy of the now verticalist-controlled and Chavez-dependent World Social Forum (WSF).[3] The chapter also examines the impact of the particularly brutal repression of the Atenco movement, the Oaxaca teachers' strike and APPO movement and AMLO's orchestrated but massive anti-fraud movement on the Other, before reaching some conclusions on the present state of anti-capitalism (autonomist, Zapatista and other/wise) in Mexico, and the implications for "the slow and laborious process of consolidating the new Latin American revolutionary left" (Cuban Libertarian Movement/CLM 2005: 1) and global anti-capitalist and alter-globalist movements.

Introduction

Mexico, as the USA's southern neighbour, is the Latin American country most directly prone to North American influence and pressure, now being virtually hard-wired into its economy through the North American Free Trade Agreement (NAFTA) since 1994. However, that year also saw the birth of the Zapatista rebellion in Chiapas in opposition to NAFTA, neoliberalism and 500 years of the racist discrimination and exclusion of the Mexican indigenous population, composed of over fifty ethnic groups each with its own language and culture, accounting for about 15% of its 110 million population. Twelve years on and the remarkably resilient and unceasingly creative Zapatistas have bounced back yet again into the centre of national political life and international mobilisation through the Other Campaign, launched by the Sixth Declaration of the Lacandona Jungle in July 2005, which marked a definitive rupture with the PRD and the liberal urban intelligentsia, once united in their opposition to the PRI dictatorship 10 years previously. The new "enemy" was identified as AMLO, the moderate PRD presidential candidate, at that time the clear favourite to win the 2006 elections. His party had betrayed the Zapatistas and the indigenous peoples in 2001 when they broke their word and supported the enactment of an unrecognisably diluted PAN government version of the San Andres Accord on Indigenous Autonomy, reached with the then PRI government in 1996. Furthermore, as Mayor of Mexico City he had shown a preference for pharaonic building projects, zero-tolerance policing against the vendors of the "informal economy," the main source of income for many of the city's 18 million population, and attempts to expel rooted proletarian communities and gentrify the historic centre in association with Mexico's richest entrepreneur Carlos Slim. The result has been a bitter division with the peasant and urban working-class grassroots of the PRD, where some wanted to support both AMLO and the Other Campaign, while many, including some former Zapatista intellectual sympathisers, considered the Zapatistas to have become the unwitting stooges of the right, as part of its plot against AMLO.

The suspicion of both technologically sophisticated cybernetic fraud and cruder old-fashioned ballot stuffing has hung over the elections of July 2, which favoured the ultra neoliberal, Christian right PAN candidate Felipe Calderon by 0.5% or just over 240,000 of the total vote of 41 million (Burbach 2006; Palast 2006). The brutal repression in May of the Peoples Front for the Defence of the Land (FPDT), and Other Campaign activists in Atenco caused a global wave of revulsion against the Fox "government of change," as brutal and fraudulent as its PRI predecessors. The Other Campaign — the first attempt in Mexican history to create a coordinated anti-capitalist network "below and to the left" among the splintered groups, movements and unaffiliated individuals to the left of the PRD — in the space of a few weeks in May transformed itself from a support network for the caravan of "Delegate Zero" (Subcomandante Marcos) and the Sixth Commission into a cohesive national and transnational (thanks to the "Otra en el Otro Lado" [Other Campaign in the USA]) movement with strong links to the anticapitalist alter-global movements. Nevertheless, compared to AMLO's multitudinous marches of a million and a half on July 16 and over two million on the 30th, hundreds of thousands of whom still remained camped in Mexico City's main square, central avenues and business district in protest against the electoral fraud, the Other's national march against repression of 15,000 in late May and only 5,000 on July 2nd seem tiny in comparison. The AMLO anti-fraud movement allegedly is financed by the local construction industry that benefited so handsomely under his mayorship, as well as by the PRD through its various state governors, senators and deputies and is — at least for the moment — directly orchestrated by AMLO and the PRD leadership, who have promised the increasingly worried press, international investors and Mexican business class to send everyone home as soon as a total recount is agreed. The Other or "Otra" has established itself as a consolidated transnational movement in less than a year, while AMLO's chances of turning the tables on the neoliberal right and its support from Bush, thanks to an impressive popular mobilization which exceeds the electoral base of the PRD, seem however ever slimmer.

Since the publication of the Sixth in 2005, a feud has raged among left intellectuals as to whether the Other is part of a rightist plot to frustrate the centre-left yet again, as happened in 1988 when fraud permitted the PRI's Carlos Salinas, later the architect of NAFTA and still seen as the *eminence grise* of Mexican politics, to steal the election from Cuauhtemoc Cardenas, son of the PRI president and "national revolutionary" General Lazaro Cardenas who expropriated and nationalized the oil industry in the 1930s. Former Zapatista sympathisers like Araujo, Poniatowska and Monsivais are now part of AMLO's entourage, which has constantly attacked the Other in the press, accusing it of naivety and opportunism over Atenco and of complicity with the Right. Others like Almeyra (2006a, b, c) Olivares Alonso (2006) and Ross (2006) have attempted to remain critically detached from both camps, claiming more sympathy with the broader Zapatista movement, while heavily criticising Marcos and the EZLN's "sectarianism," "voluntarism" and "disrespect" for the autonomy of the Zapatista communities which have been "forced" to cut themselves off from the outside world once again by the "red alert" since May. These accusations have led Marcos to criticise some intellectuals as fence-sitting cowards (Bellinghausen 2006c) and to a storm of disagreement with Ross in particular from the Other (Barrios Cabrera 2006). Others like Lopez y Rivas (2006) and Gonzalez Casanova (Bellinghausen 2006) defend the Other Campaign, while seeking to reopen relations with AMLO and the PRD. In contrast, Subcomandante Marcos has been relentless in his criticism of AMLO and the PRD as the real enemy of both the Otra and the Mexican working class, since their "alternative national project" will breathe new life and legitimacy into the notoriously corrupt Mexican political system and the orthodox neoliberal model it serves, and will inevitably break their promises to put "the poor first for the benefit of all" (AMLO's electoral slogan). Other academics close to the Zapatista movement like Harvey (2005) and Holloway (2002b, 2003) seek to defend the Zapatistas from their detractors within the global revolutionary left, while analysing the EZLN's paradoxical inability to capitalise on its enormous global political capital to help foment lasting social, economic and democratic change from below, as has happened in Ecuador and Bolivia where strong indigenous movements have helped to topple unpopular neoliberal governments.

Having established the political basis for the rupture of the EZLN with the institutional and much of the historical Mexican left as the backdrop to the Other Campaign, the following section will explore in greater detail the proposals outlined in the Sixth Declaration and how they have panned out in the trajectory of the Other and its international sister campaign, the "Zezta" or Intergalactic Commission of the EZLN.

"THE SIXTH," "THE OTHER" AND THE "ZEZTA"

In common with the first five Declarations, the Sixth as event marks a turning point in the Zapatista struggle and as text communicates to national and international "civil society"[4] the decisions of the Zapatista assemblies through the EZLN and Marcos. The Sixth was initially greeted with positive statements by the Mexican political and intellectual classes as a sign of the EZLN's further move away from armed struggle and towards non-violent democratic politics. In fact non-violence is stressed throughout the document as the basis for direct action, in common with most of the alterglobalist movement but in continued rupture with the history, ideology and praxis of both Mexican and Latin American vanguardist guerrilla movements:

> The EZLN continues its commitment toward an offensive cease-fire and will not attack any governmental force nor carry out offensive military manoeuvres; the EZLN continues, still, its commitment to insisting on the path of political struggle with this peaceful proposal that we now make. As such, the EZLN will continue in its belief in not making any secret alliance with national politico-military organizations nor those of other countries; the EZLN reiterates it commitment to defend, support, and obey the Zapatista indigenous communities that create it and that are its supreme command, and, without interfering in their internal democratic processes and in the measurement of its possibilities, to contribute to the strengthening of their autonomy, good government, and improvement of living conditions. That is to say, what we are going to create in Mexico and in the world we will create without weapons, through a peaceful civil movement, yet without ignoring or abandoning our communities. (EZLN 2005: 3–4)

The right was particularly happy about the severe criticisms made of AMLO and the PRD, which seemed to promise a divided "left." The Zapatistas and the Other, however, do not consider the PRD to be any longer a party of the "left," or at least only of the top-down variety. In fact, the Sixth has reinvigorated the debate over the meaning of this historically ambiguous political category and identity, born during the French Revolution of 1789, which anarchist, autonomist and libertarian groups in the Other generally reject as obsolete and meaningless, given the objectively pro-capitalist position of most of the historical left, whether social-democrat, institutional socialist or (ex-)communist. Another reflection on the meaning of "left" within the Sixth as "utopia" is provided by the Cuban Libertarian Movement (2005: 1–2):

> (...) left is the one that has not renounced utopia neither by word or deed, and that, in spite of everything, finds its main encouragement in a utopia that could be generally defined as a thick web of relationships among free, equal and mutually supportive beings; a utopia capable of identifying its distant and venerable beginnings and of reclaiming them for their much needed actualisation. (...) This is the left that has learned to recognize and look askance at the narrow, dry road left in the wake of the guerrilla vanguards later become some exclusive and excluding party, civil or military populism and social-democratic reformism; this is the left that doesn't feel represented by any authority and even questions the meaning of "representation," that seeks itself among the cries of "let them all go!" ["Que se vayan todos!," the slogan of the December 2001 revolts in Argentina] and the whispering promise to "change the world without taking power" [Holloway 2002a]; the left that depends on the non-negotiable autonomy of grassroots social movements as the template for a new world and that in self-management and direct action finds its truest expression. A left that surely the EZLN wants to belong to and that, in open reciprocity, finds in it one of its most visible manifestations.

However, the initial enthusiasm of Fox et al. for the Sixth added grist to the mill of the Zapatistas' critics in academic left and PRD circles. Adopting a neo-Stalinist version of the theory of the "extremes that touch," critics like Almeyra have ranted against the Sixth and the Other in their columns in *La Jornada*, the only leftist national daily newspaper and close to the PRD, as evidence that the Other is, wittingly or not, part of the Fox-Salinas anti-AMLO plot, and therefore objectively a reactionary movement, unless it corrects itself and allies itself with AMLO. However, since the repression of the movement at Atenco in May, such conspiracy-theory charges have lost the illusory credence they may initially have had.

The organization of the Other campaign began in August 2005 with a series of meetings between the different sectors of what the Zapatistas continue to refer to as "civil society" convoked by the Sixth and the EZLN in the "Caracol" of La Realidad, the traditional meeting place, in the Lacandona jungle near to the border with Guatemala, of the EZLN and its allies. Through these meetings with core organizations and groups prepared to coordinate the Other throughout the various federal entities of Mexico, the Other's strategy was discussed and decided through the direct democracy of the assembly. All groups, movements and individuals who accept the organizational principles of forming an anti-capitalist alliance "below and to the left" could become "adherents" to the Sixth and participants in the Other. "Below" implies bottom-up, grassroots self-organization among the rural and urban working class and poor, eschewing relations with more privileged strata like intellectuals, small entrepreneurs etc. whose support the EZLN once sought 10 years previously. "To the left" signifies that the Other is both theoretically and practically anti-capitalist, to distinguish it from the ambiguous and opportunist left, particularly the PRD, which in the past used an anti-capitalist discourse in the form of orthodox Marxism and socialist politics, mainly as a rhetorical window-dressing exercise and always subordinated to the discourses of "patriotism" and "national sovereignty," i.e., the interests of those sectors of the national bourgeoisie opposed to global capitalism. As for the Other's plan of action in Mexico, guidelines had already been set out in the Sexta:

In Mexico…

1. We will continue fighting for the Indian peoples of Mexico but not only for them nor only with them, but, rather, for all the exploited and dispossessed in Mexico (…) And when we speak of all the exploited of Mexico we are also speaking of the brothers and sisters who have had to go to the United States to seek work in order to survive.

2. We are going to listen to and speak directly, without middlemen nor mediations, to the simple and humble Mexican people, and depending on what we hear and learn, we will construct, together with these people who are like us, humble and simple, a national plan for struggle, but a plan that will, clearly, be of the left, which is to say anti-capitalist, or anti-neoliberal, or which is also to say in favour of justice, democracy and freedom for the Mexican people.

3. We will try to construct or reconstruct another way of practicing politics, in the spirit of serving others, without material interests, with sacrifice, with dedication, with honesty, a way that keeps it word, or, that is to say, in the same way that militants of the left — who were not stopped by violence, jail or death, and much less with offers of dollar bills — have done so.

4. We will also keep looking at ways to rise up; a fight to demand that we create a new Constitution, (…) new laws that take our demands, those of the Mexican people, into account, which are: housing, land, work, food, health, education, information, culture, independence,

democracy, justice, freedom and peace. A new Constitution that recognizes the rights and liberties of the people, and that defends the weak against the powerful (EZLN 2005:5).

Point four has been particularly controversial for the autonomist-anarchist-libertarian groups within or sympathetic to the Other, who reject constitutionalism as the gateway to institutional politics and the bourgeois "political game" of partial, retractable "human rights" and "individual liberties," always dependent on the fundamental "duty" of obedience to the "democratic" capitalist state (CLM 2005). Nevertheless, perhaps this is too narrow a reading of the word "constitution," which after all figures centrally in the thought of one of autonomism's most important thinkers, Toni Negri (1992), whose theory of "constituent power" recognises how the counter-power of historical and actual movements tends to constitute a new set of social relations, which either breaks with previous ones or forces them to negotiate a new "constituted power," following which the antagonistic force of the movement tends to be institutionalised and co-opted under the terms of the new "constitution" and its "institutions," so catalysing a new cycle of antagonist movements to struggle against the former antagonists. One needs to look no further than the history of the incessant struggle between the revolutionary and reformist left during the 20th century. Thus the Other, if it becomes the hegemonic antagonist force in Mexican politics, will have to "constitute" new social relations and political balances as one of its unwritten tasks.

The organizational principles of the Other are assembleist, horizontal, anti-electoral, anti-delegatory and directly democratic, but to what extent these principles are consistently practiced, given the overwhelming prestige of the EZLN and Marcos within the Other, remains to be seen:

> — We also announce that the EZLN will establish a policy of having alliances with non-electoral movements and organizations that define themselves, in theory and practice, as of the left, according to the following conditions:

> — No making of agreements from above to impose upon those below, but rather, they should make agreements to advance together and to listen and to organize indignation;

> — No to beginning movements that will be later negotiated away behind the backs of those who made them, but, rather, they should take into account, always, the opinions of those who participate in them;

> — No to seeking little gifts, jobs, advantages, patronage, of Power or of those who aspire to it, but, rather, they should go farther than the electoral calendars allow;

— No to trying to resolve from above the problems of our Nation, but rather, they must construct FROM BELOW AND FOR BELOW an alternative to neoliberal destruction, an alternative of the left for Mexico;

— Yes to mutual respect for autonomy and independence of organizations, of their ways of fighting, of their way of organizing themselves, of their internal decision-making processes, of their legitimate representatives, of their aspirations and demands;

— And, yes, to mutual respect and autonomy and independence and yes to a clear commitment of mutual and coordinated defence of national sovereignty, and with intransigent opposition to the attempts to privatise electricity, oil, water and natural resources. (Ibid.: 6–7)

It is evident that these conditions exclude the instrumental politics of the institutional left, but also of the "revolutionary left" that seeks state power. The second "no" is particularly topical, given the manipulation of popular outrage over the electoral fraud of July 2nd by the PRD leadership to create a "designer revolt" (Gibler 2006b), which now faces not only imminent violent repression by the protofascist Mexican state, but also the perpetual danger of betrayal through backroom negotiations by its "leaders." At the same time these organisational conditions present problems for the left-wing of the Other, uncomfortable with traditional anti-imperialist politics and notions of "national sovereignty" that do not problematise its basis in the dominance of the national bourgeois classes and it use of nationalist ideology to manipulate and divide the global working class, even when nationalism may appear to have a "progressive," "anti-Yankee" face in Mexico. It remains to be seen, therefore, to what extent the EZLN and other more historical left groups within the Other can go beyond the limitations of Guevarist "left nationalism," still the dominant ideology within the Mexican and Latin American radical left, although increasingly criticised by the growth of autonomism and anarchism in recent years.

The Other also seeks to separate itself from the verticalist traditions of Marxist-Leninist vanguardism, rejecting both the pyramid model of organization and its historical objective, the seizing of state power as the means to constitute a socialist society, organized as a mirror image of hierarchical capitalist society. From the start the EZLN made it clear that it would not be forming the "leadership" of the Other, much to the chagrin of the verticalists, democratic centralists, propagators of the Marcos personality cult and believers in "charismatic leaders" among the orthodox left:

And we don't come to you to tell you what you should do nor to give you orders. Nor are we going to ask you to vote for a candidate, since we already know that the only candidates are neoliberals. Nor are we going to tell you to do what we do, nor that you should rise up in arms. What we are going to do is ask you how your lives are going, your struggles, your thoughts about how our country is doing and about what we can do so that they don't defeat us (...) And maybe (...) together, we will organize throughout the entire country and come to an agreement between our struggles that, right now, fight alone, separated from one another, and we will come up with a plan about how we will continue with this program that includes what we all want, and a plan for how we are going to achieve this program, that is named "the national plan for struggle".... (EZLN 2005: 2–3)

Nevertheless, Delegate Zero is without doubt the *primus inter pares* of the Other, as could be observed at the First National Assembly on May 29, when he informed the Assembly, supposedly the highest decisionary body of the Other, of the EZLN's "National Plan for Struggle" up to and including election day on July 2nd to free the Atenco prisoners, leaving the Assembly to rubberstamp it, rather than debate, discuss and if necessary criticise and amend it, given the lack of time to do so (only 15 minutes of discussion time remained for each set of state and regional delegates to give their opinion on the proposal as the independent cinema where the Assembly was held was about to shut for the night).

In keeping with most of the global anti-capitalist movement, many within the Other are diffident about such "grand narratives" as socialism, communism, autonomism and anarchism or any preordained blueprint to change society "from above," although within its ranks are some of the most dogmatic Marxist-Leninists in Mexico, the Maoist "Communist Party of Mexico (Marxist Leninist)" whose huge banners of Marx, Lenin, Engels, Stalin and Mao have adorned every meeting and march of the Other's caravan, to the consternation of many within the Other and the derision of its critics (Almeyra 2006a; Sanchez Ramirez 2006).[5] In probably unintentional accordance with the autonomist theory of "multitude" (Hardt & Negri: 2000, 2004; Virno: 2004), these archaic images, once the icons of organized working class centrality, are accepted along with the hammer and sickle, anarchist and autonomist symbols, images of Zapata, Villa, Magon and Che Guevara, and perhaps even the Virgin of Guadalupe, a religious image used in the past by Zapatista indigenous women on their International Women's Day marches through San Cristobal, Chiapas, and an integral part of revived popular Latino identity in the US, as one more part of the Other's baggage, which above all contains the history of class struggle in Mexico.

The Zapatista slogan of "walking by asking" (*caminando preguntando*), i.e. moving forward in the struggle against and beyond capitalism by constantly questioning and criticizing both our own ideological and organizational assumptions, and the constantly changing and amorphous political and social environment produced by the clash between capitalist high-tech and human globalisations, has returned to Mexico in the cycles of global struggle to reinfuse the Other, via the absorption of that slogan by the alterglobalist movement since the "Battle of Seattle."

The Other Campaign officially began on January 1st 2006, exactly twelve years after the uprising against NAFTA, when Delegate Zero left La Realidad, Chiapas, on the back of a motorbike headed for the first of four months of daily meetings, speeches, protests and marches as he, the Sixth Commission and the Other Campaign caravan, made up of the groups in the Other and the Zezta close to the EZLN, like the "Disobedient" (ex-White Overalls) now global movement for example, wound their way through the southern and central states of Mexico. The Other has catalysed the organization of previously non-existent anti-capitalist movement networks, involving previously disparate struggles and rival groups, and the intensification of those already in place. It has also provoked a growing chorus of criticisms from pro-AMLO quarters, although AMLO himself has been careful to abstain from directly criticising Delegate Zero or the Other. However, the general tone of the Other had been intentionally low-key and focused on organization rather than propaganda, with Delegate Zero refusing to give interviews and the Other barring the mainstream press from its meetings and events, ignoring the total media coverage of the choreographed presidential campaigns.6 The events of May 3 and 4 in and around Atenco, a small town near Mexico City where in 2002 the local population had mobilized to defend their communally-owned "ejido"7 land and prevent the construction of a multi-billion dollar international airport, inflicting a stinging defeat on Fox and his international backers, pushed both Marcos and the Other back into the national and international limelight. By that time the Other had already reached Mexico City, its stronghold outside Chiapas due to the presence of the UNAM students' movement and the dozens of social movements and grassroots organizations spawned by the daily struggles of life in the "Monster." Since those events, Delegate Zero has remained in Mexico City to coordinate the Other's efforts to free the political prisoners remaining from the Atenco mass arrests, declared "red alert" in the Chiapas Zapatista communities and suspended indefinitely the rest of the Other Campaign's tour around northern Mexico, where both the institutional left and grassroots movements are fewer and weaker.

The organization of the "Zezta Internazional" (in mock reference, perhaps, to both Inter Milan's acceptance of Marcos' invitation last year to play a series of matches with the Zapatista football team, and to the idea of forming a "Sixth International," the "Fifth" being the centralist tendency within the WSF), also called for in the Sixth, has been conducted through meetings in Latin American and European countries, especially Spain, where the Second Intercontinental Gathering for Humanity and against Neoliberalism, or "Encuentro Intergalactico," happened in 1997, the first having been organized by the EZLN in Chiapas the year before. Both "encuentros" can be seen as among the most important steps in setting up Peoples Global Action (PGA), a global alliance of autonomous movements, in 1997 and the global justice "movement of movements" since 1999.

The final part of the Sixth Declaration begins by identifying the Zapatista movement, more as students who listen than teachers who talk, with the popular, socialist and autonomous movements of contemporary Latin America in particular, but also with the global anti-war movement:

> And we want to say to you, to the Latin American peoples, that, for us, we are proud to be part of you, although we are a small part. We remember well when years ago the continent was lit up by a light named Che Guevara, just as that light was named Bolívar beforehand, because, at times, the peoples take up a name in order to show that they carry a flag. And we want to say to the people of Cuba, who already have spent years in your path of resistance, that you are not alone and that we do not agree with the blockade against you and that we are going to look for the way to send you something, even if it is just corn, to support your resistance. And we want to say to the people of the United States that we don't confuse you with the evil governments that you have and that harm the whole world, and that we know that there are North Americans who fight in your country and work in solidarity with the struggles of other peoples. And we want to say to our Mapuche brothers and sisters in Chile that we see and we learn from your struggles. And to the Venezuelan people, that we watch very carefully your way of defending your sovereignty and your right to be a nation and to decide where you will go. And to the indigenous brothers and sisters of Ecuador and Bolivia we say to you that you are giving an excellent history lesson to all of Latin America because right now you are putting a stop to neoliberal globalisation. And to the piqueteros and the youth of Argentina we want to say that we love you. And to those in Uruguay who want a better country, we admire you. And to the landless of Brazil we respect you. And to all the youths of Latin America, it's so great that you are doing what you are doing and you give us great hope. And we want to say to the brothers and sisters of Social Europe, that is to say the Europe that is rebellious and has dignity, that you are not alone. Your large movements against neoliberal wars make us very happy. We watch, attentively, your ways of organizing yourselves and your styles of fighting so that perhaps we can learn something. (EZLN 2005: 1)

As for the programme of the Zezta, the Sixth, perhaps to distinguish the horizontalism of the Zezta from the incipient verticalism of the WSF, proposed through characteristically tongue-in-check language that:

In the world...

1. We will build more relationships of respect and mutual aid with people and organizations that resist and fight against neoliberalism and for humankind.

2. In accordance with our abilities we will send material support such as food and crafts to those brothers and sisters who struggle throughout the world....

3. And to everyone throughout the world who resists we say that there have to be other intercontinental gatherings.... We don't want to give an exact date, or place, or decide who comes or how it is done, because this is about making horizontal agreements among us all. But we don't want it with a stage from where just a few speak and everyone else listens, but, rather, that there not be a stage, that it all be at ground-level, but well-ordered because if not well organized there will just be a lot of noise and no one will understand the word. And with a good organization, everyone can listen, and they can write down in their notebooks the words of resistance that others tell so that later each participant can talk it over with their colleagues in their worlds. And we think that it ought to be in a place where there is a very big prison, because it could be that they repress us and jail us, and that way we will not all be piled one on top of another but, rather, well organized though we be prisoners. And from there in jail we can continue the intercontinental gathering for humankind and against neoliberalism. (EZLN 2005: 4–5)

The Zezta's participants are from horizontalist movements, probably disillusioned by their experience in the now verticalist-controlled WSF, from which the EZLN as an armed organization was constitutionally excluded, and the hijacking of the European Social Forum by the old orthodox left and its anti-democratic methods and obsolete political style. The Zezta is due to take place by January 2007 and the decision to organize the Zezta globally in tandem with the Other is a sign both of the continuing strength of Zapatista-instigated "new internationalism" (Dinerstein 2002) and of the presently fractured state of the alter-globalist movement.[8]

ATENCO, OAXACA AND THE OTHER

On the morning of May 3 in the town of Texcoco, a few miles from Atenco and about 15 miles northwest of Mexico City, the PRD local mayor sent riot police to evict a group of flower sellers, typical members of the informal economy, from their established pitch. The scuffle that followed quickly developed into a major conflict as members of the Peoples Front in Defence of the Land (Frente de Pueblos en Defensa de la Tierra/FPDT) from Atenco, also known as the "macheteros," (they carry machetes on demonstrations as a symbol of the peasantry in struggle) came to the flower sellers aid and blocked the main highway to Mexico City for the rest of the day, repelling various charges by riot police. During the arrest of the leader of the FPDT that day a 14-year-old boy was shot dead at close range by a police officer. Hundreds of Other activists, human rights observers, doctors, media activists and others immediately gathered in Atenco to support the people of Atenco and Texcoco. The rightist Televisa and Teleazteca media duopoly bayed for protestor blood, repeatedly showing images of a riot policeman being kicked, while filtering out images of police brutality. Early in the morning of the next day, 3,000 armed riot police from various local, state and federal forces invaded the town of Atenco in retaliation for their defeat the day before and for the political humiliation inflicted on the Fox government four years earlier over the new Mexico City airport. The centre of the town was smothered in tear gas as gangs of riot police viciously attacked, clubbed and kicked men and women, the elderly and the young, FPDT, Other activists and bystanders, photographers and human rights observers, all were badly beaten before being dragged to jeeps where the beatings continued and the sexual abuse of the arrested women began. One 50-year-old woman out shopping was forced to have oral sex with three riot policemen in the street, under threat of beating and arrest (Ballinas 2006). A UNAM student activist Alexis Benumea was shot in the head with a tear gas canister and died a month later from his wounds. Some twenty houses, identified by an informer as belonging to FPDT activists, were broken into without warrants and the occupants and others who had taken shelter there beaten and arrested and their belongings stolen or destroyed. Some 280 were arrested and taken by bus to a high security prison in the State of Mexico. During the 8-hour journey most of the women, including three foreigners, and some of the men were sexually tortured and 30 women and at least one man were raped by the police. At present, 27 people remain imprisoned in a high security jail reserved for terrorists and drug traffickers on charges of obstructing the highway and kidnapping police officers (eight police were captured — a common practice in social conflicts in Mexico — during the clashes of May 3, and were well-treated before being discovered in a safe house by their colleagues during the police operation of the following day). There have been two hunger strikes by the imprisoned. Some are not members of the FPDT or from Atenco, while others are human rights observers and doctors who were voluntarily aiding the injured from the day before. A permanent vigil was established outside the prison where they are being held to demand their release.

At the Other's first national assembly on May 29th, Marcos formalized the decision to suspend the caravan until all the remaining imprisoned are released. He proposed a campaign of artistic and political actions, including a demonstration for the release of *all* political prisoners and the presentation of the disappeared from the Seventies, as well as a second National Assembly, until and including election day on July 2nd which the assembly unanimously approved. As a result of the national and international outcry over the exceptional police brutality, the Other's profile was raised significantly, a 15,000-strong national demonstration against the repression in Atenco and for the release of the prisoners took place in Mexico City on May 30th, with smaller marches, pickets and protest actions throughout the country, in the USA and internationally during May and June. Marcos broke his boycott of the mainstream media and gave press and television interviews in which he intensified his attack on AMLO, whose response to the Atenco events was a studied silence, and on the destruction of any notion of legal order and human rights in Mexico by the political class, since all three of the main parties were involved in the repression.[9] The repression of the Atenco and Other movements in May launched the other Campaign into the Mexican and international public realms, dramatically intensifying the organization and networking of struggles. However, since election day on July 2, the decision to remain in Mexico City until the liberation of the imprisoned and suspend the rest of the Other Campaign's tour of Mexico, while humanly and ethically unquestionable, have nevertheless led to the Other's perceived stagnation and "swamping" by the media coverage given to AMLO's anti-fraud movement.

Since July 2nd, the focus of the movement has switched to the teachers and popular movements in Oaxaca City, the capital of Oaxaca state, one of the most impoverished and historically combatative regions of Mexico, along with Chiapas, Guerrero and Puebla, the states with the main concentrations of autochthonous peoples, among the most antagonist social subjects in recent years in Mexico and Latin America. The Oaxaca movement started on May 22 as the annual strike and occupation of the city's main square for a meaningful salary raise by the dissident section of the SNTE (National Educational Workers Union), Latin America's largest union and the fiefdom of Elba Esther Gordillo, the pro-Fox PRI leader widely suspected of using her union members to carry out the more traditional fraudulent activities on July 2. The movement rapidly spread throughout the middle and working classes of Oaxaca, disgusted by the despotic style of the PRI governor, Ulisses Ruiz, whose removal from power became the movement's minimum demand. The crude attempts to baton the teachers off the street on June 14th led to a battle in the city centre, resulting in the main square being retaken by the striking teachers, now supported actively by ample sections of the general population, and the formation of APPO (Popular Assembly of the People of Oaxaca). The occupation of the main square has spread to the building of barricades throughout the city and the occupation of most of the public and government buildings in the city, as well as all the TV and radio stations, rendering the state ungovernable. Ruiz survives only due to the pro-fraud post-electoral PRI–PAN pact against the anti-fraud and Oaxaca movements. The use of "state terrorist" tactics by the repressive apparatus, reminiscent of the "dirty war" fought against the guerrilla movements of the '70s, includes the murder of 5 APPO activists, the wounding of several others and the kidnapping of four APPO leaders by plain clothes police and paramilitary gunmen, who now launch nightly armed attacks against the pickets outside gov-

ernment buildings and radio stations (Gibler 2006a). The violence of the now totally discredited governor's response and the non-intervention of the Fox government has only increased the growing sense of political vacuum, destabilization and
polarization evident throughout the country, but most notable in Mexico City and
Oaxaca, as the lines for a generalised conflict begin to harden.

THE "OTHER ON THE BORDER" AND THE "OTHER ON THE OTHER SIDE"

One of the most innovative aspects of the Other has been the attempt to depart
from national Mexican politics and transcend the crumbling boundaries of the nation state to include those (non-)Mexicans who live and struggle in one of the
most extreme borderlands, where "First" and "Third" Worlds meet, clash and in-
termingle, creating a transnational space, sometimes called "Amexica." This is
the land of *maquiladoras* (corporate assembly plants for export, compared by Bowden [1998] with Nazi slave factories for their salaries, too low to permit worker
reproduction, guaranteed instead by a constant stream of internal migrants, and
for appalling work and health and safety conditions), *narco* executions (drug-traf-
ficker cartels, now the most powerful in Latin America, engaged in an increasingly deadly turf war), *coyotes* (immigrant traffickers, who will be among the main
beneficiaries of the Sensenbrenner anti-immigration bill), Mara Salvatrucha/
MS13 (a counter-cultural gang movement and organised crime cartel from El
Salvador now present throughout the US), the *Migra* (US Border Patrol), child-
sex tourism and the black-on-pink crosses to remember the femicides (some 450
mainly working-class, indigenous, internal-migrant women and girls murdered in
Ciudad Juarez and Chihuahua City since 1993, 130 of whom were raped, tortured and mutilated, over 1,000 "disappeared," only 30 cases investigated to the
victims' families' satisfaction),[10] but also of neofascist Minutemen militia and the
militarisation of "America's" soft underbelly in the "war against terrorism."

Ciudad Juarez is the region's most emblematic city and is about to host the
first Border Social Forum in October, being strategically positioned in the very
centre of the 1,500-mile long border and the twin city of El Paso, Texas, containing the CIA's headquarters for the border and global south. Bowden (1998)
despairingly calls Juarez "a laboratory of our future," a place where the now relatively low level of worker resistance allows capital to create a "posthuman" society (Berardi 2003). Beyond the borderlands lies "Atzlan," the Chicano term for
"occupied Mexico" (the southwestern states of the US ceded by Mexico after the
1847 invasion), where the Latino population has grown vertiginously in the last
25 years, as some thirty million Mexicans and Central Americans have crossed
the border, most without documents, one of the great exoduses of recent history.
Hundreds have perished from heat exhaustion in the Arizona desert, one of the
hottest places on earth and where US anti-immigration policies deliberately fun-
nel migrants with walls, border patrols, pilotless spy planes and now with armed
militias and the armoured vehicles of the National Guard. But Aztlan now also

includes Los Angeles, Chicago and New York, which have become dependent on the cheap labour of Mexican migrants, whose remittances to their home communities are now Mexico's third largest source of foreign exchange after oil sales and tourism, making organized migrant communities in Chicago and elsewhere among the most significant investors in Mexican rural communities, so much so that the Bush government now wants to tax them. The growing dependence of the US economy on migrant "prosumers" was laid bare by the May Day "Si se puede" movement's huge demonstrations and boycott of US businesses against the proposed criminalization of undocumented migrants as "potential terrorists" by the Sensenbrenner bill. This mass movement of millions of previously subordinated migrants, together with the increasingly powerful social movements of Latin America, which have forced their national oligarchies to abandon or modify their slavish obedience of the Washington Consensus, has been described as the most important generalised anti-capitalist struggle in the Americas since the Civil Rights, black nationalist, students, counter-cultural and anti-war movements of the '60s (Midnight Notes 2006).

So where and how has the Other tried to connect with these movements both in the US and on its borders? Starting with the "Other on the Border," an attempted transnational zonification and networking of struggles in Chihuahua in Mexico, with west Texas and New Mexico, activists from the autonomist Kasa de la Cultura para Tod@s (House of Culture for All), the Trotskyist LUS (United Socialist League), ejiditarios from the Valle de Juarez (the last remaining agricultural area near the Juarez–El Paso border), the indigenous movement of the Raramuri people, the FAT (Authentic Labour Front, the only independent trade union active among maquiladora workers), students, teachers and NGOs campaigning for justice for the victims of the femicides, have met weekly with a Chicano rural farmworkers union in El Paso campaigning to save their homes in the Segundo Barrio in the downtown from gentrification as part of the San Jeronimo Project, which will lead to the diversion of water, the construction of social housing and other scarce resources away from the fast growing but almost completely unplanned and unserviced urban sprawl of Juarez, and with trade unionists, migrant rights activists and teachers from El Paso and Las Cruces in the US; altogether some fifty groups as well as many unaffiliated individuals. However, the Other on the Border has been dogged from the start by a sectarian war of words carried out on its email list and aimed at the Kasa, the core movement, which had bilateral meetings with the EZLN in Chiapas at the beginning of the Other and is responsible for coordinating the Other on the Border: yet another example of the horizontal-vertical conflict within global anti-capitalism, which has resulted in a considerable waste of time, energy and motivation. As a result the actions taken in solidarity with the Atenco movement in May were very limited compared to south and central Mexico, where sizeable demonstrations and roadblocks were organized throughout May. When the Kasa was attacked by armed, masked "state terrorists" the same month and for the second time in six months (an example of the now commonplace state intimidation tactics used against the Other throughout Mexico), its computers destroyed and a member kidnapped for several hours, the response by the rest of the Other in Juarez was well below what the Kasa had hoped for in terms of solidarity and support. Once the decision was taken by Marcos, who was due to visit the borderlands in June, to suspend the rest of the Other Campaign until the Atenco imprisoned were freed, enthusiasm has gradually dropped off and the once packed weekly organizational meetings have now ceased. Even though the focus in the Other on the visits of Marcos was criticised in some quarters as reinforcing his de facto leadership, nevertheless the "Zapatour" had important organizational and mobilisational impacts, especially on areas of relatively low militant activism such as Juarez where intermovement relations were minimal or non-existent.

While some voluntaristically welcome this as a necessary self-depuration of the less committed members of the Other, others have criticised Marcos' decision to "imprison" himself in Mexico City, which has led to a sense of stagnation since the July 2 elections, concomitant with the spectacular (in all senses of that word) rise of the AMLO anti-fraud movement. Nevertheless, the Zapatistas credibility as a core movement, not only in Mexico but globally, depends on their insistence on political coherence. Thus their commitment to the Atenco imprisoned will be kept even if the remainder of the Other Campaign has to be postponed to next year and the opportunity to "shadow" the presidential campaigns in order to reveal the falsities of official politics has been lost for another six years. This is also a sign of the Zapatistas patience and different conception of political time from the more urgent, but perhaps more opportunist and capitalisistically integrated political rhythms of some urban social movement activists.

The Other on the Other Side participated in the "Si se puede" movement and has coordinated with the local struggles of the Latino community, for example the attempt to save a community urban farm and park in South Central Los Angeles from being repossessed for development. This struggle brought together activists from all the communities in LA in defence of an occupied green space, one of the few left in a highly polluted and alienated urban environment. It has also organised "free radio" workshops and alternative media skill sharing with the less-resourced Tijuana and Juarez Others. The Other on the Other Side is a vital conduit between the Other Campaign in Mexico and the increasingly powerful struggles of the Latino migrant communities in the US.

OLD LEFTS AND NEW FOES: AMLO, THE PRD AND THE OTHER AFTER THE JULY 2ND ELECTORAL FRAUD

It should be apparent by now that the contemporary political cleavages in Mexico are not only left-right, as personified by the bitter personal feud between

Fox and AMLO, but also the growing conflict between the revolutionary/anti-capitalist left represented by the Other Campaign and the substantially pro-capitalist/ "reformist" (in reality, "reformism without reforms," typical of the Latin American post-insurrectional institutional left) PRD. Taking both the political elites and the broader left parties and movements by surprise, the EZLN first attacked the presidential aspirations of AMLO and the PRD, the main centre-left party, as neoliberal and even "fascist," causing considerable consternation among the PRD's generally pro-Zapatista base. The confused resentment and outrage expressed in the letters that flooded into *La Jornada* in July and August 2005, following the publication of the Sixth, were born of the fact that most within the party view AMLO as a messianic figure, the PRD's best chance to win the presidency since its foundation in 1989, following the electoral fraud of 1988. AMLO's elevation to virtual political sainthood has been greatly aided by the clumsy conspiracy of Fox and Salinas to remove him from contention through spurious legal actions and media vilification. AMLO's right-hand man when Mayor of Mexico City, Rene Bejerano, was caught on video in 2004 receiving bribes in return for city contracts from a businessman subsequently linked to Salinas, so provoking a far-reaching scandal which showed that the PRD was very much part of the endemically corrupt, clientalist political class, although AMLO's reputation as an "honest" politician remained unscathed. The conspiracy was momentarily frustrated by a huge demonstration of over one million mainly but not exclusively PRD supporters in April 2005, forcing Fox to back down and reinstate AMLO's legal immunity as Mayor, so permitting him to continue as the PRD's presidential candidate.[11]

Marcos has since clarified the reasons for the now intense antagonism between the Zapatistas and the PRD, which in many ways had been simmering since 1994:

> the 2001 betrayal by the PRD of the 1996 San Andres Accords on indigenous autonomy and rights, signed by the EZLN and the then PRI Mexican government as well as various independent indigenous organizations and which the PRD had always verbally supported (and the enactment of which AMLO made the first of the "51 promises" in his 2006 electoral manifesto), but which it unexpectedly dropped when the majority of its senators supported a diluted PAN counterproposal which substantially maintains the racist status quo and denies autonomy.

The armed attack in April 2004 by PRD members on a Zapatista march in Zinacantán, a community in Chiapas where the local PRD government had cut off water and electricity to Zapatista families in an attempt to force them to join the PRD. Nearby Zapatistas organized a march to reconnect the services, which local PRD members then ambushed with gunfire, wounding several of the marchers. Although the PRD national leadership promised a full investigation into the incident, it has yet to happen and the local PRD leader responsible for the attack is now one of the main organizers of AMLO's non-party "Citizens Support Network" in Chiapas.

Other reasons for the breakdown of relations between the EZLN and the PRD would be:

> The EZLN's unconditional support for the UNAM students movement's strike and occupation in 1999–2000 against the hiking of fees as the first step in the privatisation of Latin America's largest state university, was a watershed in the radicalisation of the Zapatista movement, leading to rupture with Cardenas, the then PRD Mayor of Mexico City, and the radical liberal urban intelligentsia, led by Carlos Monsivais and Elena Poniatowska, once so fascinated by the EZLN. Relations also became tense with *La Jornada*, which reported the occupation objectively but whose cartoonists and editorialists joined the general media demonization of the autonomous students' movement as violent, anachronistic "Stalinist monsters," after they expelled the PRD "colonels" (official student leaders) to stop them manipulating the movement. The CGH (General Strike Council) movement was repressed in February 2000 when the Zedillo government sent riot police onto the campus of an autonomous university and hundreds of students were imprisoned or expelled, although UNAM dropped the fee hike and the movement's nerve centre, the Aula Magna Che Guevara, remained occupied and is now one of the Other's main organizational hubs.

The Chiapas state government has been under PRD control since 2000, and while the army and PRI-linked paramilitary groups no longer harass Zapatista communities to the same extent (although no action has been taken against those responsible for the 1997 Acteal massacre and hundreds of other extra judicial summary executions), the state's counter-insurgency effort has continued through discrimination against Zapatista families and communities over government aid, often administered through PRD-linked NGOs, forcing some to join the PRD and leading to conflicts over squatted land with the Zapatista autonomous "Caracoles" and "Good Government Councils"[12] in an attempt to divide and weaken the Zapatistas in their heartland. The Zapatistas ended relations with most Mexican NGOs, some of which are both PRD-linked and financed by the US State Department,[13] in 2003 when the "Aguascalientes" meeting places with "civil society" were shut down and replaced by the present "Caracoles" (seashell, an important symbol in Mayan culture and more defence-oriented), which maintain more guarded relations with a few carefully vetted NGOs and with "civil society" in general. The Zapatista autonomous communities, taking advantage of the probably only temporary lull in hostilities, have since embarked on a dual strategy of local consolidation and gradual inter/national expansion of the movement, of which the Sixth and the Other are the results. Relations with the PRD have worsened still with the choice of Juan Sabines, formerly of the PRI, as their candidate for the Chiapas governorship elections on August 20, which he seems to have won. Sabines has included in his team of advisors the ex-PRI governor Albores, responsible for the Acteal massacre and the 1998 military offensive against the Zapatista communities that left several dead, hundreds imprisoned and thousands displaced.

The failure of AMLO's Mexico City government to properly investigate the 2001 assassination of Digna Ochoa, an indigenous woman and radical human rights lawyer close to the Zapatistas, and of the UNAM student activist Pavel Gonzalez in 2004. Many suspect the involvement of the *Yunque* (anvil), a semi-clandestine neofascist group linked to the PAN, some of whose main leaders are former members, and/or CISEN, the Mexican secret service. However, the judicial arm of AMLO's government, despite hard evidence to the contrary (both were shot more than once and Gonzalez' body was found crucified in a forest outside the city) persists with the "suicide" theorem, typical of one of the worst aspects of the PRI's 70-year dictatorship when political dissidents were regularly "suicided." Given the lack of judicial independence at any level, this would seem to indicate AMLO's reluctance, as a prospective presidential candidate, to confront the Mexican "secret state," which ill bodes any prospect of justice under his hypothetical presidency for the victims of the 1968 and 1971 massacres of students and teachers, the thousands of disappearances and summary executions of the "dirty war" in the 1970s, and of the more recent massacres of peasant and indigenous movements at Aguas Blancas (1995), Acteal (1997) and El Charco (1998), the full investigation and punishment of which are the main demands of Mexican social justice and human rights movements, supported by Amnesty International and Human Rights Watch.

A disturbing tendency by both AMLO, a former member of the PRI, and of the PRD to accept into their ranks and leadership, and now in leading positions in the presidential electoral team, some of the worst PRI authoritarian "dinosaurs" such as Manuel Bartlett, one of the architects of the 1988 fraud, Leonel Cota, formerly an orthodox neoliberal on the right-wing of the PRI and now PRD party secretary, Adolfo Uribe and Socorro Diaz, close advisors to former President Zedillo and implicated in the Acteal massacre, as well as opportunists like Munoz Ledo and Camacho Solis, both former PRI leaders who have flirted with the PAN, and are now among AMLO's closest advisors.

AMLO's close relationship with top Mexican capitalists like Carlos Slim, the third richest man on the planet according to *Forbes* magazine (2006), with whom he shares a project to gentrify the historical centre of Mexico City, involving the expulsion of its working class population and the repression of the street vendors of the "informal economy," through the introduction of former New York mayor Giuliani's "zero tolerance" policy, while leaving organized crime rackets untouched. As Mayor (2000–2005) AMLO had a mixed, populist style, providing social security top up payments to impoverished pensioners and single mothers and founding a much-needed new state university with an adult education mission, the UACM, while favouring the middle-class consumerist, car and construction lobbies by building the pharaonic "Second Floor" of the city's heavily congested ring road, instead of investing in improved public transport, housing and social services, all desperate needs in one of the world's most socially polarized, congested and polluted cities.

The PRD, a coalition of competing "political tribes" brought together by PRI "democratisers," the reformed ex-Stalinists of the Mexican Communist Party and the defeated remnants of the New Left vanguardist parties in 1989, has made persistent attempts to co-opt the Zapatista movement since 1994, as part of its clientalist galaxy of ex-social movements now converted into internal party factions or NGOs, as happened to the more traditionally socialist Assemblea de Barrios of Superbarrio fame and much of the once autonomous "Colono" (community squatters) movement, enticed by the offer of parliamentary seats and organizational funding, thanks to the PRD's enhanced finances following its historical victory in 1997 when Cardenas became the first elected Mayor of Mexico City, now the party's electoral stronghold.

So gone are the days back in 1996 when Marcos, Cardenas and AMLO met in San Cristobal to discuss common strategy in the "transition to democracy," as part of the Peace Dialogue between the PRI regime and the EZLN. The EZLN's evolution as an autonomous movement has led it to break with most of its broad left and democratic allies, including the small "liberation theology" component, represented by the ex-bishop of San Cristobal Samuel Ruiz, of the otherwise deeply traditional and hard right Mexican Catholic Church.

The evidence for electoral fraud against AMLO and the PRD on the July 2nd presidential, congressional and senate elections is accumulating by the day, despite the right's pretence that nothing untoward happened and that everything is the product of AMLO's feverish imagination. The growing body of evidence for both cybernetic and traditional fraud shows that the foreign observers provided by the European Union and other organizations singularly failed in their task and that Bush, Blair and Zapatero rubberstamped fraud in one of the most important "emerging democracies" by precipitously recognising Calderon, the PAN candidate, as the winner. Although the fabulously paid judges of the TEPJF, the final court for electoral disputes, are about to make their unappealable ruling, predictably, that the elections were fair, AMLO and his "Planton" (picket) tent city, which has covered much of the city centre since July 30th, completely disrupting traffic flows and tourism (Mexico's second source of foreign revenue), will continue at least until September 15th. Under the pretext of needing to clear the central square for an army Independence Day parade, the "planton" may well be violently dislodged, given President Fox's threatening language and the creation of a militarised no-go area around the Congress building, reminiscent of the "red zone" at the G8 Summit in Genoa in 2001, in preparation for his final September 1st "Report to the nation." Such repressive action will only worsen the already profound systemic crisis caused by the fraud and the Oaxaca conflict, possibly precipitating generalised conflict throughout Mexico.

CONCLUSIONS: AN/OTHER ANTI-CAPITALISM IS POSSIBLE?

The Sixth and the Other represent the constitution of a potentially revolutionary autonomous "left," organized for the first time in Mexican history as an officially "leaderless," (although Marcos is for the moment at least its unofficial leader and spokesperson) and transnational (since it includes the "Otra en el otro lado" in the USA) grassroots network of social movements, extra-parliamentary political parties, independent trade union branches, community groups, radical NGOs and unaffiliated individuals, all linked to the networks of the anti-capitalist alter-globalist "movement of movements."

However, at the present conjuncture the Other and indeed the Zapatista communities in Chiapas find themselves facing repression by an authoritarian ultra-neoliberal president, imposed through an electoral fraud which is tantamount to a fascist *coup d'etat* and which slams Mexico's 18-year-old "transition to democracy" into reverse. The challenge to build a mass autonomous anti-capitalist alternative "below and to the left" at this moment seems huge and much will depend on developing close ties with the global networks of anti-capitalism both to defend the new movement from repression and to increase its counter-power within the Mexican political scenario. It will also be important for the Other to avoid the pitfalls that allowed President Kirchner to co-opt elements of the Piquetero movement in Argentina (see Dinerstein in this volume), a similar fate befalling parts of the indigenous movements in Ecuador and Bolivia, although the Sem Terra landless peasants movement (Latin America's largest and one of its most autonomous) has successfully resisted Lula's attempts to divide and co-opt it (Fernandes 2006). So along with avoiding cooption by the greatly expanded PRD, which won 35% of the senate and congress seats and is only slightly smaller than the PAN, with the PRI facing major internal splits and possible disintegration, the Other will need to build strong links with Latin America's growing number of autonomous anti-capitalist movements.

It will also be necessary for the Other to strengthen its links with the Oaxaca and Atenco movements and join forces with those potentially autonomous elements within the anti-fraud movement, disillusioned with the prospects for radical change through electoral politics and prepared to continue the struggle for participative democracy "from below and for below" long after AMLO and the PRD have made their peace with Fox and Calderon. All these movements will need to go beyond the region's historical tendency towards left nationalism and "popular patriotism," which view all forms of globalisation as a calamity, not just the neoliberal economic variety: an ideology which finally only legitimates the return to power of the national bourgeoisie vis-à-vis transnational capital. For the first time an autonomous, alter-globalist, anti-capitalist movement is emerging in Mexico, aided by the eclipse of neoliberalism in the region and the depth of the systemic political crisis, but its immediate fate now hangs in the balance.

NOTES

1 My sincere thanks to Carolina Ballesteros and Werner Bonefeld for their helpful comments on the first drafts of this chapter. My thanks also to Eligio Calderon, Ernesto Montes, Hector Pedraza, Carlos Morales and Claudio Albertani for the information and insights they provided in conversations and correspondence. The opinions expressed here are entirely my own and for which, of course, I take full responsibility. The paper was completed very shortly after the July 2006 national election in Mexico. All comments should be sent to: pgcuninghame@yahoo.co.uk

2 By "vertical" Left I mean those organizational traditions within the historical Left that favour a centralist, hierarchical, organizational structure (a mirror image of the capitalist firm) and that practice dogmatic, vanguardist, statist and "top-down" politics, i.e. all their political initiatives either stem from or have to be approved by the leadership, while rigid discipline and obedience is enforced on the membership by threat of expulsion. Their political ideology is usually based on an orthodox "scientific socialist" interpretation of the Marxist-Leninist canon. Left political traditions considered to be "verticalist" would be social democrats, Leninists and Trotskyists, but in the context of alterglobalism would also include (ex-) national liberation movements like Sinn Fein. A Mexican example would be the Trotskyist PRT (Partido Revolucionario de los Trabajadores/Workers Revolutionary Party), which split in the early '90s over entryism into the PRD, a path the majority chose to follow, while a minority became close allies of the EZLN and now edit the monthly magazine, *Rebeldía*, the main Zapatista publication. In fact, this is a simplification as there is a certain amount of "crossover" particularly between the leaderships of the two factions, which tends to muddy the waters of radical left politics in Mexico. An English example would be the Socialist Workers Party (SWP). In recent years the "verticalists" have increasingly clashed with the "horizontalists" (autonomists, anarchists, ecofeminists, environmentalists, independent social movements in general) over the control and future direction of the World and European Social Forums in particular and global anti-capitalism/alter-globalism in general. For a discussion of verticalist-horizontalist politics, see Levidow (2004).

3 "...what seems to be happening in Caracas — the apparent complete dependence by the local civil organisations (those who the WSF International Council has appointed to organise the particular edition of the World Forum) on Hugo Chávez and his government for organising the Forum — seems to directly contradict the spirit and soul of the Forum" (Jai Sen 2006).

4 I use inverted commas since there is so much disagreement over the term, although the Gramscian, more social movement-based interpretation tends to predominate within Zapatista and movement discourse, while the Hegelian version, based on all individuals and groups outside the state, including entrepreneurs, religious institutions and rightist interest groups, predominates in both NGO and academic discourse in Mexico. On the question of what is "civil" in "civil society" see Cleaver (in this volume) and Bonefeld (2006).

5 These same banners are now to be seen in the Zocalo, Mexico City's huge central square, adorning AMLO's bi-weekly "report assemblies," a sign that part of the Other is involved in the PRD-controlled anti-fraud movement, while the rest of the Other focuses on the increasingly violent repression of the teachers and APPO movements in Oaxaca and continuing efforts to free the 27 Atenco prisoners.

6 The Other caravan was accompanied however by members of the "Other journalism," including Hermann Bellinghausen of *La Jornada*, Indymedia, Narco News, ZNet and NACLA among others.

7 The ejidos were established throughout Mexico under the 1917 Constitution to formalize the widespread squatting by landless peasants that took place during the Mexican Revolution (1910–1917) and as a means of land redistribution, one of the principle demands of the Revolution, on the principle of common ownership. The revocation by the Salinas government in 1992 of the Constitution's Article 27, which forbade the breaking up of ejidos into private lots or their sale to landowners, was both a forbearer of NAFTA and the spark for a series of land disputes and peasant uprisings, including that of the EZLN, as corporate agribusiness, Mexican landowners and tourism projects have conducted illegal land grabs and enforced sales, with the instigation and support of the state and federal governments. This kind of struggle forms the backbone of the Other in the rural areas of Southern Mexico (Ballvé 2006).

8 See for example the recent split within ATTAC France along verticalist-horizontalist lines (Callinicos 2006).

9 The data and incidents mentioned here were taken from reports in *La Jornada* and *Indymedia Mexico*, and have since been confirmed by the preliminary report of the ongoing investigation by the International Civil Commission on the Observance of Human Rights (Comisión Civil Internacional de Observación por los Derechos Humanos) into the events in Atenco and Texcoco on May 3rd and 4th this year: http:\\cciodh.pangea.org; accessed 11th August 2006.

10 See the constantly updated bilingual website of Nuestras Hijas de Regreso a Casa (Our daughters back home), the most radical NGO working on the femicides in Juarez and Chihauhua: www.mujeresdejuarez.org.

11 Under Mexican law, a person accused of a crime or involved in a court case cannot stand for election as president.

[12] Juntas de Buen Gobierno, set up to self-govern the autonomous municipalities on collective leadership-revocable delegate principles and drawn from ordinary citizens, who then return to their former occupations, so avoiding the re-emergence of the corruption and clientalism characteristic of a professional political class with its own interests and agenda.

[13] According to Eligio Calderon, an academic of the UAM–Xochimilco, Mexico City, and former advisor to the EZLN during its 1995–96 negotiations with the PRI government.

REFERENCES

Albertani, C. (2006) "Lopez Obrador, il subcomandante Marcos e l'autonomia dei movimenti sociali," email manuscript, 12 July: claudio.albertani@gmail.com.

Almeyra, G. (2006a) "Stalin y la historia de la contrarrevolución," *La Jornada*, 26 February; www.unam.jornada.mx; accessed 26 February.

_____ (2006b) "El demonio del voluntarismo," *La Jornada*, Sunday 14 May; www.unam.jornada.mx; accessed 14 May.

_____ (2006c) "Las palabras y los actos," *Memoria*, no. 208, June; http://memoria.com.mx/node/807; accessed 27 August.

Ballinas, V. (2006) "Recibe CNDH 16 quejas por abuso sexual y 7 por violación," *La Jornada*, 10 May; www.unam.jornada.mx; accessed 10 May.

Ballvé, T. (2006) "A Day in the Life of the Other Campaign," *NACLA Report on the Americas*, March–April.

Barrios Cabrera, A. (2006) "Rechazando a John Ross," *Amate–3622*; 23 August; sextachihuahua-bounces@lists.biciverde.org; read 24 August.

Bellinghausen, H. (2006a) "'La izquierda neoliberal no resolverá los problemas': González Casanova," *La Jornada*, Wednesday 22 March: www.jornada.unam.mx; accessed 22 March.

_____ (2006b) "Toca a los adherentes a la Zezta decidir si organizan encuentro en Venezuela: EZLN," *La Jornada*, 26 June; www.unam.jornada.mx; accessed 26 June.

_____ (2006c) "Reprocha Marcos a intelectuales perder de vista la lucha continua de desposeídos," *La Jornada*, 27 June; www.unam.jornada.mx; accessed 27 June.

Berardi, F. (2003) *La fabrica de la infelicidad. Nuevas formas de trabajo y movimiento global.* Madrid: Traficantes de Sueños [online version available].

Bonefeld, W. (2006) "Anti-globalisation and the Question of Socialism," *Critique*, Vol. 34, No. 1, April.

Bowden, C. (1998) *Juarez: the laboratory of our future.* New York: Aperture Foundation.

Burbach, R. (2006) "Electoral Fraud and Rebellion in Mexico," *Latin American Perspectives*; www.latinamericanperspectives.com; accessed 15 July.

Callinicos, A. (2006) "Attac divisions reflect a shift," *Socialist Worker*, 1 July: www.socialistworker.co.uk/article.php?article_id=9120, accessed 2 July.

Cuban Libertarian Movement/Movimiento Libertario Cubano (CLM/MLC) (2005) "Reflections on the VI Declaration of the Lacandona Jungle," *UK Indymedia*: Cuban Libertarian Movement I 29.08.2005 17:22 I Analysis I Social Struggles I Zapatista; www.indymedia.org & www.movimientolibertariocubano.org ; accessed 25 March 2006.

Dinerstein, A. (2002) "Beyond insurrection. Argentina and New Internationalism," *The Commoner*, no.5, Autumn: http://www.thecommoner.org; accessed January 2003.

Ejército Zapatista de Liberación Nacional (EZLN) (2005) "Sixth Declaration Of The Lacandon Jungle: Part V. What We Want To Do" (Translated by *Narco News*, July 1, 2005). *Narco News*: August 16 2006, Issue #38: www.narconews.com/Issue38/article1371.html; accessed 16 August.

Fernandes, S. (2006) "Way forward for the left?," *ZNet*, 9 August; www.zmag.org; accessed 22 August.

Galan, J. (2006) "Alienta el abstencionismo el discurso barroco de Marcos, según académicos," *La Jornada*, 22 February; www.unam.jornada.mx; accessed 24 February.

Gibler, J. (2006a) "Scenes from the Oaxaca Rebellion," *ZNet*, 4 August; http://www.zmag.org/content/print_article.cfm?itemID=10708&sectionID=59; accessed 11 August.

_____(2006b) "Designer Uprising. Scenes from Mexico City's Post-electoral Mobilizations," *ZNet*, 7 August; www.zmag.org/content/print_article.cfm?itemID=10724&sectionID=1; accessed 11 August.

Hardt, M. & Negri, A. (2002) *Imperio*, Barcelona: Paidos.

_____ (2004) *Multitude: War and Democracy in the Age of Empire*. New York: Penguin Books.

Harvey, N. (2005a) "Inclusion Through Autonomy," *NACLA Report on the Americas (Empire and Dissent)*, September/October.

_____ (2005b) "La difícil construcción de la democracia pluriétnica: el zapatismo y la hegemonía neoliberal en el contexto latinoamericano." Paper presented at the seminar *Empire and Dissent : US Hegemony in Latin America*, Social Science Research Council (SSRC), Cuernavaca, Mexico, 4–5 March 2005.

_____(2005c) "Beyond Hegemony? Zapatismo, Empire and Dissent," unpublished manuscript.

Holloway, J. (2002a) *Change the world without taking power. The meaning of revolution today*. London: Pluto Press.

_____ (2002b) "Zapatismo and the Social Sciences," *Capital & Class*, no. 79.

_____ (2003) "Is the Zapatista Struggle an Anti-Capitalist Struggle?," *The Commoner*, no. 6, Winter 2003: www.thecommoner.org; accessed January 2004.

Levidow, L. (2004) "Making another world possible? The European Social Forum," *Radical Philosophy*, No. 128, November/December 2004: www.radicalphilosophy.com/default.asp?channel_id=2187&editorial_id=16577; accessed January 2005.

Lopez y Rivas, G. (2006) "Imágenes distorsionadas de *la otra campaña*," *La Jornada*, June 30; www.unam.jornada.mx; accessed 30 June.

Midnight Notes (2006) "Migration, movements, wages and war in the Americas: reasons for unity on May Day 2006 — and after," *The Commoner*, no. 13: www.commoner.org.uk/01–13groundzero.htm; accessed 15 July.

Negri, A. (1992) *Il potere costituente. Saggio sulle alternative del moderno*. Milan: Sugar Co.

Olivares Alonso, E. (2006) "*Zapatistas, un mundo en construcción*, visión crítica desde la solidaridad," *La Jornada*, 19 July; www.unam.jornada.mx; accessed 19 July.

Palast, G. (2006) "Why democrats don't count," *The Guardian*, 14 July; www.GregPalast.com; accessed 14 July.

Pineda, E. (2006) "La 'otra campaña' y el camino electoral: mitos y demonios que hay que exorcizar," *Chiapas al Día*, No. 504, CIEPAC, 26 April: www.ciepac.org.mx; accessed August 10.

Rabasa, J. (2003) "Negri por Zapata: el poder constituyente y los límites de la autonomía," *Chiapas*, no. 15: www.ezln.org/revistachiapas/No15 .html; accessed May 2004.

Ross, J. (2006) "A report from the Red Alert: Zapatistas at Critical Crossroads," *Counter Punch*, July 31; www.counterpunch.org; accessed 20 August.

Sánchez Ramírez, E. (2006) "¿Stalin en la otra campaña?," *Bandera Socialista*, Mexico, no. 22.

Sen, J. (2006) "Some hard questions about the upcoming World Social Forum"; social-movements@listserv.heanet.ie; 14 January,

Subcomandante Insurgente Marcos & Comisión Sexta del EZLN (2006) "Algunas consideraciones del Supmarcos sobre la propuesta de plan de acción de la Comisión," 30 May; sextachihuahua-bounces@lists. biciverde.org; read Wednesday, 31 May.

Virno, P. (2004) *A Grammar of the Multitude*. Boston, MA: The MIT Press.

Zezta Internazional/Intergalactic Commission of the EZLN (2005) "Concerning the Intercontinental proposed in the Sixth Declaration of the Selva Lacandona," Communiqué from the Clandestine Revolutionary Indigenous Committee – General Command of the Zapatista Army of National Liberation, Mexico, November 2005: http://zeztainternazional.ezln.org.mx/index.php?name=News&file=article&sid=65; accessed December 2005.

Zibechi, R. (2004) "La autonomía es más que una palabra. Reflexiones a propósito del Enero Autónomo": hwww.memoria.com.mx/183/ zibechi.htm; accessed January 2005.

13

Lessons From A Journey
The Piquetero Movement in Argentina

Ana Cecilia Dinerstein[1]

INTRODUCTION

Whilst neoliberal restructuring of the 1990s was expected to acquiesce and depoliticise labour in Argentina, the opposite appears to have been the case. The reforms facilitated the emergence of new regional, decentralised and consistently non-institutionalised forms of opposition and protest, which became paramount to the politics of the country. Since entire localities became affected by privatisation, state reforms and company closures, the unemployed and community-based organisations joined public sector workers and local trade unions at a number of roadblocks. The roadblocks, on many occasions, resulted in the prosecution and even death of their participants.[2] At the roadblocks, the unemployed, workers and their communities put forward a diversity of demands, ranging from employment programs to "genuine-job" creation and investment, accompanied by demands for political inclusion and participation in the management of social and employment programmes (see Dinerstein, 2002). At the roadblocks, the "unemployed" became Piqueteros and different organisations emerged piecemeal to constitute what came to be called a "movement."

It would be difficult to discuss protest and mobilisation in the 1990s and 2000s in Argentina without mentioning the Piqueteros.[3] However, in recent years, doubts have been raised about the significance of the movement today. Although the Piqueteros organisations were born piecemeal and the "movement" has been always heterogeneous, long-standing divisions have intensified and multiplied. For example, by February 2003 there were fifteen different organisations only in Greater Buenos Aires (Vales 2002). Another example of the tendency to disagree is provided by the celebration of the second anniversary of December

2001, when there were four commemorative acts gathering four different sectors of the movement.

Whilst it is not always clear what divides the movement, it is unmistakable that as the mobilisation capacity of different groups decreases, ruptures and further divisions increase, driven by the differences of position taken vis-à-vis state policy-making and the meaning of social change. This tendency to split and disagree over tactics and strategic action has become worse particularly after the election of President Kirchner in May 2003. Internationally, Kirchner's appointment was seen as part of a "new" political moment in Latin America, carrying out a crusade against the unpalatable consequences of neo-liberalism and organising the return of the state.[4] Nationally, too, the social mood had changed, the trustworthiness of democratic institutions was re-established, populist sentiments were re-energised and the slogan that mobilised thousands in December 2001, ¡que se vayan todos! ("out with them all!"), was almost forgotten. New policies have been introduced in a direct attempt at incorporating the spirit and practices of the community projects initiated by many groups in the Piquetero movement and at encouraging a "culture of work." In effect, these policies co-opted those who were prepared to "surrender" and isolated those sectors of the movement which were not prepared to give in. The question posed by these political and policy developments is whether the movement can still be regarded as significant or whether it has reached a dead end.

Commentators and activists have either underestimated or glorified the relevance of the Piqueteros organisations. Whilst the former have viewed them as representing a new form of mobilisation and survival strategies aimed at fighting unemployment and social exclusion, the latter considered them as an essential component of a new "revolutionary" project. Yet, neither of these positions is satisfactory, as both provide an overly narrow and misleading characterisation of the Piqueteros. As a whole, the movement inherited the historical strength and mobilisation capacity of the working class and trade unions but they also learnt how to emulate the complexity of the social reality of the world of work. Each organisation discovered their own ways to combine political, social, economic and cultural actions in unique ways that escape classifications of that sort.

In what follows I will discuss the experience of resistance of the Piquetero movement. Whilst an exhaustive evaluation of the political impact of the action of such a wide range of organisations goes far beyond the aim of this chapter, this account will evaluate the significance of their mobilisation strategies, community projects and relationship with the state. For the purpose of this discussion I will use some examples from three distinctive groups that became important in the last years: (i) the Land and Housing Federation (Federación Tierra y Vivienda, FTV), from La Matanza, which is integrated into the structure of the Argentine Workers Central (Central de Trabajadores Argentinos, CTA) and manages the unemployment programs for this region of Greater Buenos Aires; (ii) the National Piquetero Block (Bloque Piquetero Nacional, BPN), or the "duros," a conglomerate of different organisations that were created within the various political left-wing parties; and (iii) autonomous groups such as the Unemployed Workers' Movement Aníbal Verón (*Movimiento de Trabajadores Desocupados Aníbal Verón, MTD Aníbal Verón*) in Greater Buenos Aires and the Unemployed Workers' Union (*Union de Trabajadores Desocupados*, UTD), Mosconi, province of Salta, which advocate autonomy and independence from political and labour organisations.

The central argument made here is that the Piquetero Movement must be seen as vital for the politics of resistance for its capacity to mobilise the marginalised, carry out innovative community projects, and confront the state during the period of serious crisis in Argentina. Doubtless, both mobilisation at the roadblocks and the autonomous community projects helped to recover the individual capacity for mobilisation and action after the intense individualism and disillusionment of the 1990s. They also facilitated the reinvention of the political (collective) subjectivity, understood as the re-composition of identities, organisational forms and strategies capable of articulating collective action around new common ideas, such as the defence of dignity, autonomy, democracy and justice. However, the movement has reached a political stalemate in the face of the recomposition of the state since 2003.

ROADBLOCKS: SEEKING VISIBILITY

The Piqueteros have changed the socio-political shape of the country in two interconnected ways: the use of innovative mobilisation strategies (roadblocks) and the organisation of original autonomous community projects.

Their mobilisation strategies are by now well known. Since the *Santiagazo* in 1993 there has been an almost uninterrupted process of social protests against the neo-liberal stabilisation plans and economic reforms initiated by the Menem administration. The *roadblocks* were the most effective and visible decentralised and non-institutionalised form of protest run by those affected by privatisation, poverty and unemployment. These involved entire communities, local social organisations and the unemployed with the support of trade unions. These *roadblocks* were the basis for the emergence of Piquetero identity and the organisation of the unemployed into what one could, with certain qualifications, call "a movement."

While the 1997 European marches against unemployment, job insecurity and social exclusion involved a wide range of activists, from social movement campaigners to trade union activists, to community associations, in the South and North West of Argentina *roadblocks* were being organised by the unemployed "Piqueteros," public sector workers and local communities. In 1996 and 1997 the roadblock in Cutral-Co and Plaza Huincul (Neuquén) brought together 5,000 people who besieged the cities, demanding job creation and new investment. These roadblocks were followed by those in Tartagal and Mosconi (Salta) and Libertador General San Martín (Jujuy), confirming that this new

ANA CECILIA DINERSTEIN

form of protest were bound to become prominent. Between December 1999 and December 2001 the confrontation between the government and the unemployed intensified, particularly when the Piqueteros mobilised against Minister Cavallo's "zero deficit" plan, launched in May 2001, to conform to the latest IMF demand further to reduce public expenditures. The mobilisation of the unemployed contributed to the collapse of the alliance in power, led by President de la Rúa, when the ongoing controversy within the Cabinet — between those who advocated dialogue with the protesters and policy reforms, and those who prioritised the country's financial performance and advocated repressive control of the unemployed — became unsustainable (Dinerstein 2001).

The nationalisation of the hitherto provincial roadblocks marked a qualitative change in the politics of resistance: between 31 July and 17 August 2001, three national roadblocks coordinated by the First National Assembly of Popular, Territorial and Unemployed Workers Organisations brought together 50 organisations. After the financial collapse of December 2001, the Piqueteros were part of the network of resistance against institutional power and mobilised during 2002 against the transitional government led by the Peronist elite.

The roadblocks inspired debates about their significance, ranging from being seen as a cultural phenomenon, a site for identity formation, a tool for unifying and collectively expressing demands on the government, an outcome of institutional and political weakness, a post-industrial form of conflict, popular rebellion, sign of the re-emergence of the left (see Dinerstein 2002). The central feature the roadblocks will be remembered for is their power to popular mobilisation. The roads used to serve not only as the battlefield against the military police, but also the place for expressions of solidarity, connections, organisation, decision making, communication, negotiation and recomposition of identities.

AUTONOMOUS COMMUNITY PROJECTS: REINVENTING POLITICAL ACTION

The mobilisation at the roadblocks eventually served to get state resources for the development of autonomous community projects (*proyectos productivos*). These projects have reinvented politics at the very core of community life. The implementation of these projects — from literacy campaigns, to popular education programs and provision of school dinners, and from land occupation and housing construction, to the creation of work cooperatives to community farms (*huertas comunitarias*), recycling activities, negotiations for temporary jobs for the local unemployed and the creation of ad hoc job exchanges — are often accompanied by the democratic discussion among members of the short- and long-term meaning of their collective action for social change.

The projects encourage reflection and consciousness of their collective achievement and the formation of political attitudes, which may not necessarily be related to any specific ideology or traditional political organisations.

The intervention of Piqueteros organisation at local levels into situations that combined unemployment, poverty and vulnerability, have not only prevented the transition of many from unemployment to destitution, but also helped to resist isolation, depression and the loss of ability to carry out any collective action. The rationale underpinning the projects is to challenge the individualistic logic of the state-focused social policies and clientelistic relations.

Some Piqueteros organisations accept workfare assigned by local authorities to the employment programmes distributed among the unemployed and focus on the distribution and management of these. The management of the programmes is a source of financial as well as political power. It must be said that on many occasions the organisations have reproduced clientelistic relations with their members and with the government. For instance, when programmes are managed by the Piquetero organisations obtaining or continuing to receive monthly benefits by the unemployed individuals has often depended on their participation in a roadblock or an assembly, or contribution of a small amount of their monthly benefit to the organisation.

Others however, reject the workfare assigned by the state and fight for its redefinition according to their needs (Autonomous groups). Whereas in the former case, the power of the organisation is measured in terms of the amount of individual employment allowances allocated, in the latter individual employment programmes are used by the organisation for the creation of collective "productive projects," where the needs are defined collectively. Here the roadblock is used not only to fight for more programmes but also to discuss the collective redefinition of the tasks individually assigned to the unemployed (e.g. cleaning roads) in the form of community projects (*projectos productivos*). The idea is to direct state resources to the production of use values according to people's needs with the intention to create an alternative economy. Their creative capacity, demonstrated in the community work, and their strength to resist at the roadblocks in adverse conditions are slowly but surely contributing to the creation of a new social consciousness and the recovery of a social fabric.

POLITICAL PROJECT(S) AND DIVISIONS:
INCOME DISTRIBUTION, STATE SOCIALISM OR COUNTER-POWER?

The Piquetero movement brings together distinct political projects within which the Piqueteros have different roles to perform. As the Piquetero organisation within the central union, the FTV matched the institutional logic of the Argentine Workers' Central (*Central de Trabajadores Argentinos*, CTA) and together with the central demands that income redistribution and job creation should constitute the basis for a political project based on national economic development and democratisation. The FTV advocates the promotion of "Income Distribution Shock, National Autonomy and Democracy."[5] The "inclusion" of the unemployed into the labour market, as well as the increase in the number of employ-

ment programs and state welfare provision for the unemployed, would revitalize the role of the working class in resuscitating the economy.

The CTA and its Piqueteros organisations question the government's employment programmes not only in quantitative but in qualitative terms: the amount
of the subsidy must be enough to alter the dynamic of the labour market and income distribution. The union's proposal consists of a comprehensive political strategy based on income redistribution. Unlike the government's patchy employment
programmes, the CTA's project impacts on the level of demand and the development of the domestic market towards the reactivation of the economy, to overcome recession and to discipline capital to the needs of the population (see
IDEP–CTA 2000, 2001).

The organisations gathered in the BPN reject the FTV's demand for inclusion for being "reformist." Slogans such as "jobs for everyone" and "fair distribution of income" imply a deeper subordination to the capitalist logic. The BPN
claims that the Piquetero movement is a fundamental subject of the struggle for
Socialism. Generally speaking, the BPN works on the idea that in December
2001 Argentina entered a revolutionary situation and, by advocating the realisation of a revolution in traditional terms, considers the role of the Piquetero
movement within it as paramount. As a fundamental subject of the struggle for
Socialism, the Piqueteros must reject the FTV and CTA reformism. The unemployed are key agents in the struggle of the working class against exploitation:

> The Piquetero movement is the most genuine creation of the working
> class and the exploited masses of the last twenty five years... it was
> born out of a vital need of the working masses (and not only the un-
> employed...insofar as it "organises the disorganised" the Piquetero
> movement is itself a barrier to the attempts of the bourgeoisie to atom-
> ise the working class by means of unemployment (Oviedo 2001, p. 5).

The Piqueteros of the BNP share the diagnosis that mass unemployment
speaks of the incapacity of the present social regime of accumulation to reproduce labour power and, therefore, it indicates the existence of a crisis of
capitalism. Following this, the FTV's campaigns, based on the negotiation of
the so-called "genuine" job creation, and the autonomist strategies of co-op-
erativism, productive projects and self-employment developed by the MTDAV
(see below), will only help the unemployed to survive but will not eradicate the
system of exploitation.

The Piqueteros struggle must be a struggle against the "capitalist logic" led
by the vanguard party. In other words, the Piquetero movement must move ac-
cordingly to a wider strategy of the left, which, whilst being supported by the
permanent mobilisation of "the masses, must break the politics of exploitation
of the *patronales* aiming to reduce wages, counter posing anti-capitalists methods and strategies" (Oviedo 2001, p. 17). To them, the way out is not "eco-

nomic" but political, and revolutionary, with the Piquetero movement as a leading force (Rieznick 2002).

Finally, the autonomous groups aim at moving beyond the demand for "income distribution" and "social inclusion" which characterizes the strategy of the FTV but does not agree with the struggle for Socialism proposed by the BPN. For instance, the MTDAV, which represented a relatively small sector within of the movement, comprising of a dozen organisation from the south of Greater Buenos Aires, attempts to change the logic of power and money "from below" and claims that they don't want power "in a system impregnated by values which don't have any response to society" (Fernández, cited in Vales 2002).

The Movement of the Unemployed is, for the MTD Solano a source of counter-power and dignity (MTD Solano, 2002). Like the others, their work develops on territorial local bases and intends to recreate solidarity networks in each local environment, i.e. the neighbourhood. Direct democracy and participation in decision-making processes are central to this project. Popular education allows a permanent debate of the meaning of this community work, the identity of the Piqueteros, wider political issues, and links with other organisations.

The MTDAV project is driven by the will to recover the human capacity to work and create in solidarity with the intention of satisfying essential community needs within a context of hunger, crime, alcoholism, poverty and disillusion produced by capitalism and intensified by neo-liberalism. They challenge the paramount significance of money as the main determinant of social life. Work is a natural human quality or attribute directed to the production of use values and this human capacity has been, is, alienated in the form of exploitation. Dignified work would be that which is freed from exploitation, i.e. autonomous work. Dignified work means then the possibility to produce in solidarity, fighting the idea of creating surplus or profit, money, the most visible form of capitalist exploitation:

> You feel a worker when you are self-valorised, a human being who has recovered part of his/her identity. One is a worker insofar as s/he is contributing to the collective, rather than creating profit. If one thinks that a worker is a person who creates profit, then the unemployed are pariahs. Here, we work with other values, not those given by society (cited in MTD and CS 2002, p. 70)

CRISIS AND RECOMPOSITION: PIQUETEROS "IN AND AGAINST THE STATE"
TRANSITION: BETWEEN REPRESSION AND POLICY

The financial collapse of December 2001 marked a turning point as failure of neoliberal reforms promoted by the IMF and World Bank became instantly apparent. In December 2001, the country's economy collapsed, produced the biggest default in world economic history. Social mobilisation forced the resignation of national authorities demanding "*¡que se vayan todos!*" (out with them all!). Direct and radical forms of action (such as factory occupations and neighbourhood assemblies) rejected the representative and institutional politics. With the political and economic crisis of December 2001 the differences among these three sectors of the Piquetero movement became even more apparent as the recomposition of the economy and the state took place.

The politics of President Duhalde (2002) towards the Piqueteros swung between a policy of incorporation and a policy of repression — a classic example of a policy of stick and carrot. The abandonment of the dollar-peso parity advised by the IMF in January 2002 shortly after the financial crisis, aimed to contain inflation, to minimise the fall in industrial output, and re-establish trust in the financial system. Duhalde's devaluation policy simultaneously favoured concentrated economic groups with a new "rescue plan" (see Basualdo et al, 2002) and perpetuated poverty, as inflation eroded the incomes of wage earners. Thus, more than seven million people fell below the poverty line between October 2001 and October 2002. By January 2002 there were 21 million people out of a total population of 37 million who lived under the poverty line, ten million of these considered destitute. In other words, 57.5 percent of Argentines lacked sufficient income to cover basic needs.[6] Soon after the devaluation, wages continued to decline vis-à-vis the rising value of the US dollar and the constant increase in the cost of the family food basket.[7] Poverty deeply affected the young. In February 2002 the national rate of unemployment stood at 21.8 percent. Thirty-nine percent of the young had been unemployed for more than six months and more than one million of those aged 15–24 neither studied nor worked (Lozano and Hourest, 2002). Individual participation in various forms of social protest also increased in the period following the crisis from 7.6 percent before October 2001 to 16.2 percent (Fiszbein *et al,* 2002).

After declaring a "National Occupational Emergency" in January 2002, and following the advice of the "Roundtable for Argentine Dialogue," a new employment programme was launched by Decree 565 in April 2002. The plan "Male and Female Unemployed Heads of Household" *(Jefas y Jefes de Hogar Desocupados,* JyJHD) funded by a World Bank loan of $600 million and from export taxes, sought to assist heads of household with children under 18, pregnant women or disabled persons of any age, who were not beneficiaries of other social programmes. The plan intended to achieve "constitutional family rights to social inclusion" (Arts. 75 and 22, of the National Constitution) by offering a cash transfer of 150 pesos (£30) per month to eligible individuals who would register to receive it. In return, almost two million beneficiaries of the plan must engage in productive work or training, and ensure that their children are in education.

In June 2002, the confrontation between the administration of President Duhalde and the autonomous sectors of the movement entered a phase of overt and direct repression. Indeed, June 2002 was a massacre (see Dinerstein 2003a).

The deepening of the economic crisis pushed forward demands for more pro-grammes of job creation and income distribution. The mobilisation of the Pi-queteros fit well within the intense political climate of early 2002, when participants in neighbourhood assemblies, workers in occupied factories, savers' organisations, trade unions, students and human rights organisations were protesting against the IMF, international creditors and corrupt politicians. Against this backdrop, the provisional government was determined to harness protest as a condition to stabilise the economy and the country's politics.

The political project of the MTDAV was regarded by the government as particularly alarming, especially given the rebellious spirit ensuing from the cri-sis of December 2001. The MTDAV operated under the slogan "Work, Dignity and Social Change," and was qualitatively different from the rest, insofar as it was driven by notions of dignity and autonomy in achieving social change.

On June 26, the MTDAV activists blocked one of the main arteries connect-ing Greater Buenos Aires and the capital city. At the Avellaneda Bridge, the un-employed demanded an increase in the amount and number of subsidies to the unemployed, a family subsistence allowance, health and education, the end of crim-inalisation of protest and repression of the activists. Underpinning their demands around the issue of unemployment there was a clear intention to defy the Peronist elite in power and their project based on clientelism and continuing economic ad-justments. The government's response to the roadblock was blunt: brutal repres-sion. The uncontrolled police operation labelled by the government as a "manhunt" led to the murder of two young activists, Maximiliano Kosteki and Dario Santil-lán, and injury and hospitalisation of hundreds of others.[8] It was a massacre.

Its implications were profound. First, it led to new forms of class solidarity with the unemployed like, for example, the mobilisation of thousands against both unemployment and repression under the motto "Piquets and pot-banging, the struggle is one!" (*Piquetes y Cacerolas, la lucha es una sola!*). Secondly, it un-leashed a political scandal which forced the provisional administration to call for early national elections in July 2002. This call for national elections produced anxiety within the Movement of Unemployed Workers. Whereas all organisa-tions agreed that elections would not bring about real change and condemned the increasing repression of protests by the government, their attitude towards the election varied. Whereas those close to unions and left-wing parties participated in the elections of April and May 2003, the autonomous sections did not. They refused to participate and boycotted the vote, maintaining the idea of building counter power and rebellion against power as the vehicle of change.

THE RETURN OF THE POPULIST STATE:
THE "INSTITUTIONALISATION" OF PIQUETEROS ACTION?

In May 2003, Kirchner publicly recognised that employment programmes pro-vided limited assistance to those in need but that they would not work in the long term. In his view, the solution to unemployment and poverty was urgent. To provide some figures, despite an 8 percent growth in GDP since 2003 (MDS, 2004), high levels of unemployment, job problems and great social inequality persist. Open unemployment of about 1.3 million is still very high.[9] Unemployment severely affects the young: in 2004, six out of 10 people between 15 and 29 years of age (more than 5.5 million) were poor, and only 37 percent of them work (National Department of Youth in *La Nación*, 22.11.04). Only a minority of workers, that is 3.4 million, are registered as waged. Another 3.3 million workers are registered as "unwaged." Although the latter group could be seen as self-employed, in most of the cases this term is a smoke-screen to disguise unregistered employment in the shadow economy. By the end of 2004 there were five million workers with no legal rights and social security. In addition, in the last seven years there has been an expansion of child labour and child homelessness, reaching 1.5 million (MTEySS and UNICEF in *La Nación* 9.5.05).

The government implemented some strategies in the hope of depoliticising issues around unemployment, thereby neutralising the Piquetero movement. These policies were not completely rejected by most of the Piquetero organisations. Rather, a concurrence between new policy making and the Piqueteros organisations was achieved, including those with radical mobilisation strategies.

First, the government emphasised its interest in job creation, the restoration of the culture of work, and the fight against unregistered work — placed at the centre of policy-making. This matches the FTV, UTD and other Piquetero organisations' claims for the creation of "genuine" work and fair income distribution.[10] Secondly, the government launched new social programmes that sought to incorporate into a "new policy ethos" the communitarian and solidarity principles and social practices that underpin the *projectos productivos* and other forms of collective action of the Piquetero organisations. This attempt at incorporation qua institutionalisation extended also to the provision of technical and financial support to the Piqueteros. The new programmes celebrate local state intervention, promote bottom-up decision-making processes and encourage principles of the "social economy" (MDS, 2004).[11] The programmes do seem to be having the effect of disempowering the Piqueteros by institutionalising their social actions, which are an essential constituent of their politics. The success of the *proyectos productivos* — vital for the organisational growth of the Piquetero organisations — depends mainly on resources from the local and national governments, and the manner in which the resources are allocated. However, financial, material or technical support for community projects is not received directly from the government, but channelled through NGOs. This forces groups undertaking community work either to become an NGO (by legally registering, which involves a process of authentication by government inspectors, and assessment of the worth of their proposed project), or to negotiate with an existing NGO to be included in their fold to receive state funds. It allows the government to diffuse the political power of Piqueteros equating them with any other voluntary organisation and making them compete for funds with local politicians and other NGOs. This, then, decomposed Piquetero resistance on the basis of a pluralist re-ordering of social conflict, and concomitant conceptions of civil society.

Finally, president Kirchner's attempt at a "dialogue" with the Piquetero Movement led to new realignments amongst them. On the one hand, the autonomous groups held a positive yet cautious attitude towards the new government and remained firmly attached to the idea to construct counter power through community work. On the other hand, two other sections of the movement have been neutralised for different reasons. The "Kirchneristas," who have accepted the new policy line, believed that a close relationship with the government might bring more financial and political power to their organisations. They are civic associations that manage substantial projects with high social impact. Two examples of such projects are a coordinated system of housing co-operatives in La Matanza run by the FTV, and Centres for the Promotion of Literacy run by *Barrios de Pie*. Some of the Piquetero leaders have identified politically with the government (e.g. leaders of FTV). Others have been co-opted into the government and have become key figures in designing and delivering social policies (e.g. leaders of *Barrios de Pie* occupy high level posts at the Ministry of Social Development).

The "anti-Kirchneristas" or *duros* have actively opposed the government from the outset. Their way of voicing their demands for more employment programmes and an increase in the cash transfer from pesos 150 to pesos 350 per capita have been direct and radical. For example, in August 2003, the Fifth National Workers Assembly (ANT) gathered more than 3,000 delegates from different organisations to discuss a plan of action for October 2003. On 28 November of that year, for the first time under Kirchner, the Piquetero movement, with the exception of the FTV, blocked several key junctions of the capital city as well as the main access to it from its outskirts in a seven-day protest under the motto "For work against infamy." They demanded an increase in employment programmes and overdue payments, as well as an extra Christmas bonus of fifty pesos. In October 2004 the BPN occupied the building of the Ministry of Labour preventing the national authorities, including the Minister of Labour, from exiting. Whereas the Kirchneristas campaigned for Kirchner's candidates in the October 2005 parliamentary elections (being accused by opposition MPs of helping the government to buy votes by distributing domestic appliances and cash to the unemployed and the vulnerable), the anti-Kirchneristas disrupted the pre-election campaigning by "camping out" at the historical Plaza de Mayo during the "Piqueteros Week of Struggle" (*Semana de lucha Piquetera*).

Despite their forceful mobilisation, the Piqueteros were politically isolated by the government's use of police and legal threats, political ridicule and "emergency funds" being informally channelled by the key people from the President's entourage in different Departments (some of whom were former activists) who bargain directly with the leaders of social organisations. The issue at stake is that demands for more employment programmes and an increase in the amount of money allocated per capita put forward by the *∂uros* in the Plaza de Mayo contradict the government's stated medium-term plans to end employment programmes and concentrate on job creation. From the perspective of the government, the end of focused programmes would prevent the leaders managing them for their political purposes. However, there is doubt that this will happen, as focused programmes have been an important tool of social control used by the government at all levels so effectively to date.

LESSONS FROM THE JOURNEY

A capitalist crisis can "involve a *salto mortale* for capital, with no guarantee of a safe landing" (Holloway 2002, p. 204). Yet, from the account provided above, we can see how a crisis involves, likewise, a *salto mortale* for labour. In a moment of crisis, labour possesses the capacity to reveal and denounce the violence of capital openly and (re-)invent concrete organisational forms of resistance. A crisis allows labour to confront the state, capital and the law, but also to rethink and recreate the forms through which resistance is organised. In other words, crisis allows labour to challenge its mode of existence. The political implication of this is that more than "objective" opportunities to undertake a revolution against capitalism, crisis offers an opportunity for labour to reinvent itself in a dialectical fashion. It is in this deconstruction and recomposition of "subjectivity" that the "objectivity" of capital stumbles with unexpected results (Dinerstein 2005).

The Piquetero movement was created by one of the most dramatic effects of neoliberal policies in Argentina: mass unemployment. Initially, most commentators were sceptical about the ability of the unemployed workers to protest and organise autonomously. Their capacity to influence politics and policy was believed to be very limited, largely due to the prevailing idea that the "sub-proletarian" (Bourdieu, 1998) is "excluded" from the productive system and from those institutionalised forms of representation that allow workers, for instance, to be heard and to participate. My journey through the emergence and development of the movement showed that as the regional roadblocks developed into new organisational forms with mobilisation, organisational and networking capacities, they posed a real challenge to policy makers as well as existing conceptions of the politics of unemployment. The unemployed defied previous forms of mobilisation and resistance, such as political parties and trade unions.

The recomposition of the state during the period following the crisis found them deeply divided. The project of counter-power is weakening and has resulted in further divisions within the groups. For instance in September 2003, two of the main organisations joining the MTDAV, that is MTD Solano and MTD Kosteki from Guernica, Province of Buenos Aires, followed by the MTD from Allen and

Cipoletti, Rio Negro, left the CTDAV. In a document they explained that the decision was based on their discontent with the development of factions or blocks within the *coordinadora* which reproduced the logic of bureaucratic organisations and unequal power relations, weakening the *asamblea* as the site of decision-making and the construction of new social values (Interview by Lavaca.org, *Periodismo de Verdad*, to the MTD Solano, September 2003, mimeo):

> We have decided to consolidate our territorial organisations, instead of privileging the creation of super-structures. We advocate the construction of horizontal and autonomous organisations that make decision through consensus. We believe in the free articulation of diverse experiences, radically opposed to any form of domination or centralised practices. We advocate autonomy as a concrete practice wherein interests, needs and comrades' compromise define the course of action (Excerpts from Document September 2003, MTD Solano, mimeo)

The FTV leaders are not helping the movement to unify strategies. First, their "McCarthyism," particularly against autonomous tendencies, has been made unashamedly explicit. After the massacre of June 2002 a debate about the methods used by the unemployed at the roadblocks was opened, allowing the government to introduce another split within the movement, dividing the "good" and the "bad" Piqueteros, that is those groups who accepted the boundaries imposed by the government (such as the FTV) and those who had "crossed the threshold," respectively. Unlike the FTV within the CTA, the Piqueteros of the *Coordinadora Aníbal Verón* organize their own security at the roadblock, covering their faces and using sticks for self-defence. During those days when the idea that a "return to violence" in Argentina in the hands of the Piqueteros was taking place inundated the media, the FTV argued that:

> we were aware of the government's repressive plans, I have been told about the government decision to repress the roadblock...this is why we did not participate. The MTDAV is responsible for the lives of their members (D'Elía, author's interview 27.6.02).

Whereas the CTA called immediately for a general strike to repudiate police brutality, it became apparent that the leaders of the FTV did not call for participation in that roadblock. The day previous to the murders, the government had publicly threatened the Piqueteros with repression if they blocked access to the capital city. A bitter discussion within the CTA between those members who wanted to participate in the solidarity demonstration called by the MTDAV to repudiate state terror unleashed against the Piqueteros (human rights activists, left-wing unions joining the CTA) and those CTA members who preferred to organize an independent demonstration (the leaders of the FTV) followed the

June 2002 episodes. Beyond tactical matters, there had been an unfortunate "complicity" of the FTV with state repression against the so-called "anarchist" attitude of the MTDAV (Dinerstein 2003b).

Secondly, the open identification of the FTV leaders with Kirchner's politics and the state, and their concrete participation in politics as MPs, contradicts the CTA project to construct an independent yet inclusive political movement. It also contradicts the independence of the Piquetero movement.

Finally, the strategy of mobilisation at any cost of the "duros" with no serious discussion of the horizons ahead is not contributing to the strength of the movement either. Although the BPN underestimates the project of the autonomous wing of the movement and criticises the struggle for income distribution as reformist, it is itself engaged in informal negotiations with the government for more employment programmes. Leaving aside the question of the consistency of its approach, its stance reveals the internal contradictions of the movement, which the Kirchner government was able to exploit.

The Piqueteros' experience of mobilisation and community work is paramount in the history of resistance in Argentina for their capacity to mobilise the marginalised, to carry out their innovative community (political) projects, and to confront the state during a period of crisis. Doubtless, both mobilisation at the roadblocks and the autonomous community projects helped individuals to recover their capacity for mobilisation and action after a period of intense individualisation and disillusionment. They also facilitated the reinvention of the political (collective) subjectivity understood as the re-composition of identities, organisational forms and action strategies capable of articulating collective action by inventing new common notions such as the defence of dignity, autonomy, democracy and justice. However, the movement has reached a political stalemate vis-à-vis the recomposition of the state since 2003. Whether or not this stalemate is only temporary remains to be seen.

NOTES

[1] The analysis presented is based on two sources of data: the author's ongoing project "The Movement of the Unemployed in Argentina" (HS118X), funded by the ESRC within the framework of the "Non-Governmental Public Action" (NGPA) ESRC Programme, LSE, UK, and previous research carried out during the period 1997–2004, dealing with popular mobilisation and political and economic change in Argentina. I would like to thank the Economic and Social Research Council for its generous support. Thanks also to all interviewees for the information provided and for facilitating access to valuable material and documentation used here. Finally, a word of appreciation to Gregory Schwartz for his ever helpful suggestions. All the usual disclaimers apply.

2 Fatal victims of state repression at roadblocks have been Victor Choque in Tierra del Fuego in 1995; Teresa Rodriguez in Neuquén in 1997, Aníbal Verón in Tartagal in November 2000. On state repression of social protest see CELS 2003. For a "typical" roadblock see Dinerstein 2001.

3 Even school children have recently included them in a list of elements which, together with "mate" and "tango," define the meaning of "Argentinean-ness."

4 Kirchner was one among the fourteen presidents and chiefs of state invited to attend the Cumbre de Gobiernos Progresistas (Conference of Progressist Governments) organised by the Labour Party and the British Prime Minister in London on July 13, 2003.

5 See www.cta.org.ar.

6 The criteria to establish the level of poverty and indigence by INDEC is based on the value of the family basket, estimated at 193.77 pesos per adult for the city of Buenos Aires and its outskirts in April 2002. This figure varies according to age and gender as 598 pesos per month, considering indigents those who live on less than 220 pesos per month (Rameri and Raffo 2005).

7 During 2002, the price of the food basket increased by 55 percent and the prices for basic foods increased by 79 percent. Inflation affected the poorer sectors of the population who spend most of their income on food.

8 See details in *Página/12* and *La Nación* — several issues 27.6.05 and 29.6.05; Dinerstein 2003a,b. Testimonies in *Libertad*, Documental by the Grupo Alavio, 2001.

9 If the beneficiaries of JyJHD were included, the rate would even go up to 16.6 percent.

10 In addition to reclassify beneficiaries on the basis of their employability (CCNPS 2005) two new programmes have been lunched by the Ministry of Labour: the "Plan for the Promotion of Employment: More and Better Jobs" (*Plan para la Promoción de Empleo: Más y Mejor Trabajo*) and the "Plan against Unregistered Work" (*Contra el Trabajo no Registrado*).

11 Three substantial, and interlinked, programmes constitute the government's new approach. i) The "National Food Security Plan: The Most Urgent Hunger" (*Plan Nacional de Seguridad Alimentaria: El Hambre Más Urgente*); ii) "Families for Social Inclusion Plan" (*Plan Familias para la Inclusión Social*) and iii) The "National Plan for Local Development and Social Economy: Let's Work!" (*Plan Nacional de Desarrollo Local y Economía Social: Manos a la Obra*).

REFERENCES

Basualdo, E. et al. (2002), "Las transferencias de recursos a la cúpula económica durante la presidencia Duhalde" *FRENAPO*, unpublished discussion paper, Buenos Aires.

Bourdieu, P. (1998), *Acts of Resistance. Against the new myths of our time*, Polity Press, Cambridge

CCNPS (*Consejo Consultivo Nacional de Políticas Sociales*) (2005), *Noveno Informe al Poder Ejecutivo Nacional*, Marzo, unpublished report, Buenos Aires.

CELS (2003), *El estado frente a la protesta social 1996–2002*, Siglo XXI, Buenos Aires.

Dinerstein, A. C. (2001), "Roadblocks in Argentina," *Capital & Class*, no. 74.

Dinerstein, A. C. (2002), "Regaining Materiality: Unemployment and the Invisible Subjectivity of Labour" in Dinerstein, A. C. and Neary, M. (eds), *The Labour Debate. An investigation into the theory and reality of capitalist work*, Ashgate, Aldershot.

Dinerstein, A. C. (2003a), "A Silent Revolution: The Unemployed Workers Movement in Argentina" *Travail, Capital & Societé*, CDS, McGill University, Vol. 34 (2).

Dinerstein, A. C. (2003b), "Power or counter power? The Dilemma of the Piquetero Movement in Argentina," *Capital & Class*, no. 82.

Dinerstein, A. C. (2005), "Entre el éxtasis y el desencuentro. Los desafíos de la rebelión" in Bonnet A., Holloway J. and Tischler S. (eds), *Marxismo Abierto. Una visión Europea y Latinoamericana*, Herramienta Press, Buenos Aires.

Fiszbein, A. et al. (2002), "Argentina's crisis and its impact on household welfare," *World Bank Office for Argentina, Chile, Paraguay and Uruguay*, Working Paper no. 1/02, November.

Holloway, J. (2002), *Change the World without Taking Power*, Pluto, London.

IDEP–CTA (2002), *Shock Distributivo, autonomía nacional y democratización IDEP–Editorial La Página*, Buenos Aires.

Lozano, C. and Hourest, M. (2002), "La democracia y el FMI: entre la mentira y el crimen," *Realidad Económica* 187, IADE, Buenos Aires.

MDS (2004), *Lineamientos de Políticas Sociales 2004*, #1, August, Buenos Aires.

MTD (2002), "El MTD y la construcción del poder popular," *Herramienta* 21, Buenos Aires.

MTD Solano and Colectivo Situaciones (2002), *Hipótesis 891*, Ediciones Mano en Mano, Buenos Aires.

Rameri, A. and Raffo, T. (2005), "Los nuevos pobres e indigentes que arroja la inflación," IDEP–CTA, accessed 5.5.05, http://www.cta.org.ar/base/article php3?id_article=1067.

Rieznick, P. (2002), "Crítica a los Economistas de Izquierda," *PO 762*, 18.7.02 http://www.po.org.ar/home.htm.

Oviedo, L. (2001), *De las primeras Coordinadoras a las Asambleas Nacionales. Una Historia del Movimiento Piquetero*, Rumbos, Buenos Aires.

Vales, L. (2002), "Los proyectos políticos piqueteros," *Página/12*, 23.6.02.

14
For a Compositional Analysis of the Multitude

Nick Dyer-Witheford

INTRODUCTION

The web page of AUT-OP-SYS, a major site for the discussion of autonomist Marxism, takes as its introduction a classic text of the tradition in its English language variants, which first appeared in the US journal *Zerowork*, and defines the concept of "class composition":

> — Capital's "flaws" are not internal to it and nor is the crisis: they are determined by the dynamics of working class struggle. To be understood, that dynamics and cycle of struggles requires an analysis that must operate at four, interconnected and necessary levels.
> — First is the analysis of the struggles themselves: their content, their directions, how they develop and how they circulate...
> Second, we study the dynamics of the different sectors of the working class: the way these sectors affect each other and thus the relations of the working class with capital....
> — Third, we consider the relations between the working class and its "official" organizations, that is, the trade unions, the "workers' parties," welfare organizations, etc....
> — Fourth, all these aspects have to be related to the capitalist initiative in terms of general social planning, investment, technological innovations, employment and to the institutional setting of capitalist society....
> — Through these interdependent levels of class analysis we can understand the relations between the working class and capital. They enable us to specify the "composition of the working class" (*Zerowork*).

The full statement, including expansions of each point, can be found in a collection by Midnight Notes (1992, 108–14). Noting that the statement was written in 1975, aut-op-sy (nd) asks:

> How well does it stand up today, in the face of the dramatic shifts that have reshaped the worlds of waged and unwaged work since that time? What does mass struggle mean in a period when the mass worker seems to have lost its centrality? What do the struggles of women mean when the family and the welfare state have continued to fracture? What does the circulation of struggle mean at a time when millions are fleeing their place of birth? What does communism mean in the face of the "socialist" bloc's collapse and the emergence of a global ecological crisis?

This chapter responds to those cogent questions by arranging an encounter between "composition" and another idea, more recently prominent in autonomist thought, "multitude." Composition emphasizes the empirical, rigorous investigation of concrete class struggles. Multitude is a theory, to date posited mainly in very abstract terms, of the changing scope and conditions of such struggles. To connect them is, however, controversial, because analysts of class composition (including organizers of aut-op-sys) have sharply criticized multitude theorists. The argument here, however, is that while there are substantial grounds for this criticism, there are more compelling reasons for combining the two ideas to understand and expedite the class struggles of the twenty-first century.

To make this argument, I first say a little about the content and context of both concepts, go on to look at why the composition-analysts have criticized the theory of multitude, and explain why, despite these sometimes telling points, I continue to "see something in" multitude as a horizon of inquiry into contemporary struggles. After briefly mentioning some actually-existing instances of such inquiry, I conclude by revising the *Zerowork* text to outline a methodology for a compositional analysis of the multitude.

THE SCHOOL OF COMPOSITION

The concept of class composition originates with the theorists of Italian *operaismo* (workerism) (Alquati, 1974; Tronti, 1977; Panzieri, 1976, 1980) and in the factories of Northern Italy in the 1960s and 1970s. Rejecting ritual invocations of "the working class" by communist party bureaucrats, trades union officials and left academics, *operaismo* sought to understand and assist waves of mass worker militancy: strikes, wildcatting and sabotage. They bought to the task two major instruments. One was theoretical: a radical rereading of Marx's account of capital-labor relation that *started* from working class struggle and its cyclical renewal, rather than finishing with it as afterthought to some supposedly automatic historical process (see Cleaver, 1979). The other was empirical: an investigative curiosity about workers' actual experience of labour and struggle, a curiosity that found canonical support in Marx's (1880) call for "a worker's inquiry" with its list of one hundred questions about the conditions of exploitation.

In his definitive history of the "school of composition," Steve Wright (2002) documents how these theoretical and empirical elements were fused into powerful tool of militant analysis. Inverting Marx's concept of the "organic composition" of capital (the ratio of fixed to variable capital in production) *operaismo* applied the term "composition" to the dynamics of struggle against capital. They distinguished the "technical" and "political" class composition. Technical composition is the way capital organizes the work-force in production — the division of labour, supervision and discipline, and use of machinery. Political composition describes how, and to what degree, workers make the collectivity of the workplace a basis for counter-power (see Kolinko, 2001).

These concepts informed a series of empirical inquiries ("*inchiesta*") into mass-worker conflicts, combining data, observation and interviews (see Wright 2002). Most focused on the immediate point of production. Most of these workplaces were industrial — automobile plants, chemical continuous processes, and technical operations. Many of the studies aimed at identifying actual or potential leading or vanguard sectors. These analyses fed back into the strategies and tactics of the political groupings in which *operaismo* was involved.

Wright notes there was persistent tension between theoretical and empirical elements in the *operaismo* mix. In principle, theory was submitted to the ongoing re-verification of empirical finding. In practice, theory was sometimes reluctant to bow. As he observes (2002, 187), "the best work of classical workerism" was made possible by the "recognition of material divisions existing alongside the formal unity provided by the conditions of wage labor." But there was also a tendency in *operaismo* theory to idealize the working class as pure anti-capitalist (see Bonefeld, 2003). One result could be a failure to properly estimate working-class weaknesses, which was to eventually have serious consequences for the Italian ultra-left.

But, in a broad sense, composition theory *did* adjust under empirical pressures. Though *operaismo* was focused on the immediate point of production, its theorists also affirmed (even if abstractly) the importance of the "social factory" — worker's homes, schools, communities and culture. As Italy spiraled into widening political crisis, a new set of activists, associated with the social movements of *autonomia*, began to apply the concepts of composition to this wider sphere, sometimes with results its originators were reluctant to accept. Most radical of these revisions was that feminist autonomists (Dalla Costa & James, 1972) who argued that class composition had to reckon with the division between waged (male) work in production and unwaged (female) reproductive labor at home. Other "compositionists" (Berardi, 2003) brought the optic to bear on the struggles of "new social subjects" — students, casual workers and the unemployed — some heavily emphasizing the theoretical lens (see Negri, 2005), others more empirical (see Bologna, 1980).

The repression of the Italian movements in 1977 brutally truncated these experiments (and perhaps revealed some flaws in their approach). But the concept of class composition, which had itself assimilated influences from other international struggles, was relayed well beyond its point of origin, to be taken up and further altered in a complex global circulation (see Wright, 2006). Thus, for example, the work of the German collectives Wildcat (2003) and Kolinko (2001, 2002) constitutes perhaps the most direct, detailed contemporary application of *operaismo's* method to struggles at the point of production. On the other hand, the "social factory" expansion — embracing Dalla Costa and James' emphasis on unpaid labor and social reproduction — has been most fully worked through by the theorists and collectives of North American workerism (Cleaver, 1979; Midnight Notes, 1992): the *Zerowork* statement comes from this lineage, as a reading of the full text makes clear.

Theory only advances with struggle: this is central to the compositionist method. So it is not surprising that the changes this method has undergone since the 1960s were thrown into sharp relief by the eruption in the 1990s of another cycle of struggles, the great rebellion against neo-liberalism that started with IMF riots in the global South and hit public awareness in the North with the Zapatista uprising of 1994. In an analysis of this uprising, Midnight Notes member's at once recalled, and marked their departure from, the origins of composition analysis by referring to the work of one of *operaismo's* members, Alquati, who:

> ... argued that movements of working class struggles comprise a network, not just regionally or nationally, but even on the international level. A network is the unity of struggles in both their *vertical* and *horizontal* articulations. The vertical articulation is the point within the capitalist circuit of production/reproduction; the horizontal articulation is the spatial distribution and linkage. This combined vertical-horizontal articulation of struggles pivots around decisive points of interconnection: *nodal points* (Neill 1997, see also 2001).

They went on, however, to say that the Zapatistas (and many other contemporary struggles) demonstrate that this network of struggles no longer has its key nodes in the factories of the mass worker. Rather such nodes are as likely to be found in struggles of peasants and other unwaged and disposed sectors caught up in new rounds of primitive accumulation. Put alongside Cleaver's (1994) famous analysis of how news of the Zapatista uprising was circulated via Internet to form an "electronic circulation of struggle," this gives a good sense of the scope of contestation — from cyberspace to coffee plantations — a new account of class composition confronts. But doing so brings us face with a very controversial creature: the multitude.

The Moment of Multitude

The concept of "multitude" was proposed in Michael Hardt and Antonio Negri's *Empire* (2000). The timing was superb: appearing in the context of huge demonstrations in North America and Europe against the World Trade Organization, the World Bank, the International Monetary Fund and the G8, the book seemed to arise directly out of the multifarious throngs of witches, workers, hackers and greens teeming in the streets of Seattle, Prague, Quebec and Genoa; comparisons with the relation of *The Communist Manifesto* to the revolutions of 1848 were made.

The actual genealogy of *Empire*, and multitude, was of course longer and more complex. Hardt is an American activist-academic, an expert in the philosophy of Giles Deleuze; Negri a famous veteran of, and former political exile from, the Italian struggles. The ideas they presented reflected the discussions and controversies of the Parisian journal *Futur Antérieur*, whose other participants included Maurizio Lazzarato and Paolo Virno, and which had analyzed the cycles of activism in France culminating in the general strikes of 1996 (sometimes — Eurocentrically — called the "first uprising against globalization"). But as such insurgencies generalized into a "movement of movements" (Klein, 2004) it seemed that these concepts had met their world-historical moment.

Empire was exciting. It posited something new under the anti-capitalist sun. Since the book has been very extensively discussed (see Pinguin, 2003) I can treat it summarily, focusing on the idea of multitude.

The Empire (capital E) that Hardt and Negri address is that of a capitalism gone "global." This new globality emerged, they say, in response to the struggles of the 1960s and '70s. Capital sought to evade or destroy high levels of militancy in its developed centres both by becoming nomadic (free trade, *maquiladoras*) and through new technologies, particularly digital systems, that offered a more continuous and capillary penetration of space and time (bringing on the Deleuzian "society of control"). Empire is thus a condition of extreme subsumption. Spatially, there is since 1989 no part of the planet where capital is not dominant; breaking out of old national, and even imperial forms, it is coalescing a worldwide politico-judicial-economic apparatus. Temporally, there is no aspect of human life-time that it does not organize. Empire expropriates not just labor-power, but bio-power (a concept Hardt and Negri adapt from Foucault). If labour-power is human life organized through waged work, bio-power is such life organized through capitalist command the span of its social existence (Hardt & Negri 2000, 221–42).

The concept of multitude, however, posits that these very conditions can be the basis for a new contestation of capital, qualitatively different from previous cycles of struggle.

If resistant labour-power manifested as the working class, resistant bio-power manifests as the multitude.

Because capital is world-wide, the multitude's struggles are intrinsically transnational, manifesting in eruptions from Chiapas to Gaza, Beijing to Genoa. Not so much anti-globalizing as a counter-globalizing, the multitude is a force capable of seizing the positive content of planetary production and communication.

Because the locus of capitalist expropriation is no longer punctually concentrated in the workplace, but omnipresent, the sites of insurgency against it will be multiple. The era of mass-worker leadership is decisively gone, replaced by a swarming of myriad biopolitical initiatives connected in new forms of alliance, affinity and network,

Because the technologies of capitalist command are different from those of the industrial era, they offer different opportunities of subversion. Computerisation, intended to intensify control, paradoxically creates new areas of autonomy. Reversing the emphasis on sabotage of machines in Negri's earlier work, multitude theory rather emphases the potentials for reappropriation and even "spontaneous and elementary communism" (Hardt & Negri 2000, 294).

The multitude arises from conditions of "immaterial labour." This is the term Hardt and Negri (2000, 290–94) apply to work manipulating information, communication and affect, as opposed to hands-on material transformation. Such immaterial labour is, they say, associated with the high-tech and service economies of post-Fordism, as opposed to Fordist manufacturing. The pre-eminence of immaterial labour is, they suggest (in contradiction to their tendency elsewhere to shift focus away from the point of production), the basis of the emergence of the multitude — the common condition that allows the convergence of otherwise separate struggles.

Multitude is an optimistic concept. In place of the decades-long pessimism of the left intellect, it suggested the emergence of a counter-force with the capacity to make inroads against global capital. Without purporting to propose a political platform, Hardt and Negri sketched three demands they believed important to the new activism: the right to global citizenship and the planetary mobility of labour, the right to a social wage or guaranteed income for all, and the right to reappropriation, meaning "free access to and control over knowledge, information, communication and affects... the primary means of biopolitical production" (2000, 407).

Multitude is an iconoclastic idea. Its etymology runs from Spinoza and other 17th-century republicans, not Marx and Lenin. It displaces terms previously central not only to autonomists, but to all other versions of Marxism — the "industrial proletariat," the "working class." Negri (2002) insists multitude is "a class concept," albeit one of creative power exploited not just in work, but in "social cooperation... [in] the networks that compose the whole and the whole that comprises the network." But even if one accepts this argument (many do not), the linguistic innovation of "multitude," breaking with a deeply entrenched class-struggle lexicon, is startling.

Multitude is also an unfinished idea. In *Empire*, its discussion only occupies the last few pages of a long book (leading some to complain the authors had skimped on autonomism's emphasis on revolt). One of the appealing, or annoying, features of its presentation was that in contrast to customary cast-iron certainties on the left, Hardt and Negri in interview admitted the concept was a preliminary, and probably premature, attempt to grasp a new wave of struggles; multitude was not only provocative, but also manifestly under-construction, in a way that invited further development.

This invitation was, in some quarters, accepted. The idea was discussed and elaborated in the successor to *Futur Antérieur* named (what else?) *Multitude*; the Italian journal *Derive Approdi* elaborated the class analysis of multitude; and Virno published a brief, dense book, *A Grammar of the Multitude* (2004), suggesting that conditions of immateriality and total subsumption were at least as conducive to cynicism as activism. Elsewhere, however, the response was less friendly.

THE VERDICT OF COMRADES AND EVENTS

Like all else in *Empire*, the concept of multitude, while attracting great interest on the left, was also widely criticised (Balakrishnan, 2003; Passavant & Dean, 2004). Many of the condemnations came from positions antipathetic to autonomism, such as more structuralist Marxisms or post-Marxisms that had dispensed with anti-capitalism. But multitude also drew fire from the "school of composition" with which Negri had once been identified. Wildcat (2003), for example declared "the concept of the 'multitude' stands diametrically opposed to the 'workerist' concept of class composition," and condemned Negri's work as "an inversion of the concept of 'class composition.'"

Why would a theory that at first glance seems to continue and expand elements long important to autonomist thought, such as "the social factory," attract this criticism? I will focus on four points: *post-structuralist abstraction, immaterial labour, class anxiety,* and *triumphalist euphoria.*

Post-Structuralist Abstraction: Hardt and Negri's analysis is an exercise in political philosophy, and, moreover in a post-structuralist political philosophy many on the left dislike. Wright speaks of the filtration of *operaismo* insights via "French theorists such as Deleuze and Guattari" as a "melange" (2002, 2). The concept of multitude seems supported far more by discussion of biopower, rhizomes, and virtualities than by data on international division of labour, capital flows, or occupational distribution. This appearance is a little deceptive: in the background lie some quite detailed inquiries into workplaces and social struggles conducted by the *Futur Antérieur* group (e.g. Lazzarato et al., 1990; Lazzarato & Negri, 1993). But while *Empire* takes its impetus from events on the streets of Paris, Seoul and Seattle, and contains some illustrative examples, it seems far — very far — from the amassing of facts, interview and analysis that characterized *operaismo.* Wright (2002, 152–75) sees Negri's work from the 1970s on heavily exaggerating the theoretical side of the theory-empiricism balance in composition-studies. His anticipation of a new cycle of struggle, waged by a new collective subject, Wright claims, persistently outran facts on the ground — a criticism which was made at the time within Italian *autonomia,* and which looms again around the idea of multitude.

Class Anxiety: Although multitude extends social-factory analysis, it moves further away than earlier versions from the immediate point of production. To those for whom the workplace, or even a more generalized concept of "work," remains the necessary anchor for the analysis of class relations, to shift from labour-power to biopower is to go adrift. Despite the insistence of Hardt, Negri and Virno that multitude *is* a class concept, it dislodges "working class" and "workers" as the key terms; implicit or explicit in many critiques is the belief that this empties the core of Marxism. Thus, for example, John Holloway, in a critique of *Empire,* writes that "Worst of all, perhaps, is the total eclipsing of the centrality of doing in the development of the concept of multitude":

> The concept of "working class," for all its problems, for all its deformations, has at least the great merit of taking us to the centrality of human purposive activity, social doing. In the concept of multitude, this is lost completely (2003).

In return, Virno (2004, 45) characterises this type of reaction to multitude-theorists failure to use explicitly "class" language as "electroshocks for monkeys."

Immaterial Labour: The theory of immaterial labour associated with multitude is perhaps the single most contentious part of the theory. Its suggestion of the hegemony of cyborg-style high-tech labour has been criticized from numerous directions: for ignoring the obvious persistence of manual labour, manufacturing and agrarian, on a global scale (Wright, 2005); for focus on the "high" end of the capitalist value-chain at the expense of slave-like conditions at the lower end (Caffentzis, 2003); for conflating within a single category the very different conditions of say, a network system administrator, a latte-serving *barista* and a sex-worker (Dyer-Witheford, 2005). Hardt and Negri have defended their position, pointing out that when Marx claimed a leading historical role for the industrial proletariat it, too, was a tiny minority of the global workforce; they also eventually modified some of their formulations. But the many difficulties attending the "immateriality" thesis have seriously discredited the concept of the multitude.

Triumphalist Euphoria: While a refreshing aspect of multitude-theory was its hopefulness, the question was whether this resurgence of joy passed into giddy millenarianism. The power of the multitude was asserted with a confidence that made light of the problems of the movement of movements, not least those of organization. In place of the attention to the divisions of worker's struggles that compositionist analysis (at its best) allowed, multitude suggested a spontaneous coordination of struggles on the basis of the commonalities of immaterial labour — even *without* communication between different segments. This "incommunicado" thesis contradicted the manifest importance of networking, cyber-spatial and terrestrial, to the movement of movements (Cleaver, 1994; Caffentzis, 2002). It therefore overlooked the difficulties of this process. These problems were apparent even in the Seattle-era high point, with divergences around strategy and tactics between trades unionists and new social movements, North and South, direct actionists and non-violent protestors and many other fractions only thinly covered by a veneer of "civil-society" rhetoric.

But what really threw into the question the optimism of the multitude theory was the change of political landscape following the attacks on the World Trade Centre.

The events of September 11, 2001 and their aftermath raised several towering, smoky, question marks around the concept of multitude. The emergence of a reactionary, theocratic armed struggle against the centres of global capitalism terminated the simple binary, "empire versus multitude." The US invasion of Iraq, a very old-fashioned *imperial* adventure, threw in question the new global Empire from which multitude supposedly arose. Massive demonstrations around the planet against the invasion could be seen as a manifestation of the multitude, but their failure was also a sober reality check on the power of global social movements. And in the global Northwest these movements started to subside and fragment as the "war on terror" chilled activism, and narrowed the scope of what remained.

It was in these circumstances that Hardt and Negri published the sequel to *Empire*. *Multitude* (2004) discussed the new war situation, interpreted as a reactionary reflex of US imperialism against conditions of globalization that threatened its hegemony; partly defended and partly back-peddled on the concept of immaterial labour, and presented an exhaustive inventory of the grievances against capital raised by the movement of movements. A big, baggy book, *Multitude* contained many insights: writing today, as war widens from Afghanistan to Iraq to Lebanon, across the Middle East and into bombings, arrests, surveillance and civil-liberties abuse around the planet, its observations about how militarization not only violent assaults life but functions as a disciplinary apparatus of social reproduction are all-too germane (Hardt & Negri 2004, 12–25). But it provided neither a concise theoretical riposte to critics, nor the concrete evidence to shore up controversial assertions. Appearing in inauspicious conditions, when the movement of movements was in rapid ebb, it couldn't avoid the suspicion that "multitude," a concept born in the sunny aftermath of Seattle, had enjoyed its mayfly moment of celebrity, only to expire on the sudden arrival of harsher weather.

A RECONSIDERATION AFTER SEVEN YEARS

Why, then, after seven years, a torrent of criticism (to which this author also contributed), and in apparently adverse circumstances, return to "multitude"? I confess — I like the word. This may seem a small thing. But the right word concentrates into itself a world of cognition. Multitude does so, on seven counts.

1) It conveys the many-ness of revolts against commodification, the heterogeneity of anti-capitalist activity witnessed in the counter-globalization revolts, and still visible, even if often subdued and scattered. Even a quick *tour d'horizon* of the mid-sized Canadian city where I live (made easy by the local activist computer networks) reveals protests of the homeless, anti-pesticide campaigns, post-carbon planning groups, drives to unionize university research assistants, opposition to local branch plants of the US military-industrial complex, actions of transnational solidarity, support of aboriginal land rights, a (very) loose municipal coalition of such groups and a Regional Social Forum that provides a space of convergence. In all these, anti-corporate, anti-commodification and often, anti-capitalist elements are present. A similar snapshot could be taken at thousands of points around the planet. This multiplicity defies reduction to a single centre or retraction into familiar categories, and still has to be theorized.

2) Amongst these struggles many continue the global dynamics emphasized in multitude-theory. Especially salient are the planetary flows of migration, moving not to any new frontiers but from poor to rich sectors of a world-capitalist economy, and galvanizing a wave of conflict over criminalized border crossing, illicit work and the entwined social reproduction of race and class. To the major examples of Hispanic labor protests in the US and the insurrection of the French *banlieux* in 2006 can be added hundreds of other battles of *sans-papiers*, asylum-seekers, deportation- and rendition-victims (see Mitropoulos, 2006; Moulier-Boutang, 2006). Although often overlooked by critics raging against immateriality, these issues of transnational population flow and nomadic labor were central to the concept of a de-territorialized, hybrid multitude.

3) While the analysis of "immaterial labor" associated with multitude was badly mishandled, it identified crucial issues. Re-appropriations of informational work, through cyber-activism, hacking, piracy, open source and peer-to-peer networks, continue apace. Networks of indie-media and guerrilla news amount today to an autonomous activist media system circulating information and analysis on a speed and scale unthinkable thirty-five years ago (see Kidd 2003, 2004). Other, criminalized struggles over intellectual property are causing information capital serious difficulties, and not just at the high, "yuppie," end of the value chain: they will grow in intensity as "immaterial" networks more deeply interpenetrate "material" production, for example in micro-fabrication. Justified aversion to hyperbole about "immaterial labor" should not prevent analysis of such struggles, and the potentials they contain.

Similarly, the category of "affective labor" has provided an important path for reconsidering the sexual division of labor as it reappears in the context of a largely female service economy, double-shift housework and endemic precarity. In doing so, it has opened the way to the overdue re-feminization of an autonomist tradition that since the days of Dalla Costa and James has been far too male (Del Re, 2005; Dowling, 2006). Thus although the "immaterial labor" thesis was a fiasco, disaggregating its component parts — such as informational and affective work — is important in understanding the multiplicity of labors and struggles in contemporary capital.

4) However much hostility post-structuralist perspectives provoke, they bring with them issues seriously neglected by *operaismo* composition studies, especially in regard to the processes of "subjectification" (Berardi 2003). Virno's (2004, 80) consideration of the "dark side" of the multitude, and the "social individual's" ambivalence between rebellion and opportunism, raises crucial points about the ethical and affective dimensions of a capitalism whose spectacular cultural apparatus is devoted to the production of subjectivity.

5) Although the "war on terror" complicates the analysis of multitude, it also makes it even more necessary. The recent re-contextualization of the concept by the Retort group (2005) is important for two reasons. One is that it dispenses with Hardt and Negri's "Empire" in favor of David Harvey's (2003) analysis of a "new imperialism" arising from US-based initiatives for oil control, militarization, financialization and new rounds of primitive accumulation. The second is that it takes seriously Al Qaeda and its affines as movements assimilating anti-capitalist critique and revolutionary organization (the vanguard party plus networked rhizomes) for theocratic ends. In this re-mapping, multitude (*aka* the movement of movements) reappears as the antagonist of imperialism and fundamentalism in a three-way global fight (see also Dyer-Witheford, 2004); in the era of the "war on terror," the best way to organize against both war and terror may be from the perspective of multitude.

6) The move to analysis of bio-political struggles, rather than labor struggles, is a theoretical innovation consistent with Marx's accounts of capital as a social metabolism, operating not just in production but through an entire process of circulation. This process, described in the introduction to *Grundrisse* and in Volume 2 of *Capital*, provides a basis for an account of multitude's internal commonalities and differences more rigorous than that which Hardt and Negri give. Marx's original account describes only two moments in this circuit: production, where labour power, machinery and raw materials are combined to create commodities, and circulation, where commodities are bought and sold. Dalla Costa and James (1972), and other autonomists (Cleaver, 1977; Fortunati, 1995), insisted on a third moment, the reproduction of labour power, in which workers are prepared and repaired for work (or unemployment), in homes, schools, hospitals, welfare offices and, the wider community. Ecological struggles have highlighted a fourth moment, the (non)reproduction of nature, in which raw materials are ex-

tracted from the environment and wastes returned to it; while this circuit has not been thoroughly theorized by autonomists (but see Caffentzis, 1992; p.m., 1992) analysis can draw on valuable work from other schools (O'Connor, 1998). This elaborated model enables a properly Marxian account of biopower that comprehends the heterogeneity of struggles to which multitude alludes. The move was partially anticipated in social factory theory, but the shift from labor-power to bio-power removes the persistent reference back to "work," de-centers the analysis from the immediate point of production and re-posits it at the level of the circuit as a whole. It is only at this level one can grasp the dimensions of a series of ecological, energy and epidemiological struggles, such as those around global warming, "peak oil," pandemics, and other species-scale issues.

7) The optimism associated with "multitude," however dampened today, continues to resonate with an important theme in contemporary movements — renewed interest in alternatives to global capital. After the fall of the "workers' states," capital asserted "there is no alternative," and postmodern pragmatism submitted ("no grand narratives, please"). The World Social Forum's slogan "Another World is Possible" picked up the challenge, even if in weakly relativist terms. Yet the question of which "other world" to actualize remains. It becomes even more important as Al Qaeda proposes its own choice: "restore the Caliphate!" Autonomists of all stripes have, for good reason, observed Marx's embargo on "abstract utopias." But utopias (preferably practical ones) are intrinsic to struggle, and "multitude" signals, if mainly in its tone, a resumption of this issue.

I am not, it should be clear, particularly concerned with supporting or refuting the idea of multitude in its original iteration. The big, set-piece denunciations of and adjudications on multitude, and its authors' defenses, are done. More interesting now is what can be done with multitude. Deleuze says a concept is a tool; this is how Hardt and Negri intended multitude. It remains for me an open, horizon of questions about, and for, what was once, and may again be, a movement of movements in and against global capital. While groups such as Wildcat (2005) turn away towards world-systems theorists to revitalize their analysis, I look rather for more sober, rigorous and grounded account of multitude. Where I agree with the compositionist critics of multitude is that the idea needs to come down to earth. It must fall from the abstract heights at which it was proposed. It needs the shock of empiricism. *Operaismo* took the abstract, formal concept "working class," gave it concrete content and, to a degree, allowed these findings to test the initial concept. In the same way, I suggest, "multitude" is an idea that deserves not so much adoption as investigation. It requires inquiry.

THE REVIVAL OF INQUIRY

This is only to echo suggestions made before and after the concept was enunciated. In 1995, while the idea of multitude was gestating in *Futur Antérieur*, Ed Emery urged "No Politics Without Inquiry!" Observing that after the long defeats of the 1970s and '80s there were finally signs of struggle based on a new and largely mysterious class composition, he proposed a renewal of collective research to understand and accelerate the process. Eleven years later, with the movement of movements "actually at the moment quite eclipsed, but with a more or less direct impact on a number of social and political conflicts in its wake," Emiliana Amano and Raffaele Sciortano (2006) make a similar suggestion. They write in the context of the No Tav movement of community opposition to a high-speed train line traversing the Susa valley in Northern Italy, a struggle whose terrain is "the entire fabric of social reproduction." Taking this as exemplary of the conditions within and against which the global social movements must now operate, Armano and Sciortano propose a revival of "conriecerca," research conducted in and with struggle, investigating a "class composition that is not workerist" and aiming for,

> a virtuous circle of knowledge and change, that, on return puts theory itself to the test and helps find out useful questions — above all, the question of what "class autonomy" could be in changing times (2006).

And Negri (2006) also, in his own inimitable mode, has made a similar suggestion for new inquiry.

What Emery, Armano, Sciortano and Negri propose, is moreover, actually occurring. In the generally gloomy post-9/11 firmament, a handful of bright sparks is provided by several small groups working in a highly-reflexive, politically-committed inquiry into issues of composition, broadly defined.

I will just mention three. The first is the investigation of call-center work by Kolinko (2002), based on three years immersion in the "whirlpools of circulation" in Ruhrgebiet, Germany.

The second is the investigations of precarious work and the labors of the "Care–Sex–Attention" nexus made by the feminist collective Precaria a la Deriva (2003; 2004) in their explorative "drifts" through Madrid.

The third are the "encounters" of the group Colectivo Situaciones (2004) with the "social protagonists" of Argentina's protracted crisis — movements of unemployed workers, peasants and the commemorators of the disappeared.

Mention of these experiments together, in the context of multitude-theory, must be immediately qualified. Each has their specific practice and perspectives; insistence on the preservation of particularity against a fast abstraction is in fact a common characteristic. All are engaged with the debates over multitude and immateriality, but critically. Kolinko works from a perspective close to that of Wildcat, whose strong disagreement with Hardt and Negri I have cited, and their somber portrait of network hell is a salutary corrective to overestimates of immaterial labor. Precaria a la Deriva (2004) questions the way the concept of multitude can submerge the gendered specificity of struggles. So it would be misleading to enlist these names in a simple celebration of multitude.

That, however, is not the point here. Rather, it is that these groups investigate the *problematic of multitude*: that is, the question of what forms of counter-power are possible in a highly globalized capitalism, with new forms of informational and affective labor and a tight interweaving of production and social reproduction. They also, however, renew (and improve on) the best features of *compositionist inquiry*: militant, conducted in collectivities with the aim of connecting to wider collectivities, theoretically informed but empirically open, partisan but persistently reflexive, self-inoculating against vanguardism, yet aiming to expedite struggle.

Not all inquiry can, or should, emulate the projects mentioned above, each remarkable in its creativity and commitment. Those who operate in conventional academic settings will want to consider how their inquiries relate to universities, themselves a site of multitudinous contestation (see Day et al., 2006) But these three examples do epitomize something of the spirit — or style — with which I would like to approach "multitude." Only tenacious, recursive, networked, empirical and politicized inquiry can answer the question posed by Colectivo Situaciones, so relevant to the debate over multitude:

> What to do when we are faced with this mechanism of massive adhesions and rejections, which elevate and dethrone radical experiments repeating the consumerist mechanism of the society of the society of the spectacle (2005, 808).

Kolinko, Precaria a la Deriva and Colectivo Situaciones all scrupulously document and discuss their methods of investigation. There are also available other examples of proposals for inquiry, such as that from *Derive Approdi* (2002). As a contribution to this collective development of methodologies, I conclude with a re-writing of the *Zerowork* statement from which this discussion started; this with great respect to all who produced or disseminated the original. Because the scope and complexity of struggle have precisely doubled over the last thirty-five years, the rewrite has eight, not four points; it is longer than the abbreviated online original, but not much more so than the relevant sections of the full text. It too, of course, is for testing, criticism and revision by the wider networks of inquiry and struggle.

FOR A COMPOSITIONAL ANALYSIS OF THE MULTITUDE

First, again, are the struggles themselves, the struggles of the multitude, collective interruptions in the circuit of capital conceived in its widest circumference. These include struggles in production (e.g. strikes, stoppages and occupations); in circulation (e.g. against consumerism and media spectacle); in social reproduction (e.g. over health, housing, welfare, schools and university), and in the reproduction of nature (e.g. against environmental destruction and over biotechnologies). In production, make no a priori judgment about the primacy of imma-terial labor, or any other kind; the issue is how struggles against different kinds of work—informational, affective, industrial, agrarian—connect, or fail to do so. But similarly, make no assumptions about the priority of the immediate point of production; whether the struggles flow (or fail to flow) out from the work-place into the rest of the social factory, or back into it from flashpoints around social and ecological reproduction is a matter for discovery.

Second, situate each struggle in the planetary space of multitude. Ex-plore its cartography. Determine what maps, of large and small scale, ter-restrial of course, but also cyber-spatial and institutional, are needed to understand it. Locate the places (a street, a town, a factory, land) it contests and claims, however briefly or partially. But also track the flows and circu-lations of people in migration, of information in networks, involved. Chart the territorializations and deterritorializations, and how these cut into the spatial organization of "glocalized" capital (see De Angelis, 2007).

Third, study the struggles as compositions of subjects and machines. By the composition of subjects we mean the bodies (including affects and minds) wag-ing the struggle. The multitude is a multitude because it comes in two sexes, sev-eral genders and many colors, to which the mill of capital assigns varying commodity-values. Struggle is a process of becoming in which these commodi-fied identities are unmade and transformed. By the composition of the machines we mean the relation of the struggle to technology. This may be a matter of halt-ing capital's machines (stop the line, block the bulldozer, burn the GMOs) but also appropriating or refunctioning them (the recovered factory, the collective garden, the pirate network, or even inventing new ones). Marx dissected the organic composition of capital; anatomize the organic composition of the multi-tude, the ways insurgent biopower combines with technologies.

Fourth, consider the relations between the multitude and its "official" or-ganizations, which include not only the trade unions, the "workers' parties," wel-fare organizations, etc, but also the NGOs and community development groups, the local and international coalitions, the World Social Forums, its regional spin-offs, and the other institutionalizations of the movement of movements. As Ze-rowork (1975, 112) observes, it is a mistake to identify struggles with official organizations, but one cannot take a "pure" line that "analyzes struggles entirely independent of these organizations." Learn about (and circulate word of) new initiatives such as "bio-syndicalist unions" (Tsianos & Papadopolous, 2006).

Fifth, take seriously decompositionary struggles. Decomposition is "as real as recomposition," and often underestimated (Wright, 2002, 224). Capital is the dominant decompositionary force, but there are others. There are even decom-positionary struggles that attack capital but also segment the multitude. Often either ignited or recuperated by capital, these segmentary struggles are not, how-ever, just its phantom or reflex; they have their own bad autonomy. Islamic mil-itary *jihad* is a decompositionary struggle whose boldness and skill mobilizes revolt against immiseration for reactionary ends. Consider the "war on terror" as the collision of two forces of decomposition, capital and fundamentalism, and the way both "war" and "terror" are not just destructive, but modes of social reproduction that repress the capacities of the multitude.

Sixth, relate all these aspects to the "general capitalist initiative," which today includes neoliberalism, deregulation, privatization, militarization, flexibilization and precarity, command through financial markets, digital and biotechnological innovation, and new cycles of primitive and futuristic accumulation. Detecting the high-level trajectory will require corroboration between inquiries. It is important to know if we are witnessing the coalescence of a global "empire," or an acceleration of "trade blocs" ushering in new "imperialist" conflict; therefore extending transnational networks of inquiry should be a priority, especially in regard to communication with comrades in China.

Seventh, identify protagonistic as well as antagonistic features of struggles: that is, what they are for as well as against. Collate plans, platforms, manifestos, proposals and even utopias. Evaluate which move towards a feasible world of substantive equity with multiple centers. In the recent resurgence of post-capitalist imagination some of the most important is around the category of "the common." The future of the multitude depends on whether it can move not just from the circulation of capital to the circulation of struggles, but from the circulation of struggles to the "circulation of the common" (Dyer-Witheford, 2006). Therefore, while recognizing that even the best of terms can be recuperated, ask: what is the "commonist" tendency?

Eighth, finally, but also before starting, and persistently, examine the relation of inquiry and struggle. How are they differentiated, and why? Can the inquiry feed back its findings into the struggle and not into capital? How does it avoid sociologism? If it makes slogans, are they ingenious ones? If university-based, what is the inquiry's relation to struggles over academic work and campus corporatization? Is it generating categories, connections, and circulations of information helpful to the movements? Is it time to revise theoretical premises? The multitude is a composition: a convergence of singular struggles that in their combination go beyond capital. Without romanticism or cynicism, attend not just to successful transversal connections, but also to blockages, chasms and implosions. Differentiate the struggles, identify their commonalities, relay between them. Recompose the multitude.

REFERENCES

Alquati, R. (1974). "The Network of Struggles in Italy." Unpublished paper, Red Notes Archive, London, available at www.libcom.org/library/network-of-struggles-italy-romano-alquati.

Armano, E. & Sciortano, R. (2006). "Inchiesta and Global Social Movements: A Renewing? Remarks on the No Tax Struggle." Future in the Present Conference, University of Leicester, UK.

aut-op-sy (nd) "What is class composition?" http://users.resist.ca/~jon. beasley-murray/aut_01.html

Balakrishnan, G. (Ed.) (2003). *Debating Empire*. London: Verso.

Bell, P. & Cleaver, H. (1982). "Marx's Crisis Theory as a Theory of Class Struggle," *Research in Political Economy*, vol. 5.

Berardi, F. (2003). "What is the Meaning of Autonomy Today? Subjectivication, Social Composition and Refusal of Work," *Republicart* http://www.republicart.net/disc/realpublicspaces/berardi01_en.pdf.

Bologna, S. (1980) "The Tribe of Moles," in *Italy: Autonomia — Post-Political Politics*. Ed. S. Lotringer & C. Marazzi. New York: Semiotext(e).

Bonefeld, W. (2003). "Human Practice and Perversion: Beyond Autonomy and Structure," in *Revolutionary Writing: 'Common Sense' Essays in Post-Political Politics*. Ed. W. Bonefeld. New York: Autonomedia.

Caffentzis, G. (1992). "The Work/Energy Crisis and the Apocalypse," in *Midnight Oil: Work, Energy, War 1973–1992*. Ed. Midnight Notes. New York: Autonomedia, 1992.

_____(2002). "Lenin on the Production of Revolution," in *What is to be Done? Leninism, Anti-Leninist Marxism and the Question of Revolution Today*. Ed. W. Bonefeld & S. Tschler. Aldershot: Ashgate.

_____ (2003). "The End of Work or the Renaissance of Slavery?" in *Revolutionary Writing: 'Common Sense' Essays in Post-Political Politics*. Ed. W. Bonefeld. New York: Autonomedia.

Cleaver, H. (1977). "Malaria, the Politics of Public Health and the International Crisis," in *The Review of Radical Political Economics*. Vol. 9, no. 1.

_____ (1979). *Reading Capital Politically*. Brighton: Harvester.

_____ (1994). "The Chiapas Uprising," in *Studies in Political Economy*, no. 44.

Colectivo Situaciones. (2004). "Causes and Happenstances: dilemmas of Argentina's new social protagonism Research manuscript #4," *The Commoner*, no. 8, at www.commoner.org.uk/08situaciones.pdf

_____ (2005). "Something More on Research Militancy: Footnotes on Procedures and (In) Decisions." *Ephemera* 5(4).

Dalla Costa, M. & James, S. (1972). *The Power of Women and the Subversion of the Community*. Bristol: Falling Wall Press.

Day, R., C. Mark, & G. de Peuter. Eds (2006). *Utopian Pedagogy*. Toronto: University of Toronto.

De Angelis, M. (2007), *The Beginning of History: Global Capital and Value Struggles*. London: Pluto.

Del Re, Alisa (2005). "Feminism and Autonomy: Itinerary of Struggle," in *The Philosophy of Antonio Negri: Resistance in Practice*. Ed. T.S. Murphy & A.K. Mustapha. London: Pluto.

Derive Approdi, (2002) "Open letter from 'DeriveApprodi' to the European movements," http://slash.autonomedia.org/article.pl?sid=02/07/28/1845215 &mode=nested.

Dowling, E. (2006). "Formulating new social subjects? An enquiry into the realities of a (hyper)-affective worker." Immaterial Labour Conference, King's College, UK. http://www.geocities.com/immateriallabour/dowlingpaper 2006.html.

Dyer-Witheford, N. (2004). "1844/2004/2044: The Return of Species-Being," *Historical Materialism* 12:4.

_____ (2005). "Cyber-Negri: General Intellect and Immaterial Labor," in *The Philosophy of Antonio Negri: Resistance in Practice*. Ed. T.S. Murphy & A.K. Mustapha. London: Pluto.

_____ (2006). "The Circulation of the Common." Immaterial Labour Conference, King's College, UK. http://www.geocities.com/immateriallabour/withefordpaper2006.html

Emery, E. (1995). "No Politics Without Inquiry: A Proposal for a Class Composition Inquiry 1996–97," *Common Sense*, no. 18.

Fortunati, L. (1995). *The Arcana of Reproduction: Housework, Prostitution, Labor and Capital*. New York: Autonomedia.

Hardt, M. & Negri, A. (2000). *Empire*. Cambridge, Mass.: Harvard Univ. Press.

Hardt, M. & Negri, A. (2004). *Multitude: War and Democracy in the Age of Empire*. New York: Penguin.

Harvey, D. (2003). *The New Imperialism*. Oxford: Oxford Univ. Press.

Holloway, J. (2003) "Time to Revolt: Reflections on *Empire*," http://www.libcom.org/library/time-to-revolt-empire-john-holloway.

Kidd, D. (2003). "Indymedia.org: A New Communications Commons," in *Cyberactivism: Online Activism in Theory and Practice*. Ed. M. McCaughey & M. Ayers. New York: Routledge.

_____ (2004). "From Carnival to Commons: The Global IMC Network," in *Confronting Capitalism: Dispatches from A Global Movement*. Ed. E. Yuen, D. Burton-Rose, & G. Katsiaficas. New York: Soft Skull.

Klein, N. (2004). "Reclaiming the Commons," in *A Movement of Movements: Is Another World Really Possible?* Ed. T. Mertes. London: Verso.

Kolinko (2001) "Class Composition," http://www.nadir.org/nadir/initiativ/kolinko/engl/e_klazu.htm.

_____ (2002). *Hotlines: Call Center-Inquiry-Communism*. Kolinko: Ruhrpott.

Lazzarato, M., A. Negri, & Santilli, G.C. (1990). *La Confection Dans le Quartier du Sentier. Restructuration des Formes d'Emploi et Expansion Dans un Secteur en Crise*. Rapport MIRE: Paris.

Lazzarato, M & A. Negri. (1993). *Le Bassin de Travail Immateriel (B.T.I.) Dans La Metropole Parisienne: Definition, Recherches, Perspectives*. Paris: Tekne-Logos.

Marx, K. (1880). "A Worker's Inquiry," *La Revue socialiste*, April 20. http://www.marxists.org/archive/marx/works/1880/04/20.htm

Midnight Notes Collective. (1992). *Midnight Oil: Work, Energy, War 1973–1992*. Brooklyn NY: Autonomedia.

Mitropoulos, A. (2006). "Autonomy, Recognition, Movement." *The Commoner* 11. http://www.commoner.org.uk/

Moulier-Boutang, Y. (2006)."Antagonism under cognitive capitalism: class composition, class consciousness and beyond." Immaterial Labour Conference, King's College, UK. http://www.geocities.com/immateriallabour/moulier-boutangpaperb2006.html.

Negri. A. (2004). "Pour une définition ontologique de la multitude." *Multitudes* 9. Trans. as 'Towards an Ontological Definition of Multitude,' at http://www.makeworlds.org/node/104.

_____ (2005). *Books for Burning: Between Civil War and Democracy in 1970s Italy*. London: Verso.

_____ (2006) "Logic and Theory of Inquiry: militant praxis as subject and as episteme," http://www.generation-online.org/p/fpnegri20.htm

Neill, M., with Caffentzis, G. & Machete, J. (1997). "Toward the New Commons: Working Class Strategies and the Zapatistas." Second International Encuentro Against Neoliberalism and For Humanity. http://www.geocities.com/CapitolHill/3843/mngcjm.html.

Neill, M. (2001). "Rethinking Class Composition Analysis in the Light of the Zapatistas," in *Auroras of the Zapatistas: Local & Global Struggles of the Fourth World War*. Ed. Midnight Notes. New York: Autonomedia.

O'Connor, J. (1998). *Natural Causes: Essays in Ecological Marxism*. New York: Guilford.

Panzieri, R. (1976). "Surplus Value and Planning: Notes on the Reading of Capital," in *The Labour Process & Class Strategies*. London: Conference of Socialist Economists. 4–25.

_____ (1980). "The Capitalist Use of Machinery: Marx Versus the Objectivists," in *Outlines of a Critique of Technology*. Ed. Phil Slater.Highlands: Humanities.

Passavant, P. & Dean, J. Eds. (2004). *Empire's New Clothes: Reading Hardt and Negri*. New York: Routledge.

p.m. (1992) "Strange Victories," in *Midnight Oil: Work, Energy, War, 1973–1992*. Ed. Midnight Notes Collective. New York: Autonomedia.

Pinguin (2003) "The discussion about *Empire*." http://www.republicart.net/disc/empire/pinguin01_en.htm.

Precarias a la deriva. (2003). "First Stutterings of 'Precarious Workers Adrift.'" http://www.sindominio.net/karakola/precarias/balbuceos-english.htm.

_____ (2004) "Adrift through the circuits of feminized precarious work." http://www.sindominio.net/karakola/precarias/femrev.htm

Retort. (2005). *Afflicted Powers: Capital and Spectacle in a New Age of War*. London: Verso.

Tronti, Mario. (1977). *Ouvriers et Capital*. Paris: Christian Bourgeois.

Tsianos, V. & Papadopolous, D. (2006) "Precarity: A Savage Journey to the Heart of Embodied Capitalism." Immaterial Labour Conference, King's College, UK. http://www.geocites.com/immateriallabour/ tsianopapadopaper2006. html?200620.

Virno, P. (2004). *A Grammar of the Multitude*. New York: Semiotext(e).

Wildcat (2003) "The Renaissance of Workerism (*Operaism*)" Wildcat 66. July. http://www.wildcat-www.de/en/wildcat/66/w66e_ope.htm

Wildcat (2005). Wildcat Preface: Beverly Silver, "Forces of Labor." http://www.prol-position.net/nl/2005/02/silver.

Wright, S. (2002). *Storming Heaven: Class Composition and Struggle in Italian Autonomist Marxism*. London: Pluto.

Wright, S. (2005) "Reality Check: Are We Living in An Immaterial World?" Wright, S., *Mute* Vol 2 (1). London: Mute Publishing Ltd.

Wright, S. (2006) "There and Back Again: Mapping the Pathways Within Autonomist Marxism." Immaterial Labour Conference, King's College, UK. http://www.geocites.com/immateriallabour/wrightpaper2006 .html?200620.

Zerowork Collective. (1975). "Introduction." *Zerowork: Political Materials* 1, reprinted in Midnight Notes (1992) *Midnight Oil: Work, Energy, War, 1973–1992* Autonomedia, New York.

Index

208, 221, 227
San Andrés Accords 150,
205, 221
Sánchez Ramírez, E. 212,
230
Santillán, Dario 239
Santilli, G.C. 264
Saudi Arabia 197
Schnews 124, 125
Schwartau, Winn 154
Schwartz, Gregory 244
Sciortano, Raffaele 259,
263
Scott, James C. 110, 156
Scottish Highlands 17
Seattle, Washington
115–116, 135, 190, 213,
251, 253, 255
Seay, Thomas 156
self-determination 39, 120,
145, 165, 169, 171, 172
self-organization 6, 62,
99–102, 105–106, 133,
136, 138, 148–149, 156,
165, 171, 209
self-valorization 34, 142,
158
Sem Terra 225
Sen, Jai 227, 230
Sensenbrenner, James
193–195, 218–219
Seoul, South Korea 120,
253
separation of producers
and means of produc-
tion 5, 21, 28–47,
52–62, 67–74, 77–86,
91– 92, 94, 153,
167–168, 171, 173
September 11, 2001 149,
179–183, 188–191, 197,
200, 255
service economy 19, 257
Service Employees Inter-
national Union (SEIU)
188
service industries 18
service sector 146

sex industry 90
sexual exploitation of
women 90
sexual tourism 90
Shaffer, Deborah 111
Shell Oil corporation 153
Shepard, Ben 109
Shiva, Vandana 91–96
Shukaitis, Stevphen 3, 6,
99, 112–119
Si Se Puede 6, 179,
192–193, 195–196, 200,
219–220
Sikkink, Kathryn 130,
152–154
Silver, Beverly 266
Singapore 149
Sinn Fein 226
Situationists 105, 108–109
Sixth Declaration of the
Lacandona 151, 160,
203, 205, 207, 214, 229,
230
slave trade 36, 39, 44–45,
89, 154
slavery 13, 16, 26, 36, 43,
51, 64, 88–91, 158, 182,
185–189, 200
Slim, Carlos 205, 223
Slim, T-Bone 101
Smith, Adam 32, 71, 153
Smith, Cyril 46, 49,
122–123, 125
Smith, Suzanne 109
social commons 43–44
social factory 120–122,
141– 142, 144, 147,
249–254, 258, 261
social imaginary 100,
105–108
social labo(u)r 39–40,
54–55, 59–60, 120
social movements 6, 119,
121, 129, 140–141, 148,
152, 154, 157, 161–166,
171, 173, 200, 208, 213,
219, 224–226, 249, 255,
259, 263

social reproduction 48, 58,
60, 64, 87, 189, 250,
255–256, 259–262
social wage 15, 16, 252
social-democracy 15, 173,
208
socialised worker 120,
121, 144
socialism 15–20, 24, 27,
44, 61, 78, 84, 86, 127,
157, 161, 165–168, 212,
228, 235–237
Socialisme ou Barbarie
158
socialist bloc 23
socialist internationalism
19
socialist rights 15
Socialist Workers Party
116, 226
Soledad Prison 99
solidarity 8, 18, 95,
107–108, 111, 136, 143,
154, 157, 192, 214,
219–220, 234, 237, 239,
240, 243, 256
South Korea 78, 120, 192
South Wales 120
soviets 15, 16, 18, 22, 44,
74, 138, 146, 156, 161,
163, 165, 168–170
Soviet Union (*see also*
Union of Soviet So-
cialist Republics) 15,
18, 22, 74, 161, 163
Spanish Conquest 130
spatial deconcentration
20–22
Spinoza, Baruch 145, 159,
252
squatters 20, 224
Sri Lanka 20
stage theory of history 36,
45–46
Stalin, Joseph 78, 153,
195, 212, 228
Stalinism 161
Stansill, Peter 111